MASTER YOUR EMOTION

This Book Includes:

Emotional Intelligence,

Empath,

How to Talk to Anyone,

Overthinking.

Change Your Habits and Mindset
Through Self Discipline, Mindfulness
And Positive Thinking.

MIND CHANGE ACADEMY

Book 1

EMOTIONAL INTELLIGENCE FOR LEADERSHIP

A PRACTICAL GUIDE TO LEARN HOW TO IMPROVE YOUR SOCIAL SKILLS AND MASTER YOUR EMOTIONS, MANAGE AND INFLUENCE PEOPLE AND HAVE SUCCESS IN RELATIONSHIPS AND BUSINESS

Book 2

EMPATH GUIDE

A COMPLETE GUIDE FOR HIGHLY SENSITIVE PERSON, DEVELOPING SKILLS, IMPROVE EMOTIONAL INTELLIGENCE, YOUR SELF-ESTEEM AND RELATIONSHIPS. OVERCOME FEAR, ANXIETY AND NARCISSISTIC ABUSE

Book 3

HOW TO TALK TO ANYONE

LEARN HOW TO IMPROVE COMMUNICATION SKILLS AND TALK TO WOMEN, MEN, IN PUBLIC, AT WORK AT ANYTIME AND ANYWHERE WITH CONFIDENCE, INCREASE YOUR SELF-ESTEEM, MANAGE SHYNESS

Book 4

OVERTHINKING

HOW TO STOP WORRYING, RELIEVE ANXIETY AND EMOTIONAL STRESS, STOP NEGATIVE THINKING. USE POSITIVE ENERGY TO CONTROL YOUR THOUGHTS CHANGE YOUR HABITS AND MINDSET

MIND CHANGE ACADEMY

Emotional Intelligence For Leadership

a practical guide to learn How to Improve Your Social Skills and Master Your Emotions, Manage and Influence People and have Success in Relationships and Business

MIND CHANGE ACADEMY

Table of Contents

Introduction

The concept of emotions and empathy is a broad field which can be narrowed. The first step is to understand what these terms mean. Emotions can be defined as a negative or positive experience that correlates to a certain pattern of psychological doings. Empathy, on the other hand, is described as a person's ability to understand and share the feelings of other people. Empathy is a word originated from a German word Einfühlung that means feeling in.

A person is supposed to be aware of empathy so as to understand his or her emotional intelligence. Empathy will help a person respond to certain situations with ease. Such a situation will include handling a partner who came to the home with sad news from work. Therefore, it is integral parts in people's lives for over decades in begin of time. It helps people to connect and love other people surrounding them. There are several facets that are used to describe empathy in people's lives. Therefore, there are several ways identified by psychologists that people can feel empathy. These common ways include emotional, compassionate and cognitive empathy.

The emotional, cognitive and compassionate empathy have different ways of manifesting in life. The reflection they give is in different ways is always a manifestation of a person's day to day life. Life experience across family, work and friend have an influence of on the different manifestations ways.

An individual will also notice the change when handling this set of people in his or her daily life. There are numerous examples in the current globe which are documented. The documentation can be accessed with availability of technology that has made the globe a small village.

Do you want to know more? Then sit down and read as we dive deep down this topic.

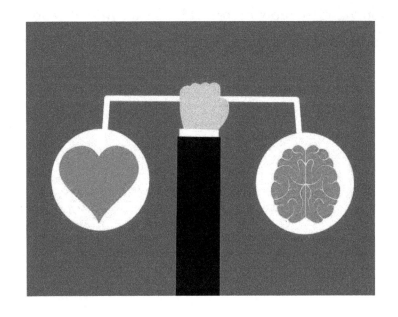

Chapter 1.   Emotional Intelligence

What Is Emotional Intelligence and The Emotional Brain

It is a common occurrence in human being lives when they look back at important decisions made and question oneself. Questions that tend to crisscross a person's mind are what he or she was thinking or why he or she had to do that. These situations bring the rise of the emotional intelligence idea. It is an important tool in the day to day life of a human being because it helps a person overcome regrets.

Emotional intelligence can easily be understood as the ability of an individual to identify, understand, use and control emotions. This process is supposed to be done in a calm manner to make it have a positive and effective impact. A person who has high emotional intelligence has various advantages in the current life. He or she is able to have better communication with people, resolve conflicts, improve his or her relationships and reduce anxiety levels in their lives. Having high emotional intelligence helps a person have high empathy levels which are critical in relationships.

People's emotional intelligence has a big potential for people having quality life. It is because it is an influential factor in how people behave. People with incredible level of good behavior are associated with healthy relationships that promote quality life a person's lives. High level of emotional intelligence is commonly associated with improved levels of self-awareness. These qualities bring different states in a person's life since a person has purpose, autonomy and intention which are components of a quality life

A greater part of the global community is heavily affected by the process of decision making. Several people make decisions anchoring them of the current happenings and circumstances. The thought that cloud people during these complicated situations is if the perception that things are beyond the ability to be changed. The impact these thoughts give is an individual's mind is the limited amount of options and solutions. Therefore, an individual is advised to take time to reflect over these scenarios. Reflecting helps a person to examine what on the issue and come up with the best ways the situation can be handled.

Developing an individual's emotional intelligence quotient has a greater influence on an individual's life to success. An emotional quotient is a standard form used by psychologist used in determining a person's emotional intelligence. The process is greatly influenced by a person's personal situation and his or her intelligence. The impact of high emotional quotient is felt in several aspects of an individual's life. It cuts through how a person makes his choices, finds solutions and creates other options when situations are difficult. There are several ways a person can improve his or her emotional quotient.

Emotional intelligence in the workplace is not just a fad that people are excited about that will go away after a while. There are true benefits to hiring an emotionally intelligent workforce.

Emotionally intelligent employees handle pressure better.

Just as the workforce of today is different from the workforce of yesteryear, the workplace has also changed. Before, workplaces tended to be more relaxed. The modern workplace looks to be more cutthroat and pressure-filled. With this in mind, hiring managers know that emotionally intelligent employees will be better placed to thrive in an environment of pressure. This is because they are able to manage their emotions even when the going gets tough. Imagine an environment where employees are unable to manage their emotions. What is likely to happen when a critical deadline is coming up? Probably lots of yelling and scapegoating. This would definitely be a recipe for disaster.

Emotionally intelligent employees are better decision makers.

Decision-making is an everyday activity in the business world. You need to make decisions about how to solve client problems, which clients to pitch to, which colleagues to include in particular teams, how to format a report for a client, how to manage your workload efficiently, and a myriad of other decisions. The more emotionally intelligent you are, the more capable you are of making good decisions. When you know how to manage your emotions, you are able to make decisions that are not simply emotional. Emotions are good and all, but they don't usually make for very good catalysts in decision-making.

Let's say for instance that you are a team leader working to deliver a project for a client. There is one colleague that is very good at performing financial due diligence, a skill that you need for this project. Unfortunately, this colleague does not really like you, for reasons best known to them. They have made this clear, to the extent of being publicly disrespectful. What do you do?

A person that is lacking in emotional intelligence might be tempted to engage in a power struggle with this colleague. After all, the colleague should respect the team leader regardless of their differences.

However, if you are emotionally intelligent, you will devise a way to deal with the colleague because you realize that getting into it with them is only going to ruin the progress of the team. You will figure out a way to play the role of team leader without giving them an arsenal that they can use against you. Instead of playing their game, you will kill them with kindness. You will be fully invested in being the bigger person, and you will not allow said colleague to drag you to their level. This is because you are self-aware, self-regulating, motivated from the inside, and well equipped with the social skills needed to handle a colleague that is behaving like a petulant child.

Employees with high EQ handle conflicts better

The workplace is a convergence of many personalities. When different personalities meet in one place, there is a high likelihood of clashing. Colleagues will not always get along. You may have potlucks or staff parties every other weekend and there still will be differences and conflict between the employees. In the face of conflict, you need employees that can resolve their differences with as little drama as possible.

Primary Emotions

- **Anger and Fear**

Anger is a strong feeling of displeasure, annoyance or hostility triggered by external provocation. Anger is associated with feelings of antagonism towards someone, something or an idea. Anger can be directed at oneself. When a person is angry at himself, the feeling of antagonism associated with his anger is directed at the person feeling the emotion.

While anger, like sadness, is a natural and often automatic reaction. Anger causes increased blood pressure, heart rate, adrenaline and noradrenaline levels. Extreme anger can substantially impair judgment.

Although anger is a primary emotion, it often occurs as a secondary emotion because it is frequently preceded by a negative primary emotion.

Anger is sometimes used as a mechanism to distract oneself from negative emotions that are self-focused. This happens when people stimulate the emotion of anger, either consciously or not, so as to avoid feelings of pain or vulnerability.

Doing this takes their attention off themselves and their unpleasant state and directs it at a person, a thing or an idea. This is considered by the person to be a better state than the state of pain. Anger by itself often does not feel bad to the person feeling it. This is because anger is associated with feelings of justification, moral superiority and pride.

Fear is an unpleasant feeling triggered by a sense of danger or a threat. It is the emotion we feel when we think something bad is going to happen. The primary trigger of fear is the perception of imminent pain. This could be physical pain: fear of bodily harm or hurt; or emotional pain: fear of loss, rejection or distress; or social pain: fear of disgrace, isolation or shame. We feel the emotion of fear not only for ourselves but for others as well. Fear for others can sometimes be more unpleasant to experience than fear for oneself. This is because we usually can't control what happens to others.

Fear ranges from a little scare accompanied by mild muscular tension to a paralyzing feeling accompanied by crippling muscular tension or numbness.

When we have a serious fear of a thing or an animal, it is called a phobia.

- **Sadness and Joy**

Sadness is an emotional pain that occurs in response to disappointment, grief, loss, sorrow, and helplessness. It is a temporary state of melancholy and is a dominant emotion. Sadness is a natural and automatic emotion but when it is extreme and persistent, it could be a symptom of depression.

Sadness is a normal emotion like fear or happiness. The death of a pet, the loss of a job or even breaking our favorite china could trigger sadness. When that feeling persists and overwhelms us permanently, it could be an indication of a mental health problem and a person experiencing such should urgently seek professional help.

Joy is a pleasant feeling of great pleasure and excitement. The emotional state of joy is characterized by feelings of contentment, happiness, gratification, satisfaction, and well-being.

- **Surprise and Waiting**

Surprise is an emotion characterized by a sudden feeling of wonder or astonishment in response to an unexpected event or information. Surprises may be pleasant or unpleasant.

A secondary emotion relating to surprise is "surprise". Tertiary emotions relating to the secondary emotion of surprise are amazement, surprise, and astonishment.

- **Disgust and Acceptance**

Disgust is the feeling of irritation. Acceptance is accepting the reality of a situation without seeking to change it.

Secondary or Complex Emotions

- **The Shame**

Embarrassed is feeling shame and discomfort.

- **Anxiety**

Tertiary emotions relating to nervousness are anxiety, dread, uneasiness, tenseness, apprehension, and worry. Another secondary emotion relating to fear is "horror". Tertiary emotions relating to "horror" include panic, shock, hysteria, terror, fright, and alarm.

- **Jealousy**

Jealous is feeling of resentment towards someone's achievement.

- **The Hope**

Hopeful is a feeling that one's desires will be met.

- **Forgiveness**

A person is supposed to forgive people who have wronged him. Learning the art of forgiveness helps a person to move on and heal from stressful relationships. Hanging on resentment has the potential of reducing a person's emotional intelligence.

- **The Offense**

Offended is annoyance due to something said or done

- **Homesickness**

Homesick is an intense longing for one's home.

- **Remorse**

Contrition is the feeling of remorse.

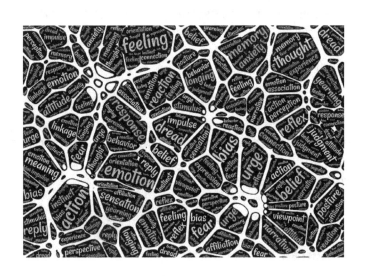

Chapter 2.   Emotion Management

How Emotional Intelligence Works

Emotional intelligence is vital to our relationship with others and with ourselves. Daniel Goleman, the author of 'Emotional Intelligence', stated that eighty-five percent of our personal and professional success will be affected by EQ. Life deals us blows unexpectedly at every turn.

Have you ever wondered why some people seem to face this headlong, and others seem to crumble under the weight of it? Have you witnessed two people who face the same misfortune but have different levels of resilience? Emotional intelligence combined with other factors can determine, to a large extent, how fast you can bounce back when faced with unsavory situations.

One method of applying EQ to our everyday life is developing the art of assertiveness. Being on planet Earth and surrounded by so many people, we are bound to get into situations that will affect our person. Assertiveness involves possessing high self-esteem and self-confidence. In situations where we feel threatened or where our integrity is questioned, the appropriate reaction is to remain calm. This is achievable when we understand the reason for the other party's behavior.

Practicing mindfulness is a good way to boost EQ in our everyday life. Taking walks, practicing yoga and meditation, can help integrate one with his/her surroundings. Be aware of yourself, of the emotions you feel, and those of others. Taking deep breaths and grounding can help pass time when caught in aggravating situations.

Feel, do not suppress. Being emotionally intelligent does not require that you stifle or dismiss your emotions. Even the calmest and most collected persons experience their own share of overwhelming emotions. The difference lies in the outlet. Finding creative and healthy outlets instead of transferring our sadness, aggression and other negative emotions to others. It is normal to feel emotions, but do not bottle them up, and do not go on a hysterical spree.

In business, EQ is indispensable in negotiation talks. By controlling your emotions, communicating effectively and figuring out the mood, limitations, and peculiarities of the other party, you can successfully close deals in your favor. Emotions are often times displayed through body language, facial expressions, and other paralinguistic variables. Possessing a high EQ makes one sensitive to these changes, and being empathetic would determine to a large extent how you would apply this information.

In our daily activities, EQ would help you decipher if a particular problem stems from you or the other party.

Sometimes we are the toxic person, and no matter how hard you try, you can't be great to everyone all the time. Man is inherently imperfect. Since self-awareness and self-regulation are thoroughly integrated into EQ, recognizing that you are the one at fault always comes handy in some conflict resolutions.

Show love and gratitude always. Appreciating what you have helps to reinforce emotional intelligence. Showing love and gratitude to those around you foster understanding and togetherness. You can demonstrate empathy by paying the bus tickets of a total stranger or reaching out to support a colleague.

In interpersonal relationships, the level of compatibility between the EQ of the two individuals along with other factors determines the failure or success of the relationship.

How to Observe and Express Your Emotions

Emotions are grouped into primary emotions, secondary emotions, and tertiary emotions.

Primary emotions are the initial emotions felt in response to a perception. These emotions are fear, anger, sadness, joy, love, and surprise. These are the emotions you feel without thinking. They are instinctive feelings we don't plan to have. Imagine you are walking down the road in the company of a friend and a reckless cyclist runs into your friend. The emotion you likely instinctively feel is fear. Fear that your loved one may get hurt.

Primary emotions are often called transient because they disappear quickly and are replaced. They are replaced by secondary emotions and can be secondary emotions themselves.

Secondary emotions are an offshoot of primary emotions. These emotions replace primary emotions. The emotion of fear you felt when you saw your loved one getting knocked down by the reckless cyclist may be replaced by the secondary emotion of anger. You feel angry at the cyclist for causing someone you love pain.

There are so many emotions that it is considered impossible to list all emotions that exist, but below is a generally comprehensive list of human emotions and their meaning. This list contains the basic emotions, their meanings, and their related secondary and tertiary emotions. As you go through this list, try to remember times when you felt each of these emotions. Also, try to remember times when you witnessed someone else express each of the listed emotions. You can take as much time as you need.

How to Learn and Improve Emotional Intelligence

There are very diverse people with different characters. Therefore, it requires one to improve their emotional interpretation of those individuals occasionally. Psychologists have gone as far as trying to interpret emotions using science like empathetic forecasting. That is where they use statistics like measuring the correlation model between an empathetic party forecast of all people concerned. Yes, in some instance, the research work but no one can measure the behavior of a person. The following are the ways of improving your EQ.

First, you should take the correspondent inner feelings and experiences like they were yours. That means you are putting the situation of a colleague on 'your shoes.' When doing that you can clearly define what the other party if feeling. You can therefore intelligently advise them on the next step to take. By doing this the respondents feel their feelings being cared and personalized.

Be attentive in listening when the other person is speaking. Always check on their nonverbal cues and try to analyze that pattern. Try also to deduce the different emotions they show like analyzing their tonal variation and gestures. Makes sure there are no distractions while listening and acquire a mental picture of what they tell you. When they notice your keenness and interest, they will reveal all their inner feelings.

Be flexible in changing and adapting to their mood. In the event of a quarrel, intelligent people will usually mitigate violence. That is done by adjusting to their partner's point of thinking and deducing some sense in it. Therefore you can even find out you are the wrong party involved. When they are wrong, do not criticize them harshly but first, credit their thoughts and market your idea politely. Leaders, judges, and mediators should possess this character in making rulings.

Deliberate on your weak point as of the other. If you are hot-tempered when wronged, you should know how to control yourself. That is because, in conflict, you should cool down to avoid further violence. Moreover, you should be quick to detect the shortcoming of the other. The person with a good EQ can manage that person accordingly. That is because they know the criteria to handle different weakness of a person. For example, if a person has a personality disorder, you can calmly handle their grievances.

Always inquire for others for feedback and information. Emotional intelligence is like a skill that needs to be learned. Therefore you cannot obtain the knowledge by yourself .consulting others for feedback help you gain more understanding of a particular area. Moreover, their response will help one notice their reactions and sentiments. Acting on their feelings will build trust and healthy relationships.

Always be motivated to learn the behavior of other people. In this context, variable people show different feelings. Learning helps one in gaining knowledge. You will also understand how to handle various emotional aspects. You will be equipped with ways you can advise such fellows. You can also use your personal experience when meeting with people of personality disorders.

Always be optimistic about every situation. There are very various scenarios that come with their difficulties and needs one to approach them intelligently. A negative attitude harms the self-belief of a person in accomplishing some tasks. You may face such a person and sometimes it is hard to interact with such individuals. However, approaching such a situation positively gives you that motivation in understanding their sentiments.

Emotionally intelligent personnel are approachable and social to others. They are free to talk to and to intermingle. They have excellent interpersonal and intrapersonal skills. They are self-aware of their conscious and do not like to engage in conflicts. They can relate to any people and are skilled in articulating their values to them. In the process of interacting, they learn the emotional patterns of many people and use that information in dealing with those victims.

Leveraging and Controlling Positive and Negative Emotions

Both the negative and positive emotions are subject to being looked at attentively, and the approaches to handle them expertly be laid down. You should let your children know that unpleasant feelings like anger should be expected in any situation because they are healthy. How you handle those feelings will determine whether there will be harmony in the family or not. An emotionally intelligent parent will teach their children the strategies to use to cool themselves down in such situations. They need to know how to determine the action they need to take to deal with a problem once they calm down. Teaching children through conversation as well as examples of how to live emotionally intelligent is vital. Teaching children emotional intelligence ways will play an important role to reduce the number of kids who wrestle with overeating. The level of destructive practices will go down because of seeing things from a positive point of view.

Nurture optimism as well as embrace realism

An emotionally intelligent family has an idea of how to take care of positivity as well as optimism. They not only recognize but also accept reality. They believe in themselves that they can go through tough times and emerge victoriously. The spirit of isolation is not given a chance in the family. They perceive they pose what it takes to set up an active family. Each one is ready to help the other in times of need and learn from their experiences. They view life from a positive perspective and do not let anything negative that has happened to ruin their harmony as a family. There is much happiness contributed by each person within the family.

Importance and Benefits of Developing Emotional Intelligence Skills

The following are the personal competencies stemming from the concept of emotional intelligence. Generally, no one would be able to score 100% of these qualities. However, you can strengthen your limitations. For you to achieve outstanding performance, you must have five essential domains including social skills of an individual, awareness of the self, self-motivation, self-regulation and having empathy.

Self-awareness

Awareness of the self basically entails having knowledge and understanding about the internal states about yourself, intuitions and your preferences. It basically involves being; emotionally aware by recognizing your emotions as well as the effects of these emotions; accurately assessing yourself

-by knowing your strengths and limited, and having self-confidence - knowing your self-worth as well as capabilities.

Self-regulation

Self-regulation involves how you manage your internal resources and impulses. This includes: Having self-control where you are able to check your impulses and disruptive emotions; having a feeling of trustworthiness where you are able to maintain high standards of integrity and honesty; having a sense of conscientiousness where you are responsible for your personal performance; and adaptability which means that you are flexible in handling changes.

Social Skills

Social Skills means that you are an individual with adeptness and you are able to provide desirable responses to the people around you. Working on your social skills means that you will be able to influence or persuade others, clearly communicate in an open and convince manner; be able to manage conflicts; participate in group works and be able to build bonds.

Empathy

Empathy means that you are aware of the feelings of other people. This means that you are able to understand others, being able to develop others, being able to leverage diversity and being able to read the current emotional currents.

Motivation

This means that you are an individual with emotional tendencies guiding or facilitating you to reach your goals. You are able to achieve an inner drive, be committed, and be optimistic.

Understanding these five essential domains emotional intelligence can help you improve the brain chemistry of emotions because you will respond rather than react even when faced with emotionally charged situations. With the five skills, you will be able to respond rather than react and get defensive. Emotional intelligence approach will tell you to keep calm, get the perspective of the situation, before judging, listen and hold yourself from reacting head-on. Secondly, you will show up with your real self. Most people tend to hide who they are especially when they are faced with hard situations or people. When you are emotionally intelligent, you will be able to present yourself with integrity and emotional transparency. Emotional intelligence will help you to think before speaking, practice self-control, look at the whole picture of an even thus you will be able handle tough or difficult situations better. These are all factors that will enable you to be in control of all your emotions thus be in control of your brain chemistry.

Negative Emotions

An inability to reduce negative emotions does not bode well for you. I understand that it is easier said than done but it is not impossible. A key way to reduce your negative emotions is to evaluate the situation that has led to the way you feel. For example, no one likes to be criticized, especially when it is in the public sphere, but not all criticisms are destructive. You need to evaluate the profile of the person speaking and the validity of their claims.

Profiling the person will help you know why the person might be telling you the things he or she is telling you. Does this person have something to gain from this criticism? If people you know care about you criticize you, they are most likely only trying to help you improve. I know you would have preferred that the criticism is not public but it is practicing humility to accept what was said and improve.

Be Mindful of Your Use of Words

You have to be careful regarding the things you say to people. You don't have to let out everything because you are angry. Words are like missiles and impossible to stop once released. You can choose to speak to people politely even when they don't rate you highly or speak less of you. They will remember your maturity when their sanity returns and will respect you for being noble when you have reasons not to be.

Put Yourself in People's Shoes Consistently

Empathy is the key to emotional intelligence. Don't you get angry because your boss speaks angrily at you and neglects the things you are going through? Don't always expect others to be as emotionally intelligent as yourself, always take the initiative. Also, learn to make excuses for other people. Instead of saying that your boss is such a terrible person, you can convince yourself that he or she might just be having a bad day.

Be Mindful of Things That Stress You Out

You need to also watch out for activities that tend to increase your stress level. Reduce these activities and you will be able to have fewer negative emotions that can cause you to make wrong decisions.

Be Assertive

It is not prideful to let people know the things you feel are unacceptable to you. Sometimes, people assume that others should know what they like and what they don't like. Making it clear to people around you that you don't like a particular thing will help them avoid doing those things to you.

They will have nothing to complain about if you rebuke them when they do those things because they have been warned.

It is true that there are people that will do things you don't like just to annoy you, but clearly defining your likes and dislikes will help reduce such occurrences.

Be Open to the Opinion of Others

When you only hear your own voice, you cannot improve the quality of your life. There are times you did something or thought about something in a particular way and felt you are right but you realized you were wrong after seeking the opinion of someone else. Learn to ask for the opinion of others and compare and contrast. You will make better decisions this way and also gain the trust of others.

Be Patient

Learn to delay your decisions for as long as possible. Decisions made in a hurry will come back to haunt you. Take your time and think through before doing anything. You can speak to people you feel are in a better position to help you whenever you can. Some decisions look like no-brainers but you will realize that they are not in hindsight. Unless you definitely have to respond instantaneously, take your time because decisions made thoughtfully always have a higher chance of being right than the ones made immediately.

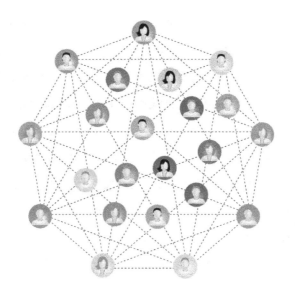

Chapter 3.   Social Skill

What Is Social Skill

Social skills and great communication abilities are some of the things that can help you to not only survive but also thrive in your everyday life and in your career. No matter how brilliant your ideas may be or how passionate or sincere you are as a person, if you fail to communicate well with those around you, none of that is going to matter because no one will be able to fully understand or connect with you. Having social skills is a very valuable asset that helps you build the rapport and the relationships that you need to fulfill the basic human need that we all have within us: to connect with others.

Social skills are skills that can be developed and cultivated over time, and there are plenty of reasons why you should do so because having great social skills can significantly work to your advantage. When you've got great social skills, you'll be able to:

- Form meaningful and lasting relationships
- Easily relate to others from all sorts of diverse cultural backgrounds and walks of life
- Easily assimilate in any social setting
- Inadvertently develop great communication skills in the process

- Communicate your thoughts, ideas, and opinions and be easily understood by others.
- Empathize better with others
- Improve your reputation and career in the workplace

Enjoy an increased quality of life because you'll find it much easier to get along with other people in your life

For your social skills to be considered a success, you must be able to get your message across clearly and undoubtedly. By the end of this book, you will be well on your way to become more confident and effective in your social and communications skills, build effective and genuine relationships with the people around you in your life, and feel good.

The social value of a person corresponds to the position she occupies in the hierarchy of society. It's linked to the richness of its network of relationships.

What are her friends, colleagues, acquaintances, professional contacts, and how much does she have? Does she have a full address book? Can she climb the ladder using privileges? Or should it rely only on its merit and the whims of its superiors?

In the same way, one will speak of sexual value to designate the power of seduction of a person relative to its social value. Social value is a changing notion. It is essentially composed of unsaid, and it allows all possible interpretations according to interlocutors. A person in search of power will, therefore, be able to divert these interpretations in his favor.

People base their perception of your social value on the interactions they have with you. In the same way, you perceive your value through your relationships with yourself; that is, your self-esteem. Therefore, we are dealing with a perceived phenomenon that depends on the subjectivity of the one who perceives it.

This is a social illusion. This is the crown you use to shine in society, your behavior, your conversation and your appearance. Depending on your social skills, your perceived social value will grow or diminish you in relation to your true worth.

Your real social value is all of your attributes that are visible to all, and that can't be questioned. These are your social skills (intellectual, athletic, artistic), your income, your physical appearance.

To try to see more clearly, we propose in this book some of the best solution on how to improve your social skills. You will be able to identify those that are most relevant to your personal and professional life. We will then give you some practical approach to improve your social skills.

Even if you do not work in customer service, sales or HR, relationship skills are an indispensable professional tool. Whether you are collaborating on a project with a coworker who is insecure or linking your company with important external agents, or in a relationship you need trust, empathy and communication to make the most of each personal and professional interaction. By doing this, you will gain support while demonstrating to your superiors that you are able to bring out the best in others. All of these are key aspects of social and career advancement.

Do you know how to get along with a colleague or in a relationship? How to hide your annoying voice when you disagree with one of your colleagues or friends; how to show a colleague or friend who is facing a stressful moment that you are there to support him? If you answered "yes" to all these questions, then congratulations: you are a person with excellent social skills. If, however, like, most of the questions, then this book may be useful for improving your social skills.

Importance of Social Skill

Social skills are underrated. To function effectively in society, you need this skill to interact. Unfortunately, despite its importance, we seem to be losing the ability to socialize instead of learning how to improve it. Kids, especially, have become too addicted to their digital devices and spend more time staring at their screens when what they should be doing instead of trying to make meaningful connections with other people. To speak more, interact more, communicate more in person rather than from behind the keyboard. This trend is extremely worrying and several studies conducted on this subject support the dangers of addiction to social media and digital devices.

In 2017, one study found that more than half a million students from the 8th through to 12th grade were showing high levels of symptoms linked to depression. Between 2010 and 2015 alone, depression and the symptoms associated with it grew by 33%. Suicide rates among girls within that age ranged surveyed around the same period increased by as much as 65%.

The University of Arizona released a study that claimed those who had difficulties and found social situations challenging were at greater risk of developing physical and mental health problems. A lack of social skills was the reason for greater stress and feelings of loneliness, both of which had a negative impact on a person's health and state of mind. Researchers in the study reinforced that it has been known for a long time now that depression and anxiety have links to poor social and communication skills.

Developing the necessary social skills needed is no longer just an option. It is a necessity. To be a part of most social groups, you need this skill. As addictive as your digital devices and the world of social media is, you still need to belong to a social group if you hope to minimize loneliness and isolation. Having great social skills can significantly work to your advantage. When you've got great social skills, you'll be able to:

- Build a support network of people you can trust and talk to when times are hard.
- Form meaningful and lasting relationships.
- Easily relate to others from all sorts of diverse cultural backgrounds and walks of life.
- Easily assimilate in any social setting.
- Enhance empathy and understanding for others.
- Inadvertently develop great communication skills in the process.
- Communicate your thoughts, ideas, and opinions and be easily understood by others.
- Empathize better with others.
- Encourage open-mindedness and seeing things from another person's perspective.
- Improve your mental and emotional wellbeing. Feeling accepted by a group and having that sense of belonging can lead to increased feelings of happiness.

From a professional standpoint, the advantage of having social skills can lead to the following outcomes:

- Improve your reputation and career in the workplace. When you can keep a conversation flowing smoothly, keep your listeners engaged and actively listen to them in return, your coworkers, clients, and supervisors will take notice.
- It contributes to the success of a business deal. A pleasant conversation and ability to get along well with your clients can work in your favor and make you more convincing.
- It helps you maintain positive and amicable relationships with your co-workers. You are going to spend most of your day working together with them, and without the proper communication skills on hand, it can be difficult to build and construct productive relationships with the ones you Social skills lend to a strong social presence, and it the career world where connections and networking matter, being able to socialize is an invaluable resource.
- It makes it easier to build teams that are productive and cohesive, which promotes cultural diversity. Today's workplace is a melting pot of diverse cultures and languages. For everyone to be able to mesh well together and work in harmony, it is important to have good social skills handy.

Self-Awareness

Develop an awareness. It can become very easy to ignore what your own thoughts are telling you. When you work on overcoming your oblivious tendencies, your thoughts can actually teach you a lot about why you might be so critical with yourself. Fear of failure usually goes hand-in-hand with a harsh inner critic. By becoming aware of what fuels you, this is your way of taking back the power. Acknowledge why you are the way you are, and work on accepting this as a fact. You do not need to try so hard to change yourself into someone that you think others want to see. Learn to accept your qualities for what they are, and think about what you most admire or love about yourself.

Emotion Management

Most of the times, there are qualities that you may seem to hate in a person. These characteristics are mostly their ill behavior. Consequently, in our daily lives, people experience bad moods and attitude. These aspects are mainly facilitated when one is wronged, or unexpected events or experiences occur. Such situations prompt victims to show negative emotions.

These emotions are hurtful to people you relate. For example, a wife may suffer from the anger and insults of the husband. These negative behaviors are the vices in the society as they result in adverse effects. Such effects may lead to committing of murder, domestic violence, and many other illicit actions. It is, therefore, upon you to control the wrong emotions so that you cannot find yourself on the wrong side. If one has to learn how to manage them, one has to know the following causes as listed below.

Societal background and teachings are some of the causes. The highest percentage of what one believes is influenced by the parents or society as a whole. Some of the vices are even inherited from guardians. They say that 'like father like son' therefore if your mentor possesses an unpleasant attitude, you are likely to inherit that emotion. Sometimes the societal teaching shapes one in whom they are.

Experiences of depraved events and situations may make one adopt negative emotions. If particular persons wronged you in the past, you would be angry with them at all cost. Whenever you pass through a painful episode, it leaves you a negative stigma engrossed with awful feelings. Therefore this results to you to blame others for your misfortunes and to be pessimistic on a particular subject.

Comparing yourself to others makes one angrier if the other colleague is better in some ways. People have to understand that people are gifted differently. Therefore, do not compare yourselves with others. In this case, you will underestimate your abilities and believe for others are perfect. That is the genesis of low self-esteem. Think of how low self-esteem persons behave because they usually are angry, envious spiteful, fearful, and hateful.

Putting your desires, in front of others, causes a negative attitude. That is where you feel you have to compete with other fellows, and you adopt a jealous approach if they succeed. You are always gluttonous in wanting to have everything at your disposal. You feel rage when others do not treat you as expected. You still want to show some pride so that others can recognize you.

First, you ought to identify the negative emotion that you possess. It may be that others say you are greedy, temperate, or pride. In particular areas, there are attitudes where only your colleagues can tell you. Do not be afraid to ask even your close friends what they sometimes hate in you. You may be thinking things are going well, whereas some of your behaviors are unpleasant. Reflect on a time you caused some chaos, what did you participate in that disputes. When you know the terrible attitude you have, you can reflect on how to change it.

You can meditate on the effect of that emotion. There may be a time when you were fully raged, and you assaulted someone. Therefore the relationship with that person broke. Or you lost your best friends because you were proud to focus on your interests than theirs. When you realize the terrible impact of that behavior, you will brainstorm on the best ways to change. Always choose to reconcile with the colleague you wronged and inquire how they expect you to behave next time.

Deliberate on the source of that attitude or disdainful character. You cannot fight something which you do not know where it originated. It is always right to think about the cause of the vice critically. You may be surprised to realize that the reason is something you never expected. Take an example of a person who is arrogant because he is the number one swimmer. Hey, there is no wrong of being a number one swimmer; however, overstating your success is wrong. Therefore, for that scenario, you have to be calm and appreciate your challenges.

By reading or sharing your resentments with other people helps one to manage a particular ordeal. You may think that you are the only one who has a personality disorder but also others do. Make a point of sharing with others on how they resolved their evil characters. You may be surprised to know that what you are passing through is less than what they are experiencing. Read journals or browse on the internet to understand how to cope with such a situation. Allow your close friends or relatives to correct your actions. In the process, they will advise on the best way to manage the emotion.

Improving your feelings is another way to mitigate unwarranted attitudes. It is not a matter of how to eliminate your distress, but a matter of how you can improve the ill emotions accordingly. For example, one may be suffering from fear and anxiety, but you can manage them. If you are shy in public address, then practice talking to a small group, and with the time you will improve in this area. Engage other friends or psychologists who can recommend you better ways to improve your behavior.

Control your attitude effectively. After learning your mood and knowing that effect, this is the best point to learn how to control. If one is temperamental, you have to learn how to cool yourself on every occasion. If possible, set the control techniques and write them down. You can even tell a person to alarm you when you have that emotion. With time you will monitor yourself and try to regulate a situation once you feel the behavior is approaching. You will develop this habit, and with time, it will end.

Look for the right company. If you stay around people, who has a negative emotion as there is no way you are going to change. However, if you hang around with mentors and emotional intelligent guys, you will absorb their character. Soon that unwanted attitude will come to an end. Through this socialization, one can inquire their approval on every action you take. If they are satisfied, know that you are in the right progress.

Stress Management

Mange your stress level. Trying to have a successful social encounter without proper stress management is just a recipe for disaster. Stress can seriously compromise your ability to converse and communicate effectively. In a state of stress, you increase your chances of misunderstanding and misreading other people's signals and vice versa. Emotions are dangerously contagious, and the way you behave and act can adversely affect the people around you.

When you're upset, you run the risk of upsetting other people. In angry, your words and actions could anger others in turn. The best thing to do in this situation is to take a break if you're feeling overwhelmed by stress. Step away from the stressful situation or conversation and come back only when you're ready and you've regained your composure.

Effective Communication

Struggling to communicate and make ourselves understood clearly enough is something many of us are all too familiar with. That's the reason it's called a "skill." If it was easy, we would all be conversationalists and social experts. Struggle to communicate the message clearly can be a real challenge, especially when you need this skill to pitch a new project at work, lock in a new client or even land yourself the job you've been eyeing at an interview.

Effective communication, like social skills, needs to be perfected through practice. Aside from your regular social interactions, another aspect of your life where social skills and effective communication are vital would be at work. A lot is going on in a professional setting. People rushing back and forth trying to get things done, deadlines that need to be met, meetings to attend, trying to work together, delegate tasks and make sure everything gets done on time before the day's end is hectic. This environment dynamic can make communication a real challenge. Even harder to keep your messages simple and concise.

Sometimes you only have a few precious minutes to get your point across, to hold someone's attention long enough to make an impact. Nobody has the time to spare and they're not interested in wasting too much time trying to decipher what you're trying to say. In a world where there is so much distraction, noise, and clutter, keeping your conversation as simple as possible is often the most effective approach to take.

Two major hurdles that must be overcome to achieve effective communication. The first is keeping your messages as succinct as possible to avoid any room for error. The second is overcoming social anxiety. Let's get to work tackling the first hurdle.

Keeping It Concise

This is going to be your best chance of keeping the attention of your audience long enough to be effective. Being understood is necessary for social interaction to be deemed successful. Especially if you find yourself in a leadership position. A leader must know how to simplify their messages because this gives them the best chance of being understood by the most (if not all) their people.

No leader can be deemed effective in his or her leadership if no one can comprehend what you're trying to say or what you want them to do. We live in a fast-paced world, and people these days have even less time than ever to spare. You only have a few precious minutes these days to make a positive social impression. Even less to communicate face to face when you're not rushing from one task to another. Keep the language simple, keep your message concise and get straight to the point. Stick to simplicity with the following techniques:

- Say It with Clarity - Speak at a moderate pace and enunciate your words. Avoid rushing and run the risk of having your words run together too much that the listeners have a hard time picking up what you're trying to say. Avoid using slang or jargon too, as not everyone may understand some of the terms you use. This one is especially prudent to be mindful of when it comes to pitching a deal with a client. Often, the client is going to make their decisions based on how well they can understand you. That is what persuades them at the end of the day.

- Communicate Like Equals - Communicate with others like they are your equals. Avoid speaking to anyone like they are beneath you. You don't have to talk to them like they are above you, either. Instead, aim to speak to them like you are talking to an equal. Before you attempt to even communicate, consider the audiences that you're going to be dealing with. What language resonates best with them? What will they respond to and connect with the most?

- Straight to the Heart of It - Having little time to spare means there's no time to beat around the bush. All great communicators have mastered one crucial skill - they know how important it is to get to the point quickly. Even if you have a lot you would like to say, trim it down to only the essentials. When you get straight to the point, you hold your audiences' attention much better, and your message gets absorbed far more effectively. The key to keeping it short is to learn how to summarize your main points, and then just stick to the main points only.

- Repeat and Reinforce - Repeating the main points of your message several times to reinforce the message and let it properly sink it. Not everyone processes information at the same right. Some people might need reinforcement and repetition several times before they finally get it. If you keep your messages short, this is much easier to do.

- Use Fewer Words - To make repetition and reinforcement easier, simply use fewer words. Fewer words, but choose the right kind of words. When you say less, you cut down the amount of time that you use, which then leaves more free time for your recipient to ask any questions that they need to clarify your points. It helps if you write down what you're going to say before you say it. When you write it down, you can see every sentence structure and make a note of which sentences you think are far too long. Where can words be minimized? Or paraphrased better so that it can be said in 3 words instead of 5?

Effective Relationships

A romance that lasts through the ages is not built overnight. It's a long road and a slow and steady process. The true test of whether a relationship is built to last is how well you talk to each other and work through the bumps and hard knocks that your relationship experiences.

Couples who have learned that being in a happy, healthy relationship is possible are the same couples who realized that effective communication skills are the key to deepening their bond and connection to each other.

Couples who have been married for years use several communication skills to successfully understand each other and they never stop using these skills as long as they are together.

Communicate is essential to the success of a relationship because you can't avoid problems the same way you try to avoid your unhappy emotions. You can't wish it will go away or pretend that it doesn't exist. Not communicating or addressing the issues you face in a relationship is a recipe for disaster and it won't be long before the relationship falls apart. The more you ignore your problems, the harder they will be to fix. In a scenario where your partner may want to talk about and address these issues but you don't, it can cause a lot of frustration, tension, and resentment over time.

Healthy Communication Habits to Practice

The happiest couples didn't magically become that way. They worked hard to get their relationship to where it is at, and they did it by engaging in healthy habits that helped to improve the way they communicate with each other. These healthy habits include:

- Expressing Appreciation - Even for the little things and especially for the things we so often take for granted. Happy couples constantly express their appreciation and gratitude towards their partner. When your partner or spouse makes you a cup of coffee in the morning without asking, thank them. When they hold the door open for you, thank them. Gestures that show your appreciation don't have to be elaborate either. Little thank-you notes or text messages throughout the day can make a big difference.

- Never Assume - Happy couples ask for what they want. They express their needs or desires and that's a healthy communication habit every couple should adopt. Instead of assuming your partner is going to pick up on the little hints or read your mind and know how to anticipate your thoughts, why not save everyone the frustration of miscommunication by asking. Assumptions are where a lot of communication breakdown tends to happen, which then escalates into fights that could have been avoided. If you want your partner to do something, don't be afraid to just ask for it.

- Work It Together - Household chores should be a shared responsibility when you live together so one person doesn't feel the burden of having to upkeep the house by themselves. Dividing the workload promotes great teamwork and a sense of happiness knowing that you can count on your partner to share in the workload with you. Rotate the chores amongst yourselves, so there's a sense of fairness and balance, and one person is not stuck doing the same thing all the time.

- Positive Language - Happy couples have learned to talk things through, especially during the stages of the relationship where one or both people may be going through a hard time. Learning to talk about the difficult things can be much easier if both you and your partner adopt the approach to only use positive language during the conversation. It minimizes the chances of things escalating and getting out of hand. Phrases such as "I hear what you're saying and I value what you have to say" or "I know this is difficult to talk about, but I'm here to support you and we can work through this together" are examples of some great positive language that can be used to help control the conversation and steer it in the right direction.

- No Judgment - Each time that you judge your partner, you make them feel embarrassed, insecure, perhaps even anxious and tense. When they experience this form of rejection from you, to protect themselves, they will close themselves off to you because they don't feel secure enough to open-up freely and be themselves. Judgment erodes intimacy, and if you wouldn't do it in any other social encounter, don't do it to your partner.

Empathy

Simply put, empathy is the ability to stand in someone else's shoes. When you have empathy for a certain situation, you can imagine if it were happening to you. This is an emotionally important skill to have because it allows you to help those around you. When your friends or loved ones come to you for advice, you will be able to consider their experience and understand what they are going through. Empathy brings people closer together; it connects you without having much to be said. As you work on improving your social skills, empathy is definitely one to prioritize.

There are different types of empathy to consider. Some come from natural feelings that you already have, while others are triggered because of the other person saying or doing something. It is fascinating to take a closer look at what allows for this understanding. By doing so, you can actually learn a lot about yourself. The following are some of the most common forms of empathy that you will experience:

- Affective: This type of empathy revolves around the idea that you can understand someone because you can understand their emotions. For example, if your friend is going through a breakup and starts crying because she misses her ex-partner, you will likely be able to identify with this emotion. When you have this type of understanding, you are able to approach the situation from a place of concern or care.

What you must be careful of is that you cannot get too emotionally involved in the other person's situation. This might eventually lead you to develop feelings of personal distress because you are able to relate so easily. When we go through things in life, it becomes easier to emotionally identify with others who are experiencing the same things that we have experienced. A careful balance is necessary in order to ensure that you are helping the other person, without hurting yourself in the process.

- Cognitive: This type of empathy is felt mentally, but not emotionally. It is the ability to allow yourself to think the way that this person is thinking without placing yourself into their emotional state of being. While it is still a form of empathy, it is more removed than affective empathy because you are simply staying on the outside of the situation.

This can be a great starting point in practicing your empathic skills. When you can listen to someone express a problem and still come up with a few solutions based on the way that they are thinking, it is a skill to be proud of. You will also be more protected because you aren't emotionally involved. Be careful that you do not come across as cold when you express cognitive empathy. Your behavior will be misunderstood if you do not incorporate some warmth in your language or your attitude.

- Somatic: This is a unique form of empathy because it is physical. This happens when you can identify with someone so strongly that your body has some kind of physical reaction. This can be in the form of a stomachache, for example. If you have ever heard about some bad news, it is likely that you felt it in the pit of your stomach. This is a somatic reaction. It doesn't always have to be a negative response. You can also feel happiness physically. Somatic empathy is a very strong form of empathy that is a great skill to have.

Out of all three forms, this one can become the most bothersome if you allow yourself to feel too much negativity at once. Feelings of sadness, fear, and embarrassment have the ability to weigh you down, even if they are not directly related to you. Know that there is nothing wrong with you or with the way that you function; you are simply in tune with your empathetic side when you can experience these feelings physically.

Whether you have felt all of these or none at all, there is room for you to improve your skills. When you are able to display empathy, you will become a better listener. No matter what type of conversation you are having, you should always be aiming to use your active listening skills. This becomes a lot easier when combined with empathy because you will be able to listen and form your own opinions a lot more quickly. Based on the information that is given to you and your perception of what should be done, your suggestions will be full of valuable advice.

Creative Thinking

Rather than talking and sharing their emotions with someone, most people with inner turmoil opt for being creative. It can be anything like making paintings, creating artifacts, writing a good poem, etc. All these creative activities help a person with a turbulent mental state to feel better and relaxed. It acts as a catharsis for them.

Critical Thinking

When you listen actively, you are being mindful of what is truly being expressed. While it is not always necessary to have a response to what the other person is telling you, active listening engages your brain differently. Instead of jumping to conclusions or feeling that you have to agree with an opinion being stated, work on simply absorbing what is being said. Pay attention to the words being spoken as well as nonverbal communication. Watch the person's stance, eyes, and expression. These cues can tell you a lot about how the topic truly makes them feel. For things that are especially difficult to express, the words themselves might not fully represent the feelings.

An example of this is when you know that a friend is having a hard time, yet they tell you that they are fine. The words that they say might reflect this sentiment, but you might notice that they are teary-eyed and shifty due to the weight of what they are going through. Being an active listener will allow you to be there for your friend if they want your support. By truly paying attention to the cues that are being given, a promise of support can be enough to turn their whole day around. Compared to a passive listening situation, you might have missed these cues and continued on like nothing was wrong. This could have potentially led your friend to believe that you do not care.

When there is a problem that needs to be solved, an active listener will find a way to chime in and offer a solution. By paying attention to the details that are being expressed, you will find it easy to come up with ideas on how to solve the given problem. Many people are under the misconception that they do not know how to talk to others when in reality, it is the listening that you must improve on. You will find that talking points become easier when you are actively listening because there are already ideas for you to consider. Being included in conversations this way can do a lot to boost your confidence. The more you are able to participate, the more comfortable you will become with your listening and speaking skills.

When you practice active listening, you are able to stay in peak mental shape. Because your brain is fully engaged in the conversation that you are having, you ensure that you exercise your critical thinking skills and your empathy. This doesn't happen with passive listening because the standards are different. By staying aware and on top of the conversation, you are becoming a part of a high-engagement experience that will allow you to grow as a person.

The next time that you talk to someone, make sure that your active listening skills are engaged. You will probably find that you can identify with the person much more easily, as well as know what you need to say to them. This also puts you in the position to consider new thoughts and ideas. When you listen to other viewpoints, you can often find inspiration that you might want to explore in the future. Overall, there are countless benefits that you will experience as an active listener. Even if you find that you mostly listen in a passive state right now, there are ways that you can transform your skills.

When someone is speaking to you, enter each conversation as though they have something valuable to teach you. Listen intently to what they are saying without passing any prior judgment or suggestions. Allow them to fully express their thoughts before chiming in with your own. If a solution is being sought, do your best to take the words that you were given with all of the non-verbal cues to come up with a response that is both empathetic and understanding. Once you master this, active listening will become second nature to you.

To Make Decisions

Be kind to yourself when bad things happen. Praise yourself when good things happen. Use this method to help yourself make decisions, both big and small. Pretend you are giving advice to a loved one. What would you tell that loved one to do in a stressful time? Tell yourself these words. Love yourself.

Remember that you are you and you are wonderful. When we ignore our own personal dreams and desires, we tell ourselves that we are unworthy. We unwittingly cause ourselves pain by ignoring what we really want to be and try to shove ourselves into someone else's idea of perfection. There is only one you. There is no reason to ever want to be anyone else, just try to be the best you possible. Being true to yourself is a powerful thing, and it comes with the added benefit of helping you to greatly improve your relationship with you.

Never feel bad about feeling bad. So many people bottle up their emotions or pretend not to feel anything so they avoid offending other people or hurting other people's feelings. But why are the feelings of others more important than yours? Why would you swallow your anger or pain just so someone else does not feel the same anger or pain? This is not to say we should deliberately make other people angry or sad just to make ourselves feel better. The key is to be honest with ourselves and our emotions. And remember that everyone is responsible for their own emotions and feelings. If you tell someone you are angry and it makes them angry, then that is their issue to deal with. You are not responsible for the way others react to your emotions. And never try to suppress your feelings forever. We all feel anger, pain, and depression. Feelings are normal. Embrace them as a part of yourself. Feel them profoundly. Wallow in them if you feel like doing so. Feelings will soon fade away as long as you do not resort to negative feelings about your emotions and cause them to be blown up in your mind.

You must tell yourself how wonderful you are and how happy you are to have yourself. It may seem silly at first, but it is necessary to know how to show yourself some gratitude. Focus on the great things you personally have to offer. When we pay attention to something, we automatically focus more energy on that thing. So, if we focus more on what is right with us, then we will spend more energy making ourselves better. But remember to spend the bulk of your time working on the inner you, not the outer you. Your outside appearance is nothing more than the shell your soul rides around in. Love your body and put your mind and soul on a pedestal.

And never forget that you are human. We are all human on this earth. We will never be perfect, any of us. We should strive to be our best, but that is all we can hope for. We have flaws and we make mistakes. And we should never be harder on ourselves than we are on other people. If your neighbor has a flaw that you forgive, then remember to forgive that flaw in yourself. We all have our little insecurities and we all feel vulnerable at one time or another. It is part of being human. Accept it, embrace it, and learn from it.

Solve Problems

So many of us are hesitant, even loathe asking for help when it comes to feelings and emotions. Confidence *is* a feeling— and at first, when you are just learning to become more charismatic, it may be as easy to lose confidence, as it is to gain it. Again, there should be no shame in this. Shame is a useless emotion and will only hold you back. By reaching out for help, you are showing, *proving,* that you are a strong person who knows when they need some assistance. Strong people solve problems—weaker people ignore their problems because of their egos or their pride.

When your confidence is flagging, reach out to a trusted friend for help. Studies show that people who receive a boost from friends or peers enjoy long-term healing effects from such a connection, which in turn boosts their overall confidence. Conversely, you can be their lifeline when your friend needs help with their own confidence.

Chapter 4.   Social Skill Management

Why Social Skills Matter in Everyday Life

Excellent social skills allow you to present your best self to those around you. They can provide you with the confidence to succeed in all situations, and the ability to get to know the people you would like to become close to. From being able to identify your strengths to knowing exactly how to carry on a conversation, your social skills will provide you with deeper social connections. No matter who you are talking to, it is a considerable boost in confidence to be able to converse, socialize, and generally get to know another person. This connectivity is what makes you feel secure in yourself and your interactions.

While socialization is profound and essential, it can be difficult for some. Working up the courage to talk to another person can often be intimidating, especially when you are unsure of yourself. Many people struggle with their social skills, wishing that they were better at the skills that come naturally to some. With practice, the techniques in this guide are meant to build you up so that you feel comfortable and confident about socializing, no matter where you are or where you go. From working on your body language to discovering how to talk to new people, you will obtain a renewed sense of confidence in yourself.

Starting at the very beginning, you will learn about the skills that you already possess. By harnessing your strengths, your weaknesses will be easier to overcome. Instead of feeling ashamed that you have weaknesses, you will learn how to transform them into traits that will make socialization easier. If shyness is a burden in your life, you will learn how to combat it in ways that still allow you to feel comfortable while also appearing more extroverted. With a simple boost to your charisma from growing your self-esteem, you will feel capable enough to handle any social interaction that comes your way.

One of the hardest parts about socialization comes when you interact with new people. Because they are new to your life, you usually do not have any sense of comfort or familiarity to rely on. By learning how to confidently begin conversations and find commonalities with others, you will see that building connections with new people is possible. No matter how difficult it feels in the beginning, socialization is always something that becomes easier the more you do it.

The current relationships that you hold in your life are essential, too. Once you have become acquainted with someone, you must make sure that you maintain this connection by putting in the effort to socialize with them. This guide will teach you how to do this by providing you with tips and tricks that you can utilize in various social settings. By the time you have adopted these new habits, you will be able to talk to anyone, anywhere; and you will no longer be hindered by your doubts or worries about socialization. The skills that you gain will stay with you for life, a permanent reminder that it is possible for you to socialize successfully.

Acquiring Social Skills

It can be difficult, even daunting, to take that first step towards socials skills mastery. There is no need to jump in feet first or tackle anything major right away. Ease yourself into being more charismatic by trying some of these techniques and tricks:

- Use music to boost your morale. If you are nervous before a social event, use classical, jazz or even chilled-out classic rock to settle your anxiety and put yourself in a calm, collected, positive mood. If you are feeling less-than-pumped, put on tunes that elevate your emotions and put your thoughts in a more positive frame. If you are feeling down on yourself, use inspiration tracks to remember that you can do whatever you set your mind out to do. Play a favorite DJ mix to move you from hermit-mode to life-of-the-party winner.
- Leave your comfort zone occasionally by trying something new. Volunteering is a fantastic way to

improve your social skills, learn new things, and practice what you've learned in a zero-pressure environment—plus, you'll good about doing something positive for the community. Take a class in something you have always wanted to learn, and take time to talk with other people in the class when you can. Go to events at your local library, another opportunity for pressure-free socializing.

- Exercise your initiative muscle by making plans, and sticking to them. Following through builds self-esteem because we learn we can count on ourselves. It also builds confidence because following through banishes fear. We begin to believe that what we say we will do, we will do—and that is a huge charisma boost.

- Tap into meditation. Try guided meditative exercises—where someone vocally guides you through the steps, a few minutes each day to cultivate a place of inner calm. Once the meditation becomes familiar, you will find you can reach that calm place in the snap of a finger—essential when finding yourself in unexpected, awkward social situations.

- Get some exercise. Even walking at a comfortable pace for 20 minutes a day can help balance the mood of your mind: your body needs those good-feeling chemicals to function properly, and so does your brain. A constant influx of happiness hormones can banish a lot of anxiety and fear about social settings. In addition, you will begin to feel better about your body, which will translate into your body language, instantly boosting your charisma levels.

- Make a goal to face one of your fears. This is a tough one, but the rewards are huge. Think of the good you feel the last time you achieved something. Facing one of your fears will teach you that you have what it takes to rise to a challenge, or overcome an obstacle. Both your conscious and subconscious mind will carry that lesson for the rest of your life. Additionally, you will foster empathy towards people who either have faced their fears or are still struggling with doing so. This one is a tough task but it is worth it tenfold.

- Tap into inner creativity. The mind does not enjoy being idle. Sometimes, instead of feeding the brain with media, news, other people's opinions, we have to put something out into the world that is made of us. Creating something is a terrific exercise to gather your mind's skills into one unified focus. It does not have to be gallery-worthy or be able to sail across the Atlantic. Take some "me" time and work on something creative, just for what it does for your confidence and inner child.

- Redesign your environment. Look at your living space. Is it dark and cluttered a place you just return to in order to crash after a long day? Now take a weekend and transform that pad into somewhere that inspires you. How would a successful, happy person keep their living space? Bring in light, tidy up, set up a workout area or meditation spot. This space is your sanctuary, where you come home to build yourself back up. Act as if you are already successful, and soon you will be.

- Use visualization every day. Before a meeting, interview, social event, date—whatever the occasion, visualize it and imagine positive results. Professional dancers must see the moves they have not yet learned in their head before they can even begin to teach their bodies to master them. It is an important trait of successful people—learn to visualize the best outcome, and you will up your odds of achieving great results.

- Practice moving your body in a confident way. Even when you're alone, or don't have a need to be "on," do it anyway! Muscle memory is a fantastic tool and essential when it comes to changing your body language. Always focus on your posture, and practice developing a relaxed, confident poise.

- "Now" is the utmost crucial time of all. It's a good practice to look back at the past and recall positive memories, and it's important to imagine a positive future, but oftentimes we can get lost in switching back and forth from past to future while completely ignoring the present. Living in the present forces us to be the best we can be right now. Being mindful of what is happening now can greatly improve your poise, confidence, and charisma.

- Keep your focus outward. When out among other people, focus on them. This will bounce back in your favor as they, in turn, focus on you. Introspection in a crowd projects awkwardness, as well as any negative emotions you might have tucked away, deep inside. So keep your mind out of itself and focused on the rest of the world. There is a lot to see, and you will be interacting, learning, and growing while you do so.

- Stick with positive people. Learn to choose whom you spend your time amongst. Positivity is contagious, but so is negativity. If you form connections to people who have a positive outlook, you will soon learn to look at life positively by proxy.

- Curate the "newsfeed" of your daily social media. Learn when to avoid negativity and bad news. Too much can wear on us like pollution or negative emotions. It is important to know what is going on in the world, but the human mind is so malleable, so impressionable, that you risk triggering anxiety or depression if you expose yourself to too much negative news.

- Resist the urge to compare yourself to other people. You are you, and there is nobody else like you. The only person you should ever compare yourself to be who you were a year, five years, ten years ago—how have you grown? How have you improved, and what areas do you need to work on? What have you accomplished, big or small, and how can you focus on making yourself feel good about that?

How to Improve Your Social Skills

Here are some highly useful tricks and exercises you can try in your free time to help you get closer to your goal of achieving greater charisma.

While a total shift of attitude: from negative to positive, unsure to confident, greedy to grateful, out of focus to present takes time and a steady amount of determination and energy, exercises can help you fine-tune and hone your skills to really shine when you need to the most.

1. Exercise to Build Rapport

Humans are largely emotion-driven beings. Very few of us use logic to guide us. When conveying charisma and confidence, you will not be successful unless people trust you. This is the essence of rapport.

Does this exercise with someone don't yet know? This may seem daunting, even scary, but they will not know it is an exercise—only you will. What is even better is that you are going to do the exercise in a low-pressure environment, such as the grocery store. This is going to take you to task regarding building instant rapport. If it does not work out the first time, try it again!

The meaning of genuine connection is hard to put into words, but it is the same way we instantly know if something is inappropriate or even obscene—it is an instinctive, almost primal reaction. When you experience a genuine connection with someone, these are a few of the signs you will be looking for:

- a sudden, genuine smile or laughter that is mirrored in the eyes
- the sharing of a personal fact, feeling, or story
- the other person letting their guard down

When you are caught in a moment with someone else—and by caught I mean you are both in the same moment by coincidence, and cannot leave that moment, such as in a checkout line at a store, in an elevator, waiting at an airport gate, or on public transport—try to make brief conversation with them. This is much easier with someone who is the employee in a situation where you are the customer, of course. You can ask them how their shift is going, how life is treating them, or what they think of a product you are buying.

In a situation such as an elevator, choosing a non-invasive question or topic is important, especially if you are male and the only other person is a woman. For the purpose of this exercise in those situations, it is best to wait for another opportunity, as women are frequently on their guard around men they do not know, for obvious reasons. We do not want to make someone afraid or uncomfortable for the sake of an exercise.

However, if the person you're with is obviously happy (if they're smiling, for instance) you can ask them, "What's your secret to being in a great mood?" Make sure you are smiling as well so that you are not accidentally misunderstood as being sarcastic.

Look for some component of their answer that will help you create a conversation. Say for instance they answer, "I just like to be cheerful. My mom raised me to always look on the bright side," you can say, "That is a good way to look at life. Where were you raised?"

They might answer with "Maine. I'm going back home to visit in a month, I can't wait!"

When someone shares something personal such as this, then you know you have scored a win in the rapport exercise.

2. Exercises to Instantly Reduce Stress

Why do I need to reduce stress, in the middle of a book about improving my charisma? You might ask. The reasoning behind this is that we all carry stress, visibly, in our bodies, in our faces, and in our eyes. Other people can sense it from a mile away, and while happiness is contagious, so is anxiety and stress. We might not even realize we are holding on to stress, it is just that natural. However, if we learn instant tricks to let it go, we can shift that stress right out of our bodies before walking through a door to a party, date, meeting, or interview.

The breath in calm, breathe out stress technique: Breathe is extraordinarily powerful. We need it to live and we breathe thousands of times a day without focusing on it or controlling it. When we choose to control it, however, breathe can be an effective tool to use in calming the mind and relaxing the body. Think about when you are at the doctor's for a simple checkup and she asks you to breathe so she can listen to your heartbeat. Unless we are feeling ill or out of sorts, this moment almost instantly calms us down, right?

In the cab, your car, the elevator, the lobby of the building—anywhere that you can do a series of slow, deep breaths without someone giving you the side-eye—breathe in through your nose, deeply. You will know you have taken in enough breathe when your stomach pushes out, and always remember to keep your shoulders still. Healthy, natural breathing has everything to do with your diaphragm and nothing to do with your shoulders.

Hold the breath for half a second. Imagine the fresh air you have just taken in surrounding and latching onto the stress in your body, then exhale through your nostrils and imagine the stress leaving your body, never to return. Do this again and feel the stress in your hands be pulled out of your body. Do it one more time, and this time imagine the stress leaving your face.

Facial exercise: Our faces can be exhausted, especially when we deal with other people all day long. Refresh your facial muscles by taking a moment in private (you can do this in front of the bathroom mirror at work or in a restaurant if you're not at home, or even in a bathroom stall), and moving your face in as many different positions as you can. It is going to look very silly when you do, but it works! Actors often do this before the director begins to shoot a scene, just to "reset" their face and deliver believable facial expressions.

3. The Instant Focal Shift

When entering a room, an instant rapport and charisma boost is to immediately shift your point of focus away from yourself and towards the others in the room. People notice when someone is giving them their full attention, and they respond positively to that. They also respond immediately to someone who seems to be distracted, disinterested, or caught up within themselves—and the response is not a good one.

This is something many of us fail to consider when we walk into a meeting or interview. We are primarily focused on a) getting there, b) finding a place to sit, and c) gathering our thoughts together. In order to make an excellent impression, you need to get your thoughts together before you enter that room. Then, when you do walk through the door, acknowledge everyone in the room with your eyes. Try a genuine smile when you make eye contact with someone. Once you've acknowledged everyone, that is when you can look for a seat—usually, someone will pull out a chair or guide you to a seat that's empty, which is a great opportunity to start things out with a "Thank you."

Focusing your attention on to other people instead of yourself has the added benefit of moving your mind away from any nervousness, insecurities, or bad habits you might have—when you stop focusing on yourself, it is easier to project confidence, rather than exude anxiety.

Improving Your Conversation Skills

This can be one of the most challenging areas for many of us to improve upon, let alone master. Speaking skill excellence often gets overlooked in schools; the naturally extroverted kids stand out and rise up, while the shyer children remain on the sidelines, never having been given a chance or a lesson on how to join their more social peers.

- Do not give up hope, however: learning good speaking skills is something anyone can accomplish, with determination and practice.
- Here are some tips regarding practicing better speaking skills:
- Do not judge yourself for being nervous; it is natural. That does not intend you have to accept it! This is where practice takes our determination to the next level. Practice speaking in front of a mirror, to the person behind the counter at the dry cleaners, to your Uber driver, anywhere you can get some practice (without delaying someone or yourself), grab it. In time, you will see your comfort level rising.
- Prepare for your audience. If you are going to be speaking to a crowd, or an important individual like a hiring manager, take some time to research them. Your words are for them, not for yourself—you can to yourself all day long at home. Discover how your audience views things, and tailor your words that viewpoint.
- If you give a speech, you have 30 seconds to hook your audience. This is also why preparation is key; do not just try to wing it. Practice before the date.

- Let yourself shine through. Your personality is the best part of public and/or social speaking, so do not hide it. Be proud of you and let your inner qualities shine.

- Ditch the "practice makes perfect" mentality. Yes, we want you to practice, practice, practice, but understand that being human involves imperfection. Do not expect perfection from yourself: expect greatness. Even the best speakers, artists, professionals have flaws and are not ashamed of them. If you stumble, just get up and keep going!

- Use humor for instant connection. Observe comedians: their stories are often based on simple, mundane aspects of everyday life. As you go through your day, take notes of moments and situations that make you chuckle, and then use these anecdotes for a clever shot of humor in a conversation.

Use Nonverbal Skills

The moment you choose to ask yourself what and how other people are feeling and thinking, you gain a chance to learn how to interact with them. This insight helps you to defuse any conflict that may appear and help guide the conversation. When it comes to responding to empathy, there is a non-verbal element added to it. When you realize that your friend is sad, and you ask them what's wrong with them, but in a cheerful way, that friend might believe that you do not actually care. If you'd decide to change your tone to one that sounds concerned and sympathetic, your friend is likely to believe that you actually care and want to know what's wrong. Like we talked about earlier in the book, your nonverbal signals and your words have to communicate together. It is important that they are in harmony.

Empathy, soon enough will become second nature to you, however, it will require a lot of work and commitment to train yourself to become aware of what another person is feeling or thinking. This can seem overwhelming when you add your very own nonverbal signals. That being said, you should not worry as nonverbal empathy is actually quite simple. Just as how body language can be whittled down to two basic signals. They are low energy and high energy.

What does it mean to be low energy and high energy?

When an individual is high energy, that person tends to be excited, loud or expressive. While someone that is low energy, tends to act relaxed, reserved or quiet.

It is imperative to note that high energy does not always correlate with being happy and low energy does not always mean an individual is sad. For instance, a lottery winner might decide to run up and down the room, shouting and whooping, or they could simply sit down, with a cheeky smile on their face. While the two responses are responses of happiness, one is low energy, while the other is high energy.

You should also note that certain people will feel low energy sometimes, while other times they feel high energy. This means when you see someone having a moment where they are excited, you should think this person is feeling high energy at the moment, rather than this person is always high energy

Empathy and Energy

While the idea behind low energy and high energy is quite simple, you might wonder how exactly it applies to empathy. If your conversation partner is high energy, it is imperative that you also try to be high energy, and if that person is low energy you should attempt to be low energy as well.

For instance, if you meet your friend over a drink and you friend has appeared to have had quite a busy day, you could notice that they are less talkative or boisterous than normal.

This translates to them feeling low energy. Conversely, you might be excited about the bar, getting to hang with your friend, the drinks and the atmosphere, basically you act excited and expressive. Your friend on the other hand could be nursing his drink, hoping you would calm down so he could have a proper conversation with you. What this basically means is that at this point your friend is low energy, while you are high energy. While you want to be outgoing and goofy, your friend would rather have a quiet drink. This causes a mismatch which makes it more difficult for the two of you to connect.

Matching Nonverbal Energy

If you decide to match the energy given off by your friend, it could make the evening to a whole lot smoother. The moment you realize that your friend has low energy, you begin to act more sedated and reserved, even if you do still feel excited. When you notice that your friend gives off a high energy, you can choose to respond by being more boisterous and expressive.

It is imperative to note that the key is to match the energy level of your partner, rather than exceed it. If your conversation partner is sedate and relaxed, you should be low energy as well. This does not mean you should be completely down in the dumps. If your conversation partner is one that is loud and boisterous, you should become high energy, but keep in mind that you do not go crazy.

Matching the energy, you are given is something that also applies to social interactions, not just to people. For example, a formal event would be one that is low energy, in other words reserved and somber, regardless of if you are feeling excited. A party in the other hand is one that is high energy, which calls for you to be more boisterous and expressive, regardless of if you feel relaxed. The very first time you find yourself in a social situation, you should take a bit of time to figure out what type of energy that situation is putting out. Once you figure that out, you should use that as a guide for your energy level.

Your energy levels are important, if you feel low energy or high energy, you should know that there is nothing wrong in expressing that, even if your conversation partner has a different energy level. That being said, it is always wiser to begin a social interaction by matching the energy level put out by your conversation partner, and then slowly move back to your energy level. Doing this enables your partner to move with you.

As you begin to monitor energy levels around you, while adjusting your own levels to match those around you, you will discover that it becomes much easier to connect with others. Additionally, you are also able to practice becoming aware of what other people are feeling and thinking. All of this feed back into how empathy is useful. When you start to master empathy, you quickly discover that by being able to comprehend empathy, you are able to understand others, reduce the number of conflicts you have, whilst building relationships that are better and deeper.

Self-Control and Self-Regulation

The bottom line here is actually pretty simple. Regardless of whether you're dealing with things from the past or things that are happening in front of you, you are always reading the situation. As the reader, you know you have a lot more control than you give yourself credit for. You read in meaning.

There is such a thing as subjective meaning. Yes, I admit that, but don't ever downplay the importance of subjective reading because things may not be as bad as you remember them. Things may not be as sad as you perceive them to be now.

Avoid the Negative Feedback loop

Given our power to read the worst into our daily activities, please understand that this really becomes almost irresistible because of negative feedback loops. We find ourselves in a situation where we end up reinforcing the very worst readings we can come up with of our daily stimuli. It doesn't have to be that way.

There is such a thing as a positive feedback loop. You can choose to flip the script. You can choose to create an upward spiral instead of a downward one. However, it is a choice.

Unfortunately, exercising that choice, knowing when to do it and how to do it requires effort and you watch repeated failures until you get good at it, but you have to do it. Otherwise, you end up with a negative feedback loop. This is how shyness becomes entrenched.

It becomes stronger and stronger because you feel that it is validated by reality. What you're really doing is you are just engaged in a negative feedback loop. You could have chosen differently. You could have flipped it around.

Here's how it normally works. You focus on your negative reading of the feedback.

For example, you see this really hot member of the opposite sex doing something seemingly directed at you. So, you give it the worst negative reading whatsoever. You interpret it as a complete and total condemnation, dismissal or rejection of who you are as a person. You feel completely unattractive, unwanted, unlovable, etc., etc.

You then feel shy because you don't want to be around other people because you feel that this is the kind of reaction you get. So, you perform badly. This can mean just running away from the social event, or this means going to and just nursing a beer, watching everybody else have a good time. Alternatively, if you at a dance club or an outdoor dance party, you're just dancing around in circles by yourself or with your narrow circle of friends.

This, unfortunately, draws more negative feedback. Well, at least you think they're negative. People will sit up and pay attention. You then interpret it the worst way again, the process repeats itself and you end up digging deeper and deeper into a negative emotional hole.

What do you think happens to your shyness in this context? It gets stronger and stronger. Basically, you're telling yourself, "This is objective proof that social settings are bad and causes me pain, makes me feel unloved, makes me feel unwanted and people can't accept me, there's something wrong with me" and on and on it goes.

There is good news here. You don't have to do it. You don't have to be stuck in that negative feedback loop.

The Importance of Empathy

Sympathy is the specialty of considering to be from someone's perspective. At the point when you have sympathy, it implies you can comprehend what an individual is feeling in a given minute, and comprehend why other individuals' activities sounded kind to them.

Sympathy encourages us to convey our thoughts such that bodes well to other people, and it causes us to comprehend others when they speak with us. It is one of the central structure squares of extraordinary social connection and, clearly, ground-breaking stuff.

Notwithstanding, how would you get sympathy? How would you comprehend what another person is feeling if that isn't occurring naturally?

To a limited degree, we are altogether intended to empathize with others usually. Our cerebrums are wired to encounter the feeling that another person is feeling. That is the reason we flinch when somebody hits their hand with a mallet, or for what purpose we're bound to giggle if another person is laughing as well.

Lamentably, just a couple of individuals have great regular empathy. Our empathic wiring exists on a continuum. A few people have extraordinary universal compassion and can get how another person is feeling just by observing them. A few people have only a little measure of universal compassion and won't see that you are irate until you start shouting. A great many people lie someplace in the middle and see how another person is feeling just part of the time.

Luckily, empathy is part ability and part training. Contingent upon your beginning level of capacity, showing signs of improvement at empathy may require pretty much work then another person - yet regardless of what your beginning stage, you can instruct yourself to be better at empathy.

Also, this area is here to show you how.

Empathy contains three lessons:

- Understanding Yourself
- Understanding Others
- Non-verbal Empathy

Understanding Yourself

Figuring out how to feel for others is crucial expertise in social collaborations. On the off chance that you comprehend what other individuals are thinking and feeling, you'll have the option to be a superior companion and have better associations.

Notwithstanding, to figure out how to understand others, you first need to figure out how to feel for yourself.

That sounds extremely sensitive inclination yet stays with me. This is significant, and inconceivably down to earth. Figuring out how to sympathize with yourself implies figuring out how to comprehend and acknowledge what you're feeling and for what reason you're feeling it.

In case you're feeling furious, you ought to have the option to remember "I feel irate" and comprehend the reasons why you feel angry. You ought to approve of feeling your feelings, and not overlook them or smother them.

On an elementary level, if something downright terrible transpired, it ought to be OK that you feel pitiful. You should authorize yourself to feel tragic. Once in a while, we get this thought we have to act cheerful consistently, or that our issues are not as significant as the issues of others, so we feel childish when we are dismal or disturbed.

In any case, that is not valid. Your issues matter, since you matter. Also, if something is occurring to hurt you or make you feel dismal, it's alright to express that bitterness and to give yourself a chance to feel that trouble. You don't need to keep that restrained.

How to Practice Empathy

You can share and recognize the emotions of other people or even a fictional character. Empathy is an emotion that is stronger than sympathy. If you can put yourself in the same situation to understand the intensity of sadness or happiness of another person, it is empathy.

For instance, you are the kind of person who can't understand the feelings of another person unless you imagine yourself in his place. You have empathy if you can put yourself in a similar situation and perceive the feelings of another individual. Unfortunately, people often confuse empathy with compassion, sympathy, or pity.

If you are feeling uncomfortable seeing someone in a distressing or depressing situation, you are feeling pity. This emotion is less engaging than compassion, sympathy, or empathy. Empathy allows you to open up your senses and let the situation affect you in a way that you feel yourself responding to the call of emotions. It is challenging to feel empathetic without facing a similar situation in your life.

Right Time to Use the Term "Empathy"

Empathy allows you to identify and understand the feelings or situations of others. For instance, you can follow the condition of a homeless family because a cyclone once demolished your house. If you can put yourself in another's situation, the word empathy is right for you. Empathy is a noun, and for the very first time, it was used in 1895. This tells us that people started becoming emotionally intelligent back then.

Right Time to Use the Term "Sympathy"

Sympathy (again a noun) was used for the very first time in the 1500s. If you have feelings of pity or grief, you are showing solidarity. For instance, you can show sympathy to a grieving mother because, even though you have not experienced this situation yourself, you have a sensitive personality that lets you feel for others. Your personality traits include feelings such as kindness, generosity, care, and compassion.

Empathy means you are identifying another person's sorrow as your own. Therefore, you will be willing to walk the extra mile to support and protect that person as if you were doing that for yourself in a similar situation. Putting yourself in someone else's shoes will not only make you feel bad about a grieving person but make you want to make some positive changes as well to improve his situation. Suppose, you are looking at your friend while he tells you his emotional experience, a painful tale of past grievances. You are analyzing his expressions and sub-textual emotions while he speaks, and you notice his eyes well up. If you are an emotionally intelligent person having a high EQ rate, you would feel for his sorrow and the extent of his grief almost instantly. Maybe you would not even have to go as far as processing each word of his narrative to reach on a conclusion that he seeks support and empathy. Just looking at his tearful eyes, you may as well feel your eyes becoming teary.

Sometimes, sympathizing and saying sorry is not enough. Sometimes, a person does not just need a shoulder to cry on, and a pat on the back as consolation that everything would be fine. Sometimes, they just want you to cry with them instead of wiping their tears. Sometimes, you just need to let the flood gates open and get rid of all the accumulated debris and emotional baggage in order to feel lighthearted.

Improving Empathy to Influence People

It's going to be hard for you to get along with and relate to the people around you if you lack empathy. Even maintaining healthy relationships with the people, you love could prove to be a struggle when you're unable to see things from another's point of view. Empathy is classified as an emotional intelligence skill for a reason. It's not easy to establish, and not everyone has it. Empathy requires you to step outside yourself. To genuine care about others and to realize that within a social context, it's not always about you all the time. Without empathy, you're at risk of being labeled selfish, egotistical, and self-centered when all you seem to care about is yourself.

How to train your empathy skills:

- Put Aside Your Point of View - At least within a social setting. That's what you need to do to become empathetic. Listen to others without enforcing your own judgment or point of view. When someone is talking to you, it's not about you, it's about them. To walk a mile in someone else's shows, you need to forget your own temporarily.

- Rise to the Challenge - Push your own boundaries and step outside your comfort zone. Mingle with people outside your regular social circle. Learn their stories, listen to their experiences and the wisdom that they have to share. Doing things, you're not comfortable with is a humbling experience. You learn so much about what you're capable of, and more importantly, you learn a lot about what other people when you actively try.

- Seek Feedback - You might get some insightful information about how you can work on improving your relationships and social skills by seeking feedback. Ask family, friends, loved ones, even colleagues about how they think you're doing. Take their comments to heart and check in with them periodically.

- Visualize - When someone tells you what they're going through, try to visualize what it would feel like if you were the one going through it. How would you feel if the roles were reversed? Would you react in the same way they did? Listen not just with your ears, but your eyes, heart, instincts, and all the senses you can engage in. Attempt to mirror their expressions and visualize what it would be like if their situation was happening to you instead.

- Keep Biases at Bay - We all have them. Biases are often focused around age, race, and gender. If you were an interviewer who prefers hiring women over men, that's a bias. If you prefer dealing with male salespeople, that's a bias. We all have them and they sometimes affect our ability to empathize. Keep your biases and bay and learn to listen with an open mind.

Learning to Trust

Trust is crucial for successful social interactions. When you don't trust the people around you, it makes it hard to let your guard down and interact successfully. All healthy relationships are built on a foundation of trust. This includes your relationship with yourself. Learn to trust what you say and do and you'll find it easier to navigate your social encounters with less anxiety. The mistakes we've made in our past can shake our belief in ourselves. We're sometimes hard on ourselves because we're afraid of repeating those mistakes. You struggle to trust your own judgment when you constantly live in fear of history repeating itself.

How to Increase Your Charisma

Boosting your charisma to become memorable public speakers and excellent storytellers. Charm and charisma are two traits that make you instantly more likable, even among people you just met. This is a major advantage to have, particularly in the career world where networking and forging new connections is very important.

Charismatic people draw other people towards them effortlessly, because they are so pleasant, charming and possess that magnetic aura that attracts others towards them like magnets. When they speak in public, they command the attention of the room. The audience hangs onto their every word from start to finish, and public speaking speeches are never boring when they're conducted by a charismatically influential individual.

If you want to connect with people, you need to connect with them on an emotional level. If you observe charismatic individuals, they seem to know just how to talk to people, how to start a conversation, how to keep it going, how to steer it in the direction they want, how to command people's avid attention with the things that they say. They seem to have insane levels of courage and have no trouble addressing a large crowd.

How did they do it? How did they seem to overcome the fear and anxiety that plagues so many others when it comes to public speaking?

They do it by sharpening their social skills and combining that with charisma to produce the winning combination.

You must be able to talk to people at the most basic level, otherwise, no amount of charisma is going to help you conquer small talk since these two elements are what is needed to achieve that overall success.

Happiness, Optimism and Positivity

Every thought that is created in your brain releases chemicals. Each time you're focused on negative thoughts, it sucks any kind of positive energy your brain might have had. Negative thoughts slow your brain down, even going so far as to limit its ability to function. Ever felt so crippled by unhappy thoughts that you couldn't do anything else except focus on how unhappy you felt? In the worst-case scenario, being immersed in chronic negativity eventually leads to depression.

But, if you turned that around and started to focus on positive thoughts instead, the cortisol begins to decrease and, in its place, serotonin takes over to create a sense of overall wellbeing. This is what your brain needs to function at its optimum capacity. Being fueled by thoughts of happiness, joy, optimism, and hope.

Thinking positive helps to support the growth and development of your brain. These thoughts can generate and reinforce new synapses in the brain, particularly around the prefrontal cortex. Findings by neuroscientists have even confirmed that those who had a happier, more cheerful and optimistic disposition had higher activity happening in the prefrontal cortex.

Practical Steps to Improve Social Skill: Tips, Tactics and Strategies

To boost your social influence, you must become skilled at adapting your messages to fit the context. This means you're going to have to:

- Be Mindful of Your Words: Always be mindful of your audience and the group of people you're talking to. Your audience needs to always be at the forefront of your mind whenever you work on your communication and social skills. What language and communicative style would they respond to best? What words and vocabulary would they connect with best? What can you do to make your message resonate with them and make a lasting impression? Only use words that you're sure the other person(s) is going to understand.

- Rephrase - Rephrasing the words that you use helps to shift your focus to what matters. One example would be to use statements like "I" instead of "you." This is useful when you find yourself in an emotional situation or a conflict. When you shift the focus, it shifts the context of the message entirely. That person doesn't feel attacked or defensive, because it doesn't sound like your blaming them.

- Changing Your Tone - Change the tone of your voice when the situation calls for it. It works on the same principles as tailoring the message to fit the audience in mind. Figure out how to use the right tone of voice too. At work, the tone you use should be professional and serious. Amongst friends, it can be jovial and upbeat. It depends on what social context you find yourself in.

- Face to Face - It is always easier to communicate when it is done in person. It minimizes the chances of miscommunication happening, and it allows you to get a better read on the situation your being faced with. It also makes it easier to determine what kind of message delivery would be best. Avoid any language that sounds like it might carry an accusatory tone behind the message. Face to face communication is always preferable, especially when dealing with important matters instead of communicating over text or email. Keep it neutral, keep it professional. Most importantly, keep it to the point. If you can't talk in person however, the best thing you can do for yourself and your message delivery is to review everything that you want to convey in your message before you send it out. If you're sending out an email, read it several times before hitting the send button. If you're about to have a phone conversation, write down what it is you want to say and have those notes in front of you so you don't miss a thing.

Chapter 5.   Leadership

Becoming a leader is not just about taking on a power position and having power to your name. Becoming a leader is about learning how to lead a team to excellence so that you can achieve your goal with your team. If you want to be a truly great leader, you need to know how to lead and manage yourself, as well as lead and manage a team of people so that you can reach your mutual goals, as well as your personal goals.

For years it has been argued about what is truly necessary in order to make a great leader. With that being said, the general consensus is that there are ten primary qualities that every single truly great leader has and that these qualities are necessary for making them a great leader. These ten qualities include: vision, courage, integrity, humility, strategic planning, focus, cooperation, compassion and empathy, self-regulation, and self-awareness. Anyone who has these eleven qualities is sure to be a great leader for their team.

Vision

In order to become a truly great leader, leaders must understand what it means to actually be a leader. Leadership is less about the power that you hold and more about your capacity to use that power to make choices that will lead you and your team toward the successful implementation of your mutual goals. In order to accomplish this, a great leader must have a vision.

Courage

If a leader is truly going to make a big impact on their team, they need to have the capacity to have courage. A leader who lacks courage is one who will find themselves easily being pushed around by their team as they struggle to gain any level of traction with the people around them. Although an ideal team would respect their leader no matter what, this is not always the case, especially with larger teams. If a leader wants to become a great leader and have their team respect them and follow what they say, they need to have courage so that their team trusts them and their guidance.

Integrity

A great leader should always act with integrity, no matter what. One of the worst things that leaders can do is act in a way that lacks integrity, as this will weaken their leadership qualities and often result in their team no longer trusting them. Think about it this way: if you had a leader who said one thing but did another, or who frequently betrayed their own values and standards in order to satisfy other things such as quotas or income levels, would you trust that person? Probably not. And what happens when someone is not trusted? They struggle as a leader.

Humility

Maintaining your sense of humbleness or humility as a leader is crucial if you want to be recognized as a great leader. A massive mistake that many people make when they step into the role of leadership is to let the role go to their heads and allow themselves to lead from a place that is egotistical and arrogant. If you are leading from an egotistical and arrogant stance, you are going to struggle to lead your team because you are going to struggle to gain their trust. Furthermore, a lack of humility also relates to insecurities and a lack of courage or confidence, which means that you are likely weakened as a leader in general, strictly based off of your egotistical behaviors.

Strategic Planning

One of the most important skills that a leader needs to have is the ability to engage in strategic planning, which allows them to create plans that are actually going to work in helping their team achieve their goals. Strategic planning means that you have the capacity to look ahead to identify what your goals are, anticipate what needs to be achieved in order for you to reach your goals, and then create a plan that will help you meet them. As a leader, this means you need to have some capacity to be able to identify likely troubles or challenges that you might face, understand what future circumstances are likely to impact your team, and anticipate anything else that may affect your team. In being able to do this, you will find yourself being able to create strategic plans that actually support you with getting toward where you want to go.

Focus

Focus is an incredibly important characteristic that leaders need to have if they are going to be able to guide their teams to success. Knowing how to focus means that a leader can identify the needs of their company and then remain completely focused on fulfilling those needs until they have been met. Through this, the leader ensures that everyone stays on track and that the team's mutual goals are met every single time.

Cooperation

Leaders who are unwilling to cooperate are often leaders who lack humility, too. All too often, leaders believe that they know what is best, and they are unwilling to receive guidance or feedback from their team along the way, which often results in problems being left unresolved. Your team is on the front lines, and they know exactly where weaknesses lie in your plans because they are enacting your plans to get the greater goal met. If your team begins to have a problem with anything, you need to be able to hear their feedback so that you can create reasonable action steps for moving toward your greater vision.

Compassion and Empathy

As a leader, you must have compassion and empathy if you are going to be able to lead your team with great success. Team leaders who lack compassion and empathy struggle to support their teams in generating any success because they struggle to connect with their team members in a meaningful way. Remember, a team that wants to cooperate with you will always work better with you than a team who feels forced to cooperate with you. Learning how to be compassionate and empathetic toward your team means that you can have relationships that are capable of building a greater level of respect and connection between you and your team members. As a result, you will find yourself having a much easier time leading your team.

Self-Regulation

Leaders are faced with large amounts of stress. At the end of the day, despite how much everyone's involvement contributes to the achievement of your mutual goal if things start to go wrong, that falls on the leader to be able to understand why and fix the situation. This means that a leader is focused on ensuring that every single person gets the job done "right," which can be incredibly overwhelming.

Self-Awareness

Self-awareness is another key quality of a truly great leader, as self-awareness is the skill that allows leaders to identify and understand their own shortcomings and prevent them from impacting their team. As a leader, it is important that you understand where your own strengths and weaknesses might impact your overall ability to lead your team so that you can proceed mindfully. The more you can remain aware of these shortcomings and lead accordingly, the more you are going to be able to truly contribute to your team's success.

Emotional Intelligence in The Workplace and in Business

There are countless ways you can successfully use emotional intelligence to improve in the workplace. perhaps the most difficult yet most effective way to do so is to honestly take stock of your own strengths and weaknesses at work. Rather than using this as an opportunity to tear yourself down, this is simply an assessment of things you do well, and therefore can find ways to do more of that at work, as well as areas that you can improve upon, so when you get feedback in those areas, you can truly take note of those.

It is also important that you find ways to healthily and appropriately deal with any stress that might come up at work. Making sure that you have a balance in your life to take time outside of work to enjoy Hobbies or get physical exercise in are great ways to help mitigate stressors at work. This also includes the ability to control any emotional outbursts that might happen while at work. Using your self-regulation skills, you can stay cool under pressure rather than letting your impulse control off the hook.

You will also find that you naturally search for positive things that happened while at work, as well as finding your internal motivation when you apply your emotional intelligence in the workplace. By focusing on why you took the job, what you enjoy about your job, the positive outcome you have in your team and in your company, as well as the underlying positive impact your company has on the world, not only will you continually refill your Reserves of motivation when times get tough, but you will also rub off on your coworkers.

When you show up to work every day and utilize your emotional intelligence to create a healthy and positive workplace for you and your team members, this can actually help them become more emotionally intelligent as well. Because you have the perspective necessary to have a healthy view of your work, this will help you choose to be respectful and assertive in creating, setting, and enforcing boundaries around work. By clarifying your boundaries and expectations, not only will you benefit from this, but your team members will have a role model of how to set their boundaries, as well as having a level of trust with you that they know when and how to communicate with you.

Emotional Intelligence in Relationships

When many people feel defensive, misunderstood, or undervalued, they come to two interactions with others from a place of negativity. That is understandable when that is the norm for much of their communication. However, to break out of the victim mentality and truly use our emotional intelligence to have better relationships with people, we have to forget about any negative patterns we are expecting from others and move forward courageously expecting a positive outcome.

A great way to go about this is by simply assuming that other people have good intentions. This is especially true when there is a misunderstanding, a ball was dropped, or during any difficult interactions at work. If an employee is not meeting expectations, rather than starting the conversation expecting a conflict or assuming that they are purposefully failing, assume that there is something important that you don't know about yet.

Most often, that turns out to be the case. Because most employees don't want to let their personal lives interfere with their professional work, there are many reasons why they might keep information from you, yet you do see the effects negatively impacting their work. This also allows you to hear the perspective of the other people on your team, which keeps you in the loop and reinforces the fact that you are open to feedback from them. This allows communication to flow freely in both directions, which improves morale exponentially.

When you go into a conversation assuming the best intentions, it will be obvious to the other person you are communicating with, and it will establish a level of trust between the two of you. You are showing compassion and empathy without the other person having to prove anything to you or share more than they are comfortable with. This will result in a profound level of loyalty and positivity on their part.

How to Use Emotional Intelligence for Leadership

Naturally, you didn't just come here to learn about what emotional intelligence is and what makes for a great leader. You came here to learn about how you can embrace the skill of emotional intelligence to help make you a great leader. Right? For that reason, it is ideal that we dig into what it means to be a great leader using the power of emotional intelligence.

Self-Awareness and Self-Regulation

Self-awareness and self-regulation are two cornerstones for emotional intelligence, and they also happen to be two important elements of leadership. As you learn how to become self-aware and learn how to self-regulate, you will find yourself improving your leadership qualities in that you can begin to become aware of how your own actions impact your leadership skills and your team. When you have a clear picture of what your strengths and weaknesses are, you can lead your team with humility and allow your team to all come together to add their own unique strengths and weaknesses to the mix.

Motivating Yourself and Your Team

Leaders who have strong EQ do not only know how to diffuse unwanted or difficult emotions; they also know how to create and navigate excited emotions. Knowing how to motivate yourself and your team is a cornerstone skill in being able to become a great leader, and it is also a skill that is largely associated with emotional intelligence. When you have the capacity to motivate yourself and your team, you create the opportunity for you to keep each of you effectively moving toward your goals rather than having everyone procrastinate or struggle to keep moving forward.

Having Empathy for Your Team

Having empathy for your team is an important part of creating team morale, motivating your team, keeping your team inspired, and collectively working toward achieving your goals. As a leader, empathy means that you can put yourself in the situation of your team members and understand what they are going through. Empathy is going to provide you with two crucial things as a leader: the ability to create better relationships with your team members, and the ability to come up with solutions for how you can still succeed while being kind to your team members.

Improved Leadership-Oriented Social Skills

As a leader, you must have excellent social skills, or you are going to struggle to connect with and lead your team. Team leaders who lack social skills find themselves having difficulty building relationships with and therefore motivating their team because they are unclear about what it takes to receive the trust and commitment of their team members. Improved social skills mean you are far more likely to actually earn the trust and respect of your team members, which means you will naturally be able to encourage them to have the same goals as you so that you can mutually reach your team goals.

Improved Leadership Skills in General

Emotional intelligence is going to improve your leadership skills in general, as well. When you increase your emotional intelligence, you will find that your skills directly related to improving your leadership and your skills related to other areas of your life improve, too. This way, you are far more likely to become a strong leader, not just for your team but in every way in your life. As a result, you are going to be far more likely to create what you desire in your life.

Build Self-Confidence

Self-confidence is both a benefit of emotional intelligence and an important part of emotional intelligence that you need to pay attention to. A person with a high EQ often also has a high level of self-confidence because they are confident in their ability to carry themselves, and they work on boosting their confidence on purpose so that they can experience healthier emotional expression.

Individuals who lack self-confidence often find themselves submitting to feelings like fear, shame, disappointment, embarrassment, regret, guilt, and other feelings that result in them holding back or preventing themselves from engaging in healthier behaviors. A person with a high EQ understands that these are the driving emotions behind low self-confidence, which is why they intentionally navigate these emotions and heal them so that they can move back into a space of having a heightened sense of self-confidence.

As you work on boosting your EQ, you also want to work on boosting your self-confidence. As a leader, having a higher sense of self-confidence means that it will be easier for you to stand in front of your team and actually lead them without doubting yourself or showing signs of fear or weakness that may lead to your team not trusting in you.

One great way that you can begin to build your confidence as a leader is through visualization. Each day, engaging in about 10 minutes of visualization and affirming to yourself that you are a strong and capable leader with a clear vision and an important mission can help you boost your self-confidence. Many leaders also engage in a practice where they do one thing that scares them every day as a way to become used to facing and navigating fear, so that fear no longer has the ability to hold them back from acting as a leader.

As a leader, and as an individual who is increasing their EQ, another important thing that you need to practice is questioning your inner critic or your inner voice to see if what it is saying is, in fact, real. In many cases, you will discover that the inner voice that is attempting to hold you back is actually being ruled by fear, which means that you are not actually lacking confidence so much as being driven by the emotion of fear. When you learn to identify this and work through it, you give yourself the opportunity to move past emotions that may be holding you back so that you can begin creating a deeper sense of self-confidence and self-assurance.

Improve Your Leadership Skills

A high emotional intelligence gives you such a leg up when it comes to being a leader. Because you are in a role in which you are in charge of your employees, and you assigned the tasks that they spend most of their day on, it absolutely matters how you treat them, how you support their work, and how you respond to them. It is well understood that a happy employee is a productive employee. Your ability to appropriately communicate and celebrate the accomplishments of your team will go a long way in improving your leadership skills.

Having higher emotional intelligence will not only help you understand why it's important to be respectful to your employees and co-workers, but it will instill in you an innate sense of respect for others. This is crucial to keeping your employees satisfied and engaged, which has a direct correlation to their participation and success in work.

It also improves your leadership skills because you are more able to quickly adapt and change on the Fly. I do not know of many leadership roles that have no sudden situations that have to be dealt with or fires that need to be put out. Your ability to see the bigger picture, be aware of yourself and the team, regulate your own emotions and those of your team, and then implement a plan that keeps the long-term success in mind are all aspects of emotional intelligence.

Practical Steps to Improve Leadership Skill: Tips, Tactics and Strategies

Increase Your Self-Esteem

If you want to increase your self-esteem, you can establish certain steps in your routine to help yourself. Here are a few to begin!

- Re-affirm your positive traits. Just as we often think negative things about ourselves, we must learn to affirm positive traits as well. Tell yourself that you're a good friend, a good daughter, a kind person, or a generous person. Just like you've learned to associate negative thoughts with yourself, take the time to repeat to yourself positive thoughts. This way, those will become a new part of you. You know that common exercise of looking in the mirror and talking positively to yourself? Well, it works just like that.

- Avoid comparisons. One of the toughest parts of developing your self-esteem is realizing that you cannot compare yourself to others. Too often, we compare ourselves with people around us like family, co-workers, friends, or people we don't even know thanks to the exposure to social media. Whether it's about looks, money, personal possessions or whatever it may be, the trap of comparing is that you never feel good enough. But the truth is that you have no one you should be comparing yourself too! Self-esteem is feeling the best you can about yourself and comparing yourself only to you. It's about being the best person you can be in a process of discovery and self-growth.

- Identify your unique gifts. Everyone has something that they excel at. We all have our strengths and our weaknesses. Instead of focusing on your weaknesses, focus on what your strengths are and what skills you possess that make you feel confident. Whether it's your skills at work, your creative outlets, your skill on the guitar or how well you cook, it's important that you are not ashamed of what you do well and channel that energy, so you feel confident about yourself. Don't focus on your failures - focus on your successes! Be proud of your accomplishments. Focus on self-care. Whether you are exercising, treating yourself to a spa day or getting a good night's sleep, it's important that you take care of yourself physically to take care of your mental health. Exercise is proven to release serotonin, a neurotransmitter of the brain that creates feelings of happiness and contentment.

- Help others. Studies show that helping someone else or volunteering can help you feel better about yourself. It takes you out of your mindset and urges you to think about someone else. The best way to increase your feelings of self-worth is volunteering face to face such as at a homeless shelter or a soup kitchen.
- Remind yourself that you are not your circumstances. Tell yourself over and over that even if you are going through a tough time right now, you may not be soon. Circumstances occur in our life that is sometimes out of our control.

Managing Stress

A crucial part of self-management is also the ability to handle the everyday stress properly. In the beginning, let's clear one thing up – there IS such thing as positive stress. That kind of stress can even motivate us and push us in the right direction towards our goal.

Aside from that, here are a couple of tips that might help you to deal with stress:

- Meditation
- Regular exercise
- Time to relax outside of work

- Time you will spend alone doing the things you like
- Laughing and smiling
- Good night sleep
- Healthier eating habits

Chapter 6.   Manage People

Leading and Managing People

Sensitive information is essential for people in leadership positions as it helps relate to the people that they lead. A leader with high emotional intelligence is likely to excel in the job, as he or she has acquired the basic requirements for success in the work they manage.

They are able to manage their thoughts, feelings, and emotions in a way that they do not affect the productivity of the people around them.

Leadership is a very crucial role in an institution. You find that the performance of the people entirely depends on you. If you are unable to work on your character as an individual, then managing other people becomes difficult.

Taking a close look at the most successful companies today, you will notice that the majority of the success is influenced by the top of the institution. Bosses who have high emotional intelligence have managed to boost the performance of those around them.

Self-Awareness

The ability to know and understand who you are based on evaluating your emotions, thoughts, and feelings is very vital, especially if you assume a leadership role. One of the most common questions in an interview is describing who you are.

"Tell us about yourself," this is a question we are always aware of, but most of the times we have artificial answers for the question mainly aimed at pleasing the interviewer and earning you a job.

Aside what you tell other people about yourself, what is the genuine and accurate description of who you are?

At times, it is good to conduct a self-evaluation. Get to know who you are and how you perceive things and life in general. While at it get to understand how this affects those around you.

It is also good to be aware that while doing this you will discover some negative things that you may not be happy about, but realize that you can always make a change and do what is right.

You recognize that some leaders tend to be easily provoked. Any slight mistake done leads to him or her acting with rage, and this affects the performance of the people they lead.

This can be avoided when a person learns how to manage their emotions and realize the effects of those emotions around the people that they lead.

As a leader who has acquired EI, you tend to relate well with the people mainly because you have reached a point of knowing yourself and understood how to work well with others.

Self-Regulation

As a leader, personal accountability is something that you will need to poses. You need to be in control of your emotions, desires, feelings, and thoughts. Liability is not always accessible, but you can train yourself to embrace it.

As a leader, you may find that at times, you are the one at fault. In this case, you will need to identify that you need to own up to your mistake and apologize or do the right thing.

This will make the employees realize that you are bold enough to acknowledge that you are human, and sometimes, you make mistakes.

This earns you more respect and boosts your performance.

Motivation

Are you inspired beyond acquiring social status and money? Do you have a passion for what you do or you do it because you have to and not because you want to?

Motivation is contagious, and you find that in a group of people that has a person who feels motivated and energized, and they are likely to pass over the same to the people around them.

The people follow suit because they desire to share in the kind of energy that you have. Motivated leaders often lead to inspired colleagues. You find that employees execute the tasks handed to them with a lot of enthusiasm.

This is one of the most critical aspects that help businesses to have a competitive advantage over their competitors. Work is done well and fast by people who feel motivated to produce good results.

Empathy

This entails viewing things from other people perspective. Being in a leadership position will involve regularly placing yourself in other people's shoes, to understand why they do things the way they do. This is not an easy task as it requires that you exercise a lot of patience, but it is worth it.

You get to study people's emotions and observe how they handle them, which gives you an understanding of how best you can treat them. For instance, if you notice employees who find it difficult relating to other people, you could try to engage them more.

Be friendly towards them; make them know that they can trust you. You could also boost their confidence levels by giving them challenging tasks. Place them in positions where they need to work with other people and show them that you believe in their abilities.

This will help them learn how to relate with others and increase their performance.

Social Skills

One of the core tools ineffective leadership entails having the skills to relate with others. This involves the simplest things, like holding a small conversation with the people around you.

You need to be able to talk with almost everyone and get to know who they are. In a company, this will influence the productivity of employees as you have shown that you care about them.

They get inspired when they know that you are willing to go an extra mile into having conversations with them that do not necessarily entail work, but you show that you are concerned about their welfare.

Empower and Delegate

With high levels of emotional and situational awareness, a leader has a detailed image of every individual in his/her team.

Great believers in a team effort, they are able to effectively dissect every task and challenge and fully utilize each person's abilities in meeting that challenge. Leaders are rarely selfish when it comes to the desire to steal the spotlight and get all the credit and fame. Research has demonstrated a clear orientation towards group activities like brainstorming, sharing knowledge and focusing the collective mind power towards the achievement of a goal. This entails employee empowerment and delegation.

Achieving great things is never a one-man show, so both teams and individuals are allowed degrees of freedom to independently assess and decide on the outcome of particular tasks in their field of expertise. That way a leader ensures that every subtask is met with the highest degree of experience and knowledge available in the team. In addition, implementing a practice of shared work and delegation sends a message that the leader believes in his subordinates. As a result, effective delegation can increase the enthusiasm, morale and confidence of team members in their own abilities.

The Delegation Process

The following techniques may help you to become better at delegating:

Evaluate the tasks which take up your time during the average week. Consider how much time they take and what skill level is required to so the job properly. Then think about what else you could be doing with that time. You will realize that the time can be far more productively spent and this should convince you to delegate this task to a member of your team. The most difficult part may be deciding which team member should be entrusted with this task.

Instruct your chosen team members carefully, you must be certain that they fully understand what is expected of them and that they will continue to do the job as you have done it. You should be open to the idea of them changing the method, providing the results are still accurate and within the parameters given. However, no employee should change a system without having first used it for an appropriate amount of time; this will ensure they understand all the ramifications of changing it.

One task should be delegated at a time. This will help you to feel more comfortable about someone else doing one of your tasks and will allow you to keep a close eye on the results. As the first task is shown to be completed successfully then you can start to plan the next item to delegate; gradually the pace of delegation will increase as you hand over all the daily tasks, and you will find yourself as busy as ever. The key to delegating successfully is ensuring that the chosen team member understands fully what is expected from them and works towards the same goal as you and the rest if the team.

Delegating anything is probably not a skill that many business owners have in abundance. However, it is an essential skill to master and will allow you to focus on the things that are relevant to your project.

The Difficulties of Delegation

If followed through, you are most likely to achieve success in delegating responsibilities within your teams. However, it is important you avoid these two things after you give delegated tasks to your team members;

Reverse delegation: This happens when; even though you have assigned a task to a person; they still expect you do most of the work involved; as a way to supposedly "show how" things should be done. A good leader would avoid this; encourage your people to think through their responsibilities; take on tasks and own their outcomes.

Micro Management: A leader cannot be too far from her people; but she should keep a safe distance from constantly interfering with their work. At certain times you may not understand what they are doing and what stage they are; you can ask questions to seek understanding not that you take on command and begin trying to get people to do things just like you would. Give people the opportunity to succeed and sometimes the experience of failing before you interfere with their processes. Sometimes this cannot be afforded and you would have to step in and take on the wheel; ensure this is rare and only used when it is absolutely necessary.

The Benefits of Delegation

There are many different aspects of coaching and delegating effectively; used properly these skills can be developed and improved to establish a group of people which will assist you in leading your team and reaching your goals:

Understanding the Current Skill set of your Team

In order to fully appreciate and drive your team forward it is essential to understand them and what motivates them. This is the best way of establishing a good knowledge of their skill set and of which approach is best to obtain results.

Once you understand what your team is capable of you will be able to identify where improvements can be made and the best method for achieving these improvements. This is stage one of coaching, identifying their needs and building on their current abilities; this will ensure your team is constantly challenged and open to new experiences and goals.

In the majority of cases your team will welcome the additional responsibilities and opportunities. Pushing your team to be the best they can be will ensure that they are always providing maximum effort at work. This means that both you and your project will benefit from their personal growth.

Understanding your team and their skill set will also ensure that you allocate them jobs within or near their comfort zones whilst gradually coaching them into a new area, or improving their existing skill set.

Providing Opportunities to Grow and New Challenges

The natural follows on from identifying the current skill set of your team is creating the opportunities and challenges for your team. There are many tasks completed daily which can be handled differently and it can be a great learning experience to allow someone, with the right experience and attitude, to tackle these tasks and find their own way of competing the challenge.

People Skills: Pay Attention to Other People's Strengths and Weaknesses

It is not enough to give people tasks and say "you do this". It is important how the task is communicated. In communicating a task, a leader should pay attention to expressing two key things; 1) Your trust for the person to carry out the responsibility excellently and 2) the relevance of that task to the overall project goal. People like to know that are part of something big; and that their contributions are integral to the success of the entire project. A leader does not assume that people automatically know these things as such she takes out time to effectively communicate the relevance of each task to team members.

Now take note that this is carried out with clear integrity and you are not merely working people's emotions to somehow influence them to work better. The task assigned must mean something to you and this is what is communicated. If people perceive that you are merely trying to make them feel good with nice words about their „supposed" relevance; they begin to distrust you. And trust, you would find, is one of the leader's greatest assets. So communicate clearly; without deception; the actual relevance of a task to the entire team. This may require you as the leader to think more deeply about how to get your people to make an emotional connection with their tasks. It would require thinking through ways things can be said to maximum effect. It is not automatic; it is an art driven by skill which can be learnt.

Be Available for Follow Up

After the tasks have been broken down and duly assigned; the job of the leader is not yet done. Understand that in delivering their responsibilities, your people can make certain assumptions that may prove to be wrong and then get stuck in carrying out their tasks. You would be responsible for untangling such situations for them; usually by guiding them to think of new ways to approach the task.

Encourage your people to reach out to you for help when things are getting complicated. If they make a mistake; correct them without condemning them. Focus on the task and never attack the personality of a team member who makes a mistake. This would encourage people to speak up when they are unsure and own up when they have made a mistake.

As a leader you are a helper; and you should ensure you are within reach. Some leaders create walls of processes that make it difficult for people to reach them; this is what is often called bureaucracy. While a single leader should not be made to respond to every problem within large systems; teams should be structured in a way that direct subordinates have access to the leader; and can get quick responses from her; especially in a crisis situation.

Coping with Negative Emotions in People

The thing is, emotional management is difficult to do, especially when it comes to stressful situations at work. Unfortunately, it is also much more common. But this doesn't mean that you need to allow yourself to be controlled by negative feelings. So, why don't you start by trying to identify the calm and negative emotions that can be found in the workplace first?

Remember that being aware of your emotional state is the first step to controlling your emotional state, just like we have laid out in the mixed model for emotional intelligence.

Now, coming back to the negative emotions that we are faced with, one of emotional stress in the workplace arises from frustration or irritation. This is generally stemming from the form of helplessness.

Say, you have a boss who is deliberately sexist or racist. If you want to get out of this situation, you first need to stop and evaluate if such labels are truly applicable for your superior. Then, ask yourself if that is why you are feeling this way. Is there a better more tactful way to deal with this issue?

Take your time to think things through. After doing so, you will find that you feel calmer and more in control. Now, you can move on and look for a positive way to deal with the situation. One suggestion is to recall the similar incidents that you or your peers have been in and see and learn from how those situations have been tackled.

Nevertheless, this is not merely about frustration and irritation. Every other negative emotion that you may experience in the workplace, such as worry or anger, nervousness or aggravation, dislike or disappointment, and unhappiness or dissatisfaction, can be resolved in the exact same manner. It's all about understanding what negative emotions you have and finding a rational and effective way to deal with them.

It is important to keep in mind that introspection is a major part of running any business. As a leader, the ability to examine your own motives and feelings matters not only because it will give you a clear vision of what you see yourself doing in the future but also because it will allow you to lead the people who follow you with much more clarity.

Exploiting Positive Emotions in People

Quick question: On a scale of one to 10, how happy do you feel when you go to work - a five, maybe a six, if we're lucky?

Now, ask yourself, "How long do you spend at work?" Most of your waking hours, right?

Do you feel that regret building in your chest? Imagine, if you could fix that, if you could do something that made going to work in the morning to look forward to. How much more productive do you think you would be? According to corporate studies, a lot!

Why don't we teach you a few tricks of the trade?

Express Gratitude

One easy way to increase the positive emotions in your employees and team is by creating a culture of positive recognition. Think about it; just saying something like "thank you" can make the recipient feel recognized and valued. By learning to count your blessings, particularly in a business atmosphere, you are fostering positivity in every individual team member. Because positivity is a reflective emotion like empathy, it tends to reflect back and add value to the team as a whole.

Ideally, a great technique to inject gratitude into daily business dealings is by starting meetings with a positive feedback session. Meaning, talk about the good and reinforce it before you even touch upon the problems that need to be addressed.

Build Connections

Another important way in which leaders can build positivity into their teams and companies is by encouraging the employees to build connections among their own teams. Happiness research has shown that positive moods are practically contagious, which means that even if you are personally not in a good mood, simply being in contact with someone who is can help with your mood and those around you.

You need to encourage staff to celebrate little successes or personal achievements; small companies and family-owned companies tend to do this by employing "employee of the month" or "manager of the week" strategies, which can entice employees to do better. It also gives the staff a sense of community; that, in turn encourages, workplace friendships, which is very beneficial to productivity and company growth.

Embrace Strength and Values

Another pro tip is to use goals and opportunities to attract employees to work on their strengths. Goals give employees a sense of purpose, particularly since the big picture isn't always easy to imagine. By allowing employees to do what they are good at and giving them more opportunities to shine, we are effectively strengthening organizational goals and facing developmental challenges with the best possible candidates for the job. Doing something well in itself is a good feeling; as such, it makes it easier to make people feel good about themselves as well.

How to Talk to Anyone

Sometimes, it is inevitable to deliver tough news. This is something all leaders must face no matter how uncomfortable it is. It requires a high level of emotional intelligence to be able to skillfully deliver unpleasant news or have a tough conversation with the people you lead. For example, how do you tell a team member that they are not going to get a pay raise after all their hard work without dampening their morale? How do you provide critical feedback to a colleague who has been recently falling short on their duties without making them feel worthless?

Having to face your colleagues, peers, employees, or business partners and address issues that many see as very difficult can be quite a delicate task. This is why many people easily make one of two mistakes when issues arise:

1. Being too blunt: Although this may address the issue, it hurts feelings and effects morale while creating misunderstanding in the process, and may cause one party to detach emotionally and mentally, leading to less effective communication. Also, it shows that the person bluntly addressing the issue probably lacks emotional intelligence. Of course, some occasions call for directness but resorting to that as your go-to approach does not show empathy at all.

2. Putting it off: This is the easier option to take, but it will likely make the situation worse. Dodging a difficult conversation is the hallmark of leaders who either don't have a clue on how to go about the situation, or who are too busy worrying about the feelings of others that they let that worry overpower their vision and the goals of the organization.

Being able to handle difficult conversations is a core skill that you must possess and master to become a successful leader. And although no one (leader or not) enjoys having a tough conversation, the following tips will help you reduce the awkwardness and hurt usually associated with tough conversations.

Teamwork

It is easy for people to work together when they have high emotional intelligence.

Collaboration is not an easy task since it involves people who share different opinions and view. Human beings are made to function differently. You realize that the way people reason is very different.

To be able to work together, one has to be accommodative and respect that in spite of having varied opinions, they can still execute tasks well without having their differences in mind. By acquiring emotional intelligence, teamwork will be successful in the following ways:

Creating Passion Within the Team Players

Having emotional intelligence will enable team participants to know themselves and those around them. This gives an insight into what inspires them and makes them feel motivated towards achieving a common goal.

In spite of having differences, we can identify a common unifying factor that helps us work together. The way we treat each other will directly affect our productivity and determine whether we are inspired or demotivated.

Identify Your Strengths and Weaknesses

While working together, it is essential to recognize other people's strengths and weaknesses. This directly affects helps you determine where people can perform best and at the same time, show where their performance is likely to be compromised.

In businesses, it is essential to position each employee in a place where they can best be productive. This reflects on the overall performance of the company.

Getting a Leader

Individuals with high emotional intelligence tend to make very great leaders. They can relate well with the people around them. Such individuals tend to be in control of their emotions and are well aware of the feelings of others, which, influences the way they handle them.

A leader is significant in connecting people and increasing the productivity of the team. You find that in every organization, there is always someone in charge for people to work well and succeed.

Often, while selecting a team leader, you look at the qualities people have since they affect or influence the way they will lead other people.

In this case, a person with high emotional intelligence often makes a perfect choice and can relate with people to achieve incredible team success.

Being Innovative

Excellent communication skills are essential for the success of any team. You need to allow everyone to have a voice and speak their mind.

This contributes to sharing ideas and being creative. People get to say what they think and explain what leads to such kind of thoughts, and you can share their reasoning.

When you discuss ideas together, you can enhance them as you try to devise ways in which you can make the concepts better. To achieve this, members of the team need to have high emotional awareness so that they can give everyone a chance to express themselves.

Know Your Goal and Have a Plan

Get to set some goals which you can work hard towards achieving. Ensure that the goals are realistic and achievable. These goals act as a source of motivation and help one in acquiring smoothing to work towards.

Grab a paper and write down your aims and ambitions. Place it somewhere you can access every day so that it acts as a reminder for what you are working hard towards. This will have a positive impact on increasing your emotional awareness.

Stop Procrastinating

When procrastination knocks on your door, purpose tells it you are not in. When fear of failure stares straight in your eyes, it is your purpose that gives you the courage stare it down. And when the situation and the people in your workplace appear unmanageable, it is purpose that whispers, "You can do it."

Can You See It and Feel It? Then You Can Achieve It

Just like the pregnant mother who drew strength from the mental image of her unborn child, if you can see yourself clearly in your mind as having overcome whatever challenging situation you are faced with, you are going to triumph over that situation. In other words, no matter the difficulty you face, you must visualize yourself as a success long before any physical appearance of success shows up in your current reality. If you hold that picture of success in your mind's eye and never back down from it, success is the only possible outcome you can experience.

Visualizing is a bit different from mere imagination or wishful thinking in the sense that visualizing contains one vital ingredient which wishful thinking or mere imagination do not have. That ingredient is feeling or emotion. When I suggest that you visualize yourself as a success, it means you should add emotions to your vivid imaginations. Do not just see it; feel as though it is happening, or it has happened. I know this may sound like some psychic or extrasensory mumbo-jumbo, but the results are fascinating when you apply these simple techniques.

Conclusion

I hope it's clear to you by now that there is only one person for you to hold accountable for your success or failure: you. Not many people see the world through that lens, why?

It's hard. It's hard to accept that you bear the full weight of many of the negative things that happen to you. It's easier to accept the responsibility only for the good, and spin stories about the wicked world working against you when things don't go your way. I'm not suggesting that bad things won't happen, nor am I suggesting that you can stop all of those things from happening. But what you can do is be prepared for the changes and trials that life will inevitably throw at you. You can shoulder them with grace and not allow them to throw you off-course of your goal.

The components that make up a successful mindset are not limited to those I have written about here, there are more, many more. Part of that mindset is seeking others who share your perspective, or better yet, those who challenge it. Seek new knowledge, test it, throw out what doesn't work, keep what does.

Remember too that failure is an integral part of success, if you are trying your best, you should be failing sometimes, that's normal, it builds your character and resilience, it can teach you gratitude. Life will constantly hand you lessons, pay attention to them. Tenacity breeds success. Keep striving, keep moving.

I wish the best of luck.

EMPATH GUIDE

A complete guide for highly sensitive person, developing skills, improve emotional intelligence, your self-esteem and relationships.
Overcome fear, anxiety and narcissistic abuse.

MIND CHANGE ACADEMY

Table of Contents

Introduction to Empathy

Is it accurate to say that you are affected by the sentiments of everyone around you? Do individuals portray you as compassionate? Maybe you have consistently could feel the feelings and physical manifestations of others as though they were your own. On the off chance that this sounds accurate in your life, you might be an "empath."

Just 1 to 2 percent of the populace experience this sort of affectability, being able to feel and assimilate the feelings encompassing them. They likely view the world through their feelings and instinct instead of putting a lot of rationale behind their basic leadership. While this trademark can be a wellspring of individual quality, it is additionally critical to realize how to oversee regular difficulties of being an empath.

What is an Empath?

While there is critical research behind the sentiment of compassion, there are not very many examinations concentrated essentially on empaths. What is known is that empaths likely have hyper-responsive mirror neurons — the gathering of synapses answerable for activating emotions like sympathy — as per explore discoveries. This makes it workable for somebody to feel particularly touchy to electromagnetic fields produced by an individual's cerebrum and heart and intuit the feelings felt by everyone around them. On the off chance that there is an energized group or a gathering of individuals in grieving, the vitality can be felt profound inside an empath's body.

For the individuals who are increasingly thoughtful empaths, they might be progressively touchy to the mind concoction liable for feeling joy — dopamine. In occurrences where an excessive amount of incitement happens, an empath can feel overpowered. After some time, empaths can become modified to keep away from outside incitement or need almost no of it to feel glad. Regardless of whether an individual is withdrawn, some basic reactions of touchiness can incorporate fatigue, over-burden, misery, and uneasiness. Regularly, when these emotions emerge, it's useful to have some space to withdraw to at home or a most loved open air spot you can revive in.

At the point when overpowered with distressing feelings, empaths can encounter tension, alarm assaults, sadness, and weariness and may even show physical side effects, for example, an expanded pulse and cerebral pain. This is on the grounds that they disguise the emotions and agony of others without the capacity to recognize it from their own. To help deal with these staggering minutes, it is significant for empaths to distinguish their own contemplations and emotions, however much as could reasonably be expected, and isolating them from those of others.

Signs You Are an Empath

1. You are independent

Regularly, empaths become overpowered when in enormous gatherings of individuals. Instead of feeling decidedly affected by everyone around you, you likely decide to be increasingly contemplative and lean toward coordinated and little gathering collaborations.

2. You are effectively affected by pictures and motion pictures.

Maybe tears come rapidly and effectively when you watch a motion picture, or you may encounter the feeling behind the subject of a photo. In these occasions, minutes on screen and in print bigly affect how you feel.

3. You fear losing all sense of direction seeing someone

Empaths likely have a background marked by getting totally consumed by new connections and are frightful of not having the correct sort of limits set up. You may feel totally gobbled up and obscure the lines between your emotions and those of the individual you are involved with.

4. You retain others' feelings

Being on top of what others are encountering, both great and terrible, is a sign you are an empath. You may feel surrounding feelings around you as though they were your own and become depleted genuinely and even physically.

5. You are profoundly natural

It is safe to say that you are driven by your own premonitions about individuals? Empaths regularly tune in to their internal contemplations with regards to making a decision about individuals, spotting positive connections that assist them with feeling their best.

Utilizing Your Emotions as a Strength

For the about 15 to 20 percent of the populace who are named "profoundly delicate," they feel more profoundly and strongly than people around them. Their minds are preparing data and considering it in an incredible, nuanced way. While this conduct can be viewed as being excessively touchy, mindful, or excessively mindful, these capacities can likewise be seen as alluring — being astoundingly discerning, instinctive, and hyper-perceptive. Try to figure out how to oversee and channel those (occasionally) awkward feelings.

To make preparations for disagreeable or overpowering feelings, empaths can worker various sorts of methodologies to make every day encounters progressively attractive.

Adopting a methodological strategy to time the board, and defining firm limits with individuals who channel your vitality, gets important. Furthermore, knowing when reflection and stillness is required can be a significant method to pull together. The key is to discover approaches to deal with yourself and deliberately react to elevated emotions as they emerge.

While more research is required with regards to understanding the science behind empaths and the motivation behind why a few people retain sentiments more promptly than others, there are still approaches to distinguish whether you experience empath-like propensities. By understanding the signs and triggers for empaths, it is simpler to use these capacities as qualities, while better dealing with any negative effects. In any occurrence, it is imperative to comprehend your enthusiastic needs and impart them to people around you.

Types of Empathy

Empathy is defined as the capacity to understand or feel the emotions of others. It can also be described as the ability to share the feelings of others. Empathy, for the most part, is a beautiful attribute. It's one of the finest qualities a human being can possess. It is associated with goodness, charity, compassion, care, and self-sacrifice. Empathy makes it easier to identify with those who are suffering, and consequently, take action to remedy the situation. The world can always do with a little more empathy.

Empathy is mostly classified into three groups:

Emotional Empathy

Here you experience the feelings of other people: sadness, anxiety, joy, pain, and so on. An emotionally empathic person catches the sensations of others, which strengthens relationships with those around her/him. Emotional empaths can do well in fields like medicine, nursing, and counseling since they deeply identify with the suffering of others and go out of their way to alleviate that.

The downside to emotional empathy is that your emotions fluctuate up and down, depending on the situation of those around you. That can be exhausting. In other instances, you feel the pain of others so deeply, yet there's nothing you can do to change their situation, and you're left suffering as well.

Cognitive Empathy

This is the ability to know the thought process of other people, and in the process, understand their perspective. It mostly involves thoughts, intellect, and understanding. Cognitive empathy helps you appreciate different viewpoints. You're able to accommodate people who hold different opinions and beliefs from those of your own. This ability also comes in handy during discussions since you understand the thought process of others and engage them appropriately.

Compassionate Empathy

In this case, you do not only identify with the suffering of others, but you're also moved to take an extra step and lend your help. This is the ideal form of empathy, where you actually take action to make a difference.

However, precaution should be taken so that you do not run yourself dry, trying to donate to every cause. A donation here refers not only to finances but also time, expertise, skills, goodwill, and so on.

Empathy isn't just towards people. It applies to situations as well. An empath will be drawn towards the state of the environment, economy, politics, international relations, animal welfare, and such other matters that eventually affect the quality of human life. People without empathy find it easy to look away, especially when others are suffering.

First, all empaths are born with the ability to experience what other people are going through, either through emotions or even their feelings. Secondly, no empath is born already skilled. They all have to learn the skills, and if not, they are prone to suffer a lot. This should not get you worried if you have no skills yet, this book will help you learn some new skills that you need to know as an empath. To your surprise, you might even be more than one kind of an empath, so if you find yourself falling into various kinds of empaths, count yourself talented. These types are also referred to as the many gifts of empathy.

Physical Intuition

These are the kind of empaths who are able to know what exactly is happening in another person's body. For example, this type of an empath can easily tell when you have a stomachache or a headache. Being a skilled empath will make you able to help other people through this correct knowledge.

Physical Oneness

The way these empaths get information is always personal. These are empaths who can feel other people's physical way of being in their own body when around or with them. For instance, this kind of empath, when with Betty, they will always develop a stomachache, like this stomachache belongs to Betty. This is a confusing type of empath, but if you are a skilled one, you will be able to assist those around you with the messages you get into your body. You ought to be skilled to avoid confusion or any form of suffering.

Intellectual Empath Ability

These types of empaths are able to get into people's intellectual abilities. For example, they might find themselves using long words while speaking to Joy, but then later, they come to realize that Joy also likes using long words.

Emotional Intuition

These types of empaths are able to tell what is going on in someone's body, specifically their emotions, even when other people are trying to hide or fake their emotions. For instance, an empath will note that Betty is always cheerful, but she is hiding worries behind her smiles. Skilled empaths will know how to cut through the fake and real emotions since they all have the ability to differentiate what is real and what is fake. This helps you become a better friend since your friends get to realize you know them better.

Emotional Oneness

This is the type of empath where you get to learn the reality about what is cooking in other people's feelings. The difference of this kind of empath with the Emotional Intuition is that an empath in emotional oneness is able to feel what others are feeling. Your emotions and those of your friends will tend to merge. And as a skilled empath, you should not be carried away by the absorbed emotions since most of them are always negative. Instead, you should help your friends come out of this negative emotion or feeling, for instance, worries or anger. Being skilled means, you will have a stable emotional foundation to help out.

General Types of Empaths

Spiritual Intuition

This is a kind of empath where you get to experience how someone else connects to God or other spiritual beings. For instance, accompanying Betty to church and getting to hear what her pastor preaches about God, you get to feel the flavor that Betty gets from the teachings about God. This can happen in the case where you know nothing about your friend's religious views. Skilled empaths use this chance to know the many faces of God and even develop interests for religions and spiritual lives.

Spiritual Oneness

This kind of empath is different from that in Spiritual Intuition in that, in Spiritual Oneness, an empath will experience directly how their friends are connecting to their Supreme Being. This can be through the hymns that are being sung and relating the inspiration behind them. This helps skilled empath grow more spiritual in various ways.

Animal Empath

An animal empath will experience what it feels like to be a certain animal. A skilled animal empath is totally different from an animal lover in the sense that an animal empath is able to tell the difference between two animals that an animal lover thinks are identical. A skilled empath will help animals locate their groups or even help pet owners.

Environmental Empath

Environmental empaths are able to tell the difference between landscapes in certain environments. To them, each landscape is scenery. Skilled empaths enjoy walking through forests, and this can even make them emotional.

Plant Empath

Plant empaths get to feel what it is like being a certain tree, leave, or even flower. Skilled empaths use this gift in their agricultural farms or even in gardening.

Mechanical Empath

Mechanical empaths experience what it is to be a certain machine and their needs. This can even make them fix machines without the necessary qualifications due to the increased interest in machines. As a skilled empath, you are advantaged because you will not need a mechanic to identify what your machine needs, you will be able to tell it yourself. It may lead to more research into machines and technologies.

Medical Empath Talent

This gift helps identify any sickness or anything about your own or other people's health matters. Skilled medical empaths help give support, can even end up developing professional skills and become nurses, or even help in preventing any burnouts.

Empath Talent with Astral Beings

These empaths have direct experiences with astral beings such as angels and fairies. Skilled empaths will use the experience to grow themselves or enjoy more of these adventures.

The Difference Between Cognitive Empathy, Emotional Empathy, Compassionate Empathy

Empathy is one of those buzzwords continually put on everyone's lips. There is no doubt about it, but the continuous use of this wonderful quality that facilitates relations between human beings causes, on occasion, there is confusion regarding the term, which ends up losing meaning.

We probably all know that through empathy, that ability that allows us to recognize and identify with otherness, we are able to perceive what the other can feel and think. But what surely know of this quality which has been so positive over centuries of evolution for unity and survival of the community, it is that there are three different types of empathy: the emotional, cognitive, and compassionate.

Firstly, we have emotional empathy. It is a dimension that can be contagious and even dangerous when we do not know how to impose limits, and we are impregnated" with the suffering of others. It is to feel what others feel and to understand their personal reality. In this process, mirror neurons, our feelings, and even our physiological response come into play.

Cognitive empathy, in turn, implies making use of the intellect, cognitive processes such as attention, reflection, communication, inferences, etc. It basically means knowing how the other person feels, why they feel this way, and figuring out what ideas and thoughts might be in the other's mind.

Also, we have this great unknown, this dimension that is often overlooked: compassionate empathy. With this kind of empathy, we not only understand what the person feels and what their problem is, but we mobilize to help them if we believe they need help.

However, when we apply emotional empathy, there is an emotional reaction through which we identify so much with the feelings of the other person that we can feel them in their own flesh. Sometimes, if this emotional empathy is extreme and the identification with the other person is total, it can paralyze us and prevent us from being able to advise and be a useful help for the other. However, emotional empathy is about a noble and deep feeling that, beyond compassion, allows us to give sincere support without being condescending.

On the other hand, through cognitive empathy, we can understand and recognize what the other person is feeling, but always from the intellect, never from the emotion itself. In this type of empathy, there is, therefore, no emotional reflex and can be learned through social imitation. Psychopaths, who by definition are unable to identify themselves emotionally with another person, could fake emotional empathy for a manipulative purpose; to get what they want from others.

Thus, this is the kind of empathy that allows us to offer others a useful response since with it, and we take action: we propose or execute a plan to help the other. Usually, when we put empathy into practice, we usually apply a balance between the two, being able to recognize the feelings of another person in us and to understand what happens to them to give them effective help.

Empathy is a fundamental quality in communication and, therefore, it is a skill that we work continuously in point of discussion. We often associate it exclusively with the peaceful resolution of conflicts, in which knowing how to understand all the parties involved and addressing them as assertively as possible is essential to mediate successfully.

On the other hand, the role of empathy in communication goes much further: it is essential to really reach those who listen to us, connecting with their feelings and their needs. Being empathic with our audience guarantees us to opt for the only possible way to have communicative success: to carry out an intervention adapted to the interests of the audience, making it the protagonist.

Empaths, Intuition, And Perceptions

Being an empath is a beautiful gift. You are wise and caring, insightful and perceptive. You take care of those you love and have a deep consideration and respect for all life on earth.

It is important when looking into how you can live your best life and thrive psychologically and spiritually that you first have a sound inner standing of what it truly means to be an empath. There are different levels to being an empath as we will explore in the next section, however, for now, let's break down the empath personality so you can inner stand it holistically.

All of the following are aspects to the empath personality however in varying degrees. For example, there may be elements you strongly resonate with and others which you only see a small part of yourself embodying. This knowledge is not taught in school, nor is it widely accepted, and many unique abilities that accompany being spiritually aware and connected and existing in a higher frequency or vibrational state of being are intuitively felt. Your empath nature connects instinctively to something beyond the everyday 'I' and often separation based reality which many people still reside in. Looking at the varying aspects to being an empath, therefore, can be a healing journey in itself.

It is OK if you only resonate with a few. Not all empaths display all of these qualities or characteristics. As you read the different aspects of the empath personality, spark your awareness back to memories or a memory where you may have been displaying some of these abilities without being conscious of what was occurring at the time. With each, there is a description of what it means, followed by how you may have been subconsciously or unconsciously displaying and embodying it.

The Artist, Creative, and Visionary

You are an artist. Due to your ability to connect to something above and beyond you through your deep and rich emotional wisdom and intuitive sight, you can also tune in to universal archetypes, ideas, concepts, and often ingenious images and thoughts in a unique way. This makes you a natural artist, creative, and visionary. Whether you choose to express yourself through song, dance, art, painting, drawing, poetry, writing, photography, film making, or directing, you can achieve great things. The visionary aspect to your nature can, literally, connect on an unseen level to some concept or archetype beyond the physical realm, and further bring it forth into the physical. Alanis Morissette is one of the most well-known empaths and even if you have not yet heard of her, her music inspires many people around the world.

Practical Implications of being the Artist, Creative and Visionary: If you embody the artist, creative, or visionary you may have found yourself as a child daydreaming and letting your mind wander to unseen worlds and ideas. Your imagination was rich and you may have been bored in social or overly externally stimulating situations. You also may have naturally had a strong inner knowing that you could come up with better or ingenious ideas and solutions to ones being presented in school, or by your teachers and peers. Your abstract and creative ways of thinking may not have been appreciated or understood by others.

Importance of Empathy

Without empathy, people would go about their lives without considering the feelings and thoughts of other people. Every person has differing perspectives on life; therefore, if we did not have something that made us accommodate each other, life would be very complicated. We all experience moods, joy, sadness, pain hurt et cetera, and if we focus only on the things happening in our lives, we will limit our capabilities. It is easy to jump into conclusions if we do not take a moment to truly understand what the other people stand for. Lack of empathy normally leads to bad feelings, misunderstandings, poor morale, conflict, and even divorce.

When one uses empathy in real life to understand why a person is angry, or a child is throwing a tantrum, he/she might learn about things in their lives that trigger the behavior. For example, one might find that something happened at home, thus pushing the angry person to act out or that the child did not have a meal in the morning thus they are not okay.

Empathy enables one to ask questions about the situation or behavior of another person before taking a defensive stance or reacting to some emotions. There may still be the need for disciplinary action, but one should use empathy first. Empathy makes a person feel valued and understood even if they are punished for the wrong deeds, and as such, they will accept responsibility for their action. Empathy is currently the missing link in schools, families, workplaces, and the world at large.

There are a few misunderstandings that arise when one is applying empathy in real life. Some people believe that being empathetic involves agreeing with the opinion of everybody else. That is wrong and will only lead to exhaustion. Understand the perceptions of the other person, acknowledge them but you do not have to sing along every tune.

Other people believe that being empathetic involves doing what everyone else wants or doing anything to make others happy. That is wrong. You are not obligated to please everyone; you do not have to cooperate in every other situation. Just because you fail to accommodate every other matter does not mean that you are evil. The world is complicated; therefore, use empathy but do not agree with everything.

Empathy does not mean being there for someone for a lifetime. After listening to a person and offering a solution, you do not have to always be there for them, you have other tasks to accomplish and if you feel that the person is just using you, walk away. Empathy does not mean you should have no ego or intention. Once you assist someone, allow your ego to help you walk away or change the discussion.

Applying empathy in real life can be challenging therefore, there are investments that one needs to make and they include time, patience and proactivity.

Time

It takes some time for one to listen to others, pay attention and not jump into conclusions. Coming up with good solutions also takes time. In most cases, we want to arrive at an answer very first without taking the time to understand; this only leads to more problems. Empathy is like watching sand draining in an hourglass; it takes time, but not that much time, and it is very satisfying.

Patience

Empathy does not only take time; it requires a lot of patience. Paying attention to someone, listening to everything they are saying, and selecting a comprehensive solution takes a lot more than just jumping into conclusions, listing arguments and repeating an opinion. Normally people fail to give the patience and attention required when making conversations; therefore, it becomes harder than it should be.

It takes proactivity

Some people think that empathy should only be given when both parties have something to gain. In the real sense, we should show empathy even to people who show no sign of understanding our perspectives and opinions. This can be very frustrating, and one might find it very unfair, but empathy begins with you. It will not work if both of you wait on each other to start the conversation.

Be the role model, set the example, be a good listener and do not talk until the other person is done. Understand the opinions of other people but remember you do not have to agree with them. Being empathetic can be a tough challenge but still, there are many people that practice it. Apply empathy every day and enjoy the benefits.

Many equate the terms sympathy, compassion and empathy. Some even confuse love with these terms. There is one essential difference:

Sympathy

This is when you feel bad when you see others suffer and maybe even express bad feelings (such as donating to Christmas or writing a card to a bereaved person for funerals). It is often confused with compassion because it perceives that the other person does not feel well, but only briefly and not deeply or really becomes active. The difference to compassion is thus the duration or the depth and, above all, the non-existent "bad conscience." You accept the situation just like you do and what you cannot change it and not get involved. But one does not ignore the situation, but perceives it and makes a small contribution to the comfort or the relief and expresses its regret.

Compassion

Compassion is more than that, and it really cares - actively "empathize," the grief, the pain, the pain, take in the arms, be there constantly, even if the other is in despair or has pain, but nothing can do. Having compassion means exactly what the word expresses: to suffer with oneself, to put oneself back, to be there and to accompany and endure. It's hard, and that's why constant compassion is rare. Since many sympathize with the situation and remain in the present, compassion can also be self-destructive to the helper. Escape here can be a form of self-protection for those who have previously felt what is difficult for observers to understand and comprehend, especially if they only feel sympathy.

Empathy

Real empathy is one step ahead because it combines compassion with action. It is the common solutions for searching and finding. It is understanding and accepting the inevitable, but looking forward and working together to improve what can be improved. This can be the loss of suffering, an elaboration and accompaniment in finding a solution from the problem situation and the accompaniment on the way out of misery. It is the right mix - the help for self-help, also the involvement of other helpers - but always in the sense of the one who needs help.

Empathy is a multi-dimensional construct consisting of cognitive (understanding mental states, Theory of Mind) and affective (emotional responses to another's state of mind) proportions. A lack of empathy is considered central to the autism spectrum disorder Asperger's Syndrome (AS), although there is no systematic and simultaneous exploration of cognitive and emotional empathy.

Empathy is strongly associated with acceptance. The indirect message of any empathy is, how you feel understandable and normal - you're OK the way you are. Empathy cannot be expressed at the touch of a button. Much more important than any formulation is the attitude. Can I empathize with the other person? Emotional as well as cognitive, accepting the other person as it is? Can you see her as an equal individual?

Empathy is a precursor to compassion. It does not motivate you to help others. Depending on whether you separate your experience from the experience of the other, empathy leads to compassion or compassion. When you develop compassion for someone, you feel caring for that person. This sense of caring is not stressful for the compassionate but rather transforms the negative-feeling feelings into positive emotions such as love.

The Psychology Behind Empaths

In everyday life, among the people around us, you can see various behavioral reactions in similar life situations. For example, some are very sympathetic to hungry, homeless cats and dogs, trying to shelter and feed them, they cannot pass by a crying child, they will always help those in need, or they will think and empathize for a long time about it. Others, on the contrary, do not care about all this. To understand this, to find the reasons is very interesting. People say about such people - Sincere, Kind, Soft, Or Soulless, Callous. But how does psychology explain this science? An answer will help this work.

Empathy Is a Psychological Concept

Communication is a complex and multifaceted process that can act at the same time as a process, interactions of individuals, and as an information process of their interaction on each other, and as a process of empathy and mutual understanding of each other. In the process of communication, there must be a mutual understanding between the participants in the process. In the process of knowing another person, several processes are simultaneously carried out: the emotional assessment of another, an attempt to understand the motives of his actions. At least two people are included in these processes, and each of them is an active subject. Consequently, the decision of oneself with the other is carried out as if from two sides: each of the partners likens itself to the other.

The perception of man by man offers a special process: identification. Identification literally means assimilation. Close in significance to identification is another mechanism of cognition of another - empathy. And from how people will relate to each other, to be able to empathize, to feel the pain of another, this is how relations will form in society. Therefore, good relations in society and good communication depend on the level of development of empathy. Consider empathy in more detail.

Empathy is a comprehension of an emotional state, penetration into a feeling in another person's experience. It has been established that the empathic ability of individuals increases, as a rule, with the growth of life experience. Empathy is more easily realized in case of similarity of behavioral and emotional reactions of subjects.

Therefore, the role of empathy in communicative activity is very large. Since social interaction is actions that are focused on the semantic perception of them by other people, speaking of the emotional sphere, one should understand the concept of emotion.

Emotions are a psychological reflection in the form of a direct biased experience of the vital meaning of phenomena and situations, due to the relationship of their objective properties to the needs of the subject. In the process of evolution, emotions arose as a means of allowing living things to determine the biological significance, condition of the body, and external influences.

The highest product of the development of human emotions is stable feelings for objects that meet his highest needs.

Emotions can cause changes in the overall emotional background, the so-called mood. The development of emotion in ontogenesis finds expression in the differentiation of the qualities of emotion to the complexity of objects, causing an emotional response.

Development of the ability to regulate emotions and their external expression. The emotional experience of a person changes and is enriched in the process of personality development as a result of empathy, empathy, arising in communication with other people during the perception of a work of art, under the influence of the media. Emotions act as regulators of human communication

The Appearance of Empathy in Children of Different Ages

Having picked up and studied the relevant literature, understanding the essence of this problem, we began to study the manifestation of empathy in students and pupils of our educational institution. To get the answer to the question: Does empathy appear in young children?

They were observed in the younger group of kindergarten. To cry the baby in a group of 10 children, they reacted as follows; 4 people came and began to calm, stroking the head, 4 people stood nearby and looked, 2 did not react to what was happening. In this regard, we can assume that already in young children, empathy manifests itself; that is, they are able to empathize. Having attended the classes of the "Fairy Tale," fairy tale open the door" in the first grade and having analyzed the reaction of children to the actions of the heroes of fairy tales, we got the following result. Of the 10 children listening to the tale, 6 people actively reacted to the events described in it, 2 of them most acutely, 4 outwardly did not manifest a reaction.

Empathy is more evident in elementary school students. With age, its level of development decreases. WHY? This remains to be seen. I think that empathy as a sign is genetically embedded in a person, and since the environment will influence the manifestation of this sign, it will also appear, and the environment is the education of moral principles in the family and school.

Background data showed varying degrees of empathy.

First of all, empathy manifests itself to old people, then to younger people, animals, and last of all to peers since empathy also depends on upbringing, we can say that our school does not pay enough attention to the education of interpersonal relationships between peers.

After all, as the popular saying How It Comes Around, It Will Respond. On the other hand, if the level of empathy is very high (a person is very worried about others), there is a possibility of getting a nervous breakdown and getting sick. In our opinion, students after graduation when choosing a profession should take into account the level of their empathy. Doctors, teachers, educators, social workers, service workers must have a high level of empathy.

7 Phases of Becoming a Skilled Empath

Examining anything as far as stages is constantly somewhat of a hit-and-miss. Stages can cover, and there is no set in stone request to things. By the by, I've discovered that there frequently is a sure request to how customers go from being an overpowered empath to turning into a gifted empath. The stages sketched out beneath are proposed as a supportive sign, however they are not at all exacting principles about how things "must go".

1. The Burdened Phase

Your affectability feels like a lack, a weight, something you have to get freed off. You make a decent attempt to demonstrate to the world and yourself that you can toughen things out, not think about how no doubt about it, "resemble others". You're battling yourself since that is the thing that you learned you should do by one way or another. You could possibly think about empaths now be that as it may, in any case, you're persuaded its fate and misery from here on out.

2. The Basic Self-Care Phase

You've taken measures to care more for yourself. These measure are especially in accordance with the sort of self-care for the most part suggested for HSPs (empath or not). You set aside some effort to rest and process things. You abstain from overstimulating situations. You're doing what you can to make harmony with your "self preoccupation" and your affectability.

You might be acquainted with the idea of Highly Sensitive People now, or you may just, naturally have come to perceive that you work better and are all the more beneficially when you limit your day by day portion of incitement. (note, most empaths are additionally HSPs, however not all!)

3. The Energy Research Phase

You're examining vitality wonders and vitality instruments and practices. You may have a contemplation practice that encourages you, representations that you use to rinse your vitality field and "root" into the ground. You may even be exploring different avenues regarding protecting trying to keep others' vitality out of your own space.

A portion of your practices might be to some degree accommodating or effective. However, you're left with a mind-boggling sense that it's insufficient. You can't see yourself jumbling on like this a mind-blowing remainder, and you sure as *bell* would prefer not to do a wide range of representations throughout the day just to get by. Regardless of your expanding attention to what is up with you, things are likewise looking to some degree distressing.

4. The Empath Training Phase

You realize despite everything you have far to go, yet are beginning to see distinct enhancements. You may feel more clear and less foggy, feel less overpowered in gatherings, progressively OK with yourself, or essentially reinforced by the information that you are figuring out how to assume responsibility for something that recently felt so totally crazy.

5. The Gaining Control Phase

You've rehearsed the empath instruments to the point where you can apply them rapidly. As the day by day vitality load on your framework diminishes, you are beginning to get looks at manners by which you have one of a kind endowment that could help other people. You likewise come to comprehend that you have no commitment to the world everywhere in any capacity. The endowments inside your empathic capacity are yours to utilize, or let be, as feels right to you.

You are assuming responsibility for your everyday life, and your long haul life plan. You are never again a moon circling around others. You've seen your very own internal spot As.

That feeling of your own center may at present be to some degree temperamental, however it's unquestionably coming into center.

6. The Increasing Clarity Phase

You've drilled the empath apparatuses and done the subliminal reinventing to the point where you would now be able to be in swarms without being overpowered by any stretch of the imagination. You can be available to others' exceptional feelings without taking those feelings on. You may need to check in with yourself after introduction to exceptional energies from others in any case, in the event that you picked something up, you're ready to relinquish it effectively and rapidly.

As you continue applying these abilities, you find that you retain energies from others less and less in any case. To an ever increasing extent, you are as yet mindful of the vitality around you, however just in the manner in which you'd know about the cooling murmuring a way off, out of sight.

On the off chance that you need to (re)- open your own training, you currently can. Customers will profit by your capacity to remain present with them without enduring alongside them, but you'll likewise have the uncanny capacity to feel precisely what they are experiencing. You currently can intentionally choose whether you need to strongly "feel along" with individuals, to assist them with bettering comprehend what is happening, or whether it's ideal to remain increasingly confined and be a steady impartial grapple.

The majority of the day, you don't need to intentionally consider being an empath, by any means. The greater part of your old wiping propensities has been totally reworked to the point where you can simply concentrate on being you, without getting occupied and de-railed by others' energies.

7. The "Gracious better believe it, I completely overlooked I am an empath" Phase

You keep on dealing with any territories in which you might be retaining others' feelings. At present, it's a greater amount of a coincidental practice than an extremely standard one. Most days, you don't have to do any vitality work whatsoever. From time to time you'll experience an inward cleanse of sorts where profound intuitive energies come up to be discharged. The work isn't totally finished however, it's increasingly a matter of "up-leveling" as opposed to "endeavoring to remain above water".

Since you have quite a lot more time to "simply be" you're progressively keen on figuring out how to show signs of improvement at getting a greater amount of the great stuff that life brings to the table. The conciliatory days are finished. You are never again carrying on of a profound feeling of blame. Or maybe, you need to find progressively

39

about how you can utilize your vitality aptitudes to make and get a greater amount of what you love.

Practical Steps to Improve Empathy: Tips, Tactics and Strategies

There are three important strategies which empaths can use to help those in distress. These techniques help empaths normalizing and maintain their gift without putting themselves in problems.

Liquid Empathy

Before working with empathy, utilize this procedure to help deal with your inexperience. At whatever point you feel mysteriously pitiful, apprehensive, or angry out of the blue, you can utilize the liquid sympathy procedure to free yourself of these feelings and help you become accustomed to working with enthusiastic vitality.

Empaths are intended to fill in as the core of mankind. They can feel the feelings of others since we are intended to heal and work with them. Looking at the situation objectively, this implies they can work with and control emotional energy. They can take in emotional energy, yet that does not imply that they need to get a hold of it.

So, take a full breath and look inside yourself. Know about any negative feelings keeping you down. Negative emotional energy will, in general, be substantial, cloying, and dim. The weight is the sign. To state that a feeling is substantial infers that it reacts to gravity. It does.

So now grab hold of all the substantial, negative energy within yourself, and send it where it needs to go. Send it to the focal point of the Earth. The Earth's center is hot and liquid. It can separate and dissolve any component into its most perfect structure. On the off chance that the core can soften overwhelming metals, it can positively liquefy down negative vitality.

So push, channel, and siphon any negative energy inside you down into the Earth. See it move through the ground past the roots and earth, past layers of fossil and coal, lastly arrive at fluid hot magma. The negative energy is disintegrated with extreme heat and light, and the antagonism blurs away to discover just harmony. You in the interim, feel lighter than you would have suspected conceivable.

Practice this strategy regularly. The more you do, the better control you will pick up the emotional condition you live in. When you deal with it, you can attempt effectively depleting negative feelings surrounding you before they even touch you.

Projective empathy

This procedure is valuable when somebody is experiencing negative feelings and you need to enable them to feel good. If somebody feels disappointed, angry or furious, you could dissolve or flush the negative feelings and help them quiet down. If somebody is disturbed, you could enable them to feel tranquil. On the off chance that somebody feels despair, you could extend trust straight into their heart. You could share and enhance your most joyful sentiments to make an emotional atmosphere of unadulterated satisfaction.

This procedure depends on the hypothesis that an entryway once opened might be ventured through in either bearing. On the off chance that you feel another's feelings, at that point, you have a connection legitimately to their heart. So for what reason should you feel the feeling? Some portion of the reason you get they are communicating that they wear not have any desire to feel that way. So help them feel something better by turning around the feed and anticipating a feeling through the connection rather than just accepting it.

To do this, it is fundamental to develop ammunition stockpile of happiness, tranquillity, peace, confidence and cherishing memories in your brain. To extend a feeling, you need to feel it. To find or gain a couple of experiences, empathy needs to be kept in the cutting edge of your psyche. When have you felt joyful, successfully cheerful? When have you felt so quiet and loosened up that you could have remained as such until the end of time? Construct an information stockpile of these recollections in your psyche. Record them if it causes you to show them. Work on inclination them regularly. This will do some incredible things in a larger number of ways than one.

So on the off chance that you go over somebody whose feelings are shouting for assistance, do the following. Take a full breath and settle on what feeling you wish to extend. In the wellbeing of your psyche, review the memory that inspires your picked feeling. Make the memory as solid as conceivable in the present. Give the feeling of that memory a chance to fill your heart. At the point when your heart is overflowing with your picked feeling, send the abundance enthusiastic vitality you've created towards your objective. Give the vitality a chance to saturate the connection between your souls. Your passionate projection will gradually overpower and change their negative enthusiastic state until it mirrors your inspiration.

Showing with Empathy

Energy streams where feeling goes. Empathy gives a genuine lift with regards to showing the empaths' deepest longings in all actuality. To show, you can utilize your creative mind, you can make a dream board with pictures of what you need, and you can record what you need in the request structure. The majority of that is fine, yet what truly makes it work is the feeling.

The feeling is a widespread language that the universe comprehends at a base level. Sentiments have so much vitality and power in our lives that it just bodes well that they assume such a significant job in showing.

One minimal known favorable position of being an empath is that since we are associated with the core of the universe so personally when we feel something, we feel it into reality. So when you compose your petitions or make your vision sheets, utilize the full intensity of your feelings. Whatever you are drawing into you, feel what it resembles to have it now. Task how astonishing it feels to have what you need most, regardless of whether you don't have it. With regards to showing, empathy is an exceptional blessing!

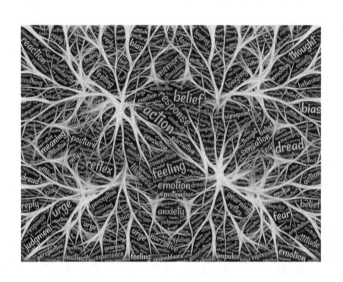

Chapter 1.   Emotion Management

What Is an Emotion

In many years, psychologists and philosophers have been having a spirited debate on emotions and its various types like happiness and sadness. They have been trying to determine their nature if perceptions about various philosophical dynamics or cognitive judgments that are about the satisfaction of set objectives. Various theories in neuroscience explain several suggestions on how a human being's brain can generate emotions by combining bodily perceptions and cognitive appraisals. If something thrilling in your life happens to you today, it is natural and very normal to develop an array of emotions such as happiness or sadness if it is a paining situation. There is a dualist view, traditional, that explains that a human being's body consists of a soul and a body. In this case, the soul is believed to be the one that experiences all mental states and emotions. However, this view can be disregarded and just termed as a motivated inference or a wishful thought since there is no substantial evidence that immortality and the soul exist.

Today, there exist two main approaches, scientific approaches, that can be employed in coming up with an explanation of what emotions are and their nature. Cognitive appraisal theory is one of the approaches and it explains that emotions can be said to be judgments on how the situation you are in currently meets the goals you have set. According to this theory, emotions such as happiness are believed that they are an expression of goals being fulfilled. On the other hand, sadness and such emotions depict unfulfilled goals and disappointments in life and can refer to a form of anger towards a stumbling block to your goals. Another theory that tries to explain what emotions are is that of William James together with others. They came up with an argument that emotions are just perceptions of various changes that take place in your body in different situations. These body changes that depict emotions include mental reactions and physiological stages in life.

These two theories, psychological perception, and cognitive appraisal can be integrated to come up with a unified definition of emotions. With an understanding of these theories, it is crystal clear that the mind is what controls and determines all sensations and perceptions based on the different situations we are in. We can, therefore, describe emotions as one's mental state that is associated with their nervous system linked to the chemical changes that take place in the body. These chemical changes are usually linked to your feelings, thoughts, degree of displeasure or pleasure and behavioral responses. Emotions can also be termed as negative or positive experiences that are linked to certain patterns of physiological functions in the body. The bottom line is that emotions are responsible for all the cognitive, behavioral, and physiological changes that we undergo in our bodies and how we react to them.

Basic Emotional Responses

There are various types of emotions that have different natures and also varying influence in the way that we conduct ourselves when with other people and even generally how we live. These emotions if not controlled they may tend to control us. They can even harm the choices that we make in life. Apart from that, these emotions are a determiner to what our thoughts are in different situations that we face daily. Having an understanding of these emotional responses will also give us a strong foundation to later discussing how we can use them to rewire our bodies and minds to attain a better and healthier life. These emotional responses are discussed below;

Happiness

This is one of the emotions that people have used different approaches to attain it thus tends to be vital. Happiness is referred to as a nice emotional state which depicts feelings of joy, contentment, well-being, gratification, and satisfaction. This emotional state is usually expressed through facial expressions like smiling, body languages like a relaxed stance and even a pleasing voice tone.

Sadness

This is another emotional state that is the opposite of happiness and is depicted by feelings such as grief, hopelessness, dampened mood, disinterest, and disappointment. This is a very common emotional state due to different stressful life experiences that we undergo daily. Having prolonged sadness might be hazardous to your health, specifically mental health since it can advance over time to become fatal depression. Its severity usually varies as it depends on the cause and the extent at which you can cope up with it.

Fear

Fear is a very powerful emotional state that plays a vital role in one's survival. When faced by danger or any situation that seems threatening, you will get into a flight or fight response situation. At this point, you will find that your muscles become tensed and with an increased heartbeat and respiration rate. This will trigger you to either fight the danger or run away from it instead. This emotion is usually depicted by widening eyes and other psychological reactions like rapid breathing and heartbeat.

Disgust

Disgust is an emotional state that happens in situations when you are disappointed or bored due to failure to achieve something. It can also be as a result of unpleasant sight, smell, or taste. This emotion can be depicted by the tendency to move away from what is disgusting you, other reactions like retching or vomiting and even facial expressions like curling your upper lip. This emotion might even make you to forever hate something that once disgusted you which can be hazardous.

Anger

Anger is one of the greatest and most powerful emotions which is depicted by agitation, hostility, antagonism, and frustration. Just as fear, it is also capable of triggering your flight or fight response. There are various ways in which anger is usually displayed and they include facial expressions like frowning. Body languages like turning down someone in a harsh manner can also be a sign of anger.

Identifying Emotions

For you to use your emotions the right way, you need first to identify the emotions the right way. Let us look at the best way to identify the emotions:

Understand the Trigger

The first step towards identifying the emotion is first to know what caused it. This will help you to describe the events that led to the emotional event. In this step, try to stick to facts alone.

You can write down the event that led to the emotion so that you have it clear in your mind.

Why Do You Think It Happened?

The next step is to identify the possible causes that led to the emotional event. This is crucial because it determines the meaning that you give to the situation that happened. The type of emotional event that led to the issue will determine the way you react to the event in question.

How the Situation Made You Feel?

The next step is to determine how the emotional event made you feel both physically and emotionally. This will help you see whether the emotion resulted in a positive or negative reaction.

You need to notice both the positive as well as the negative emotional and physical reactions that you felt when it happened. Notice any physical feelings that you experience, such as tightness in the body.

What Was Your Reaction

You need to ask yourself this question so that you understand your urges. However, for the process to be effective, you need to make sure you are completely honest. It might be painful to admit some of the urges that you felt when the event happened. When we face some situations, we at times get strange urges to react differently. Some of the emotions that we go through might make us regret later on.

You need to compare your reaction at the moment that things happened and how you usually react normally. This will tell you whether you managed to control the urge or you failed to do so.

What Did You Do and Say?

The next step would be to understand what you actually said or did due to the emotions. Even though you didn't manage to respond the right way, you need to be honest with yourself about how you handled the situation. You also need to understand how the decision you made impacted on the situation. This can be a good learning experience for you.

Once you evaluate your reaction, you can then use the situation to learn how to handle another situation that might arise.

How Did the Reaction Affect You Later on?

The final step in identifying the emotions is to understand the consequences of the actions that you took. If you said some words during the event, how did they affect you? On the other hand, if you acted in a certain way, how did it affect you later on?

So, if you find yourself being overly attached to your emotions next time, you need to ask yourself what happened and take the time to observe how you react when it happens. Go through these steps so that you can recognize your emotions. Once you practice and get used to these steps, you will be able to identify your emotions the right way and then choose the best way to respond to situations.

5 Common Emotions Experienced by Humans

Jealousy

Jealousy is a combination of different emotional reactions against the success of another person. The responses include; anger, fear, and anxiety brought about not being the primary owner of the privilege. Research has it that both women and men tend to be jealous because of various reasons. For example, when a woman believes her rival is more beautiful than her, it is likely to spark some jealousy. However, it is normal for practically everyone to experience some level of resentment. When caring about someone or something important, you may become anxious with the thought of losing the person or that something to somebody else.

What is Depression?

Being depressed involves your body, moods, and thoughts you will be having from time to time. When one is affected by depression, the way they deal with life becomes different. The way you eat, how you feel, and interact with people becomes different. Depression is a disorder, and it is tough to deal with it all by yourself.

If you notice you have depression or someone is affected by it, advise them to seek medical help. When you get the right support, everything will be fine. Being depressed means, you will experience feelings of sadness that will last for an extended period. You will eventually lose interest in things that shape your life. Remember that people who are depressed do not acknowledge who they are. When one is depressed, it does not mean you have a weakness, or you are experiencing inadequacy. It is an illness that requires professional medical help.

What is Anger?

Renown investigators like Berkowitz, who spend most of their time dealing with psychology, defines anger as a strong feeling of annoyance, displeasure, or hostility. It is also considered as a normal, healthy feeling that allows one to convey a message of reaction to a given situation. As much as it is reasonable to feel angry, the same attitude can be harmful if you express it in a way that upset you or the people around you. Everyone has had a feeling of anger, and everybody has a way of dealing with the sentiment.

The bible has covered the topic of anger comprehensively. The verses that talk about anger are numerous, but we will only mention a few. We should avoid responding to people with a negative attitude since it stimulates anger. Another famous verse about anger is proverbs 22:24 that strongly condemn us not to befriend hot-tempered people.

What is Fear

Fear is a natural feeling that everyone experiences frequently. It is something that you cannot avoid because it is a way of responding to severe sensations. It is easy to confuse fear with worry, anxiety, doubt, panic, and apprehension. The feeling of being afraid is the worst feeling that anybody would want to feel. It is uncomfortable, unpleasant, distressing, and at that point, you consistently try to come out of that situation. Everyone experiences fear in different ways; everyone is afraid of different things. This makes it challenging to come up with the right definition of fear.

Stress and Worry

Stress is a natural human response when faced with challenging situations. Same as fear, the fight or flight action is triggered by the mind when stress is experienced. Stress might be positive or negative. It is positive when one's objectives are to be met; hence, more adrenaline is produced. For negative stress, depression is always experienced, and one might go to the extent of killing himself or herself.

Why Do You Need Emotions?

We may have evolved to living in comfortable homes and not having to hunt for our livelihood, but emotions continue to remain a necessity. Psychology expert Kendra Cherry couldn't have said it better when she summed up the five main reasons why we still need our emotions:

- To act
- To survive
- To avoid danger
- To decide
- To understand

Not only does becoming a master of your emotions help you better understand yourself and others, but it also helps others understand you. The emotions displayed by others can affect your own based on the information being conveyed. For example, when you see the fear in another's expression, you're instantly on high alert and looking around for the danger. When you see someone so happy, they can't keep the smile off their face, it's infectious and you can't help but feel happy when you're around their presence.

Our emotions exist to let us know change is happening within our immediate environment or us. Sometimes it alerts us that change could be happening within both. Our emotions supply us with the information that we need about what we're experiencing and how we should respond to it.

Imagine if your emotions shut down and you felt nothing. How would you know when to feel when there was a danger present? Or to comfort a loved one when you see them upset? These basic emotions are classified as "basic" because they don't apply to us humans alone. Even animals experience these emotions, like when your dog wags its tail vigorously with happiness each time you come home. What about the times when you've caught them doing something naughty and they looked so adorably guilty?

Any emotion that you experience is going to affect your body and your mind. This is a perfectly natural occurrence, given the environment and stimuli we're exposed to are constantly changing too. Your brain is the organ in your body responsible for creating these emotions. Specifically, the limbic brain.

The limbic structure of the brain comprises of several parts. Several chemical messengers that work to transmit messages to your limbic structure.

This is referred to as neurotransmitters, and what happens is messages from your body are sent to the brain. These messages will then be responsible for telling your brain how it should feel.

When someone cuts in front of you as you're waiting in line, the messages that get sent to the limbic structure tell your brain that you should feel annoyed or angry about this.

What Is Emotional Intelligence

Emotional intelligence is the capacity to monitor your emotions as well as to be able to handle the emotions of other people. For you to be emotionally intelligent, you need to be able to distinguish between the different emotions then label them the correct way. Once you do this, the next step is to use the information that you have gathered to guide your behavior and to think as well as to influence the behavior of other people.

Emotional intelligence is whatever we use when we put ourselves in the shoes of other people, have deeper conversations with our spouses or manage a child that is unruly. It allows us to understand ourselves better, connect well with others, and live a happy life that is full of good decisions.

Components of Emotional Intelligence

Before we can look into anything else, it is vital that we understand the components of emotional intelligence. As a person, I have gained a lot of insight into emotional intelligence after I mastered the components of emotional intelligence.

Let us look at these components because they also form the skills that will allow you to interact better with one another.

Self-Awareness

Self-awareness has smaller components that make it one of the best components of emotional intelligence. First, emotional awareness means you get to recognize another person's emotions and its impact on the environment. Additionally, you need to have accurate self-assessment so that you know your limits and strengths. You also need to have self-confidence, which is the ability to be sure of one's capabilities and self-worth.

Self-Regulation

Self-regulation is all about being able to manage your emotions and how they affect you. For you to manage your emotions the right way, you need to maintain high levels of integrity and honesty, as well as take full responsibility for your performance as a person. You also need to be flexible in handling change that comes both professionally and personally.

You also need to be innovative, so that you are comfortable with and open to new information and novel ideas that come your way.

Self-Motivation

As the name suggests, emotional intelligence requires you to have the drive to meet standards. You have to try and improve so that you meet a certain standard of excellence.

You also need to be committed to what you do. We are always committed to other things, and we leave what means a lot to us. The commitment that you have needs to be aligned with the goals of the organization and the group. You also need to be ready to grab any opportunities that come your way.

Self-motivation needs a lot of optimism, as well. You need to be persistent when pursuing goals despite the setbacks and obstacles.

Empathy

When you are empathetic, you have the ability to place yourself in another person's situation and understand it. You are able to sense what the other person is going through, and you can see their perspective, and you take an active concern in what they are going through.

As business owners, we are tasked with the responsibility of understanding our customers the right way. When it comes to being empathetic, we are able to recognize, anticipate, and meet our customers' needs the right way.

Empathy doesn't stop at knowing what other people are going through and understanding them; rather, it also begs us to sense what other people need so that we can develop and improve their abilities. To do this, we need to understand what diversity is all about then cultivate the various opportunities through the people that we meet.

Social Skills

Social skills beg us to have influence, which refers to the use of effective tactics to be persuasive all the time. We also need to be able to communicate clearly and in a convincing way. It also encompasses leadership, being agents of change, and being able to manage conflict the right way. We also get to build bonds and collaborate with other people.

The Dimensions of Emotional Intelligence

According to the theorists Mayer and Salovey, there are four unique branches of emotional intelligence that guide us in knowing or emotional abilities and skills. These include:

Perceiving Emotion

Perceiving emotions is all about being able to identify and label the emotions that you come from other people. For instance, if I am in the office, and I call someone that needs to get disciplined, I need to read their emotions so that I understand what they are going through. At times you have to look beyond the mistakes a read the emotions of someone before you get to know what to do.

You also need to express your own emotions the right way. When you express the emotions, you will be able to label them then distinguish between the ones that are honest and dishonest.

Utilize the Emotions

Once you perceive the various emotions, the next step is for you to use them in making decisions. Most of the times, we fail to utilize emotions because we don't know that they are vital to our survival. Instead, we experience them; identify them, and that is that.

For you to utilize emotions, you need to prioritize your thoughts based on the emotions that are associated with different thoughts. You have to learn about and come up with thoughts that will allow you to make better judgments later on. You also need to capitalize on the mood changes so that you appreciate the different points of view, and then use the different emotional states so that you can make better decisions when faced with problems.

Understanding Emotions

You also need to understand emotions the right way. To do this, you need to make sure you identify the emotions the right way then sees the connection between all the emotions. You also have to look at the various causes and consequences of the emotions and then understand the complexity that surrounds them. You also need to look at how the various emotions change from one state to another.

Managing Emotions

This is the final dimension of emotional intelligence. Here, you have to manage both the pleasant as well as the unpleasant emotions, as well as to monitor them then reflecting on them. You need to understand how to prolong your attachment or detach yourself from the emotional state and learn to manage your emotions both within you and in other people.

Importance of Emotional Intelligence

One of the most enduring stories of life in the United States takes place in a small town in Alabama, as penned by Harper Lee. To Kill A Mockingbird is standard teaching in many schools across the United States because it deals with issues that impacted Americans in the early 19th century but which still affect us today. In To Kill A Mockingbird, one of the characters says (to paraphrase) that a person can never be really understood until you walk a day in their shoes. That adage has become a common phrase that people use in parlance but it illustrates how important empathy, and by extension, emotional intelligence, can be in creating communities where individuals understand one another and are able to work well together.

You do not have to live in Monroeville, Alabama to understand the importance of emotional intelligence. It was Harper Lee's experiences living in this town in the 1930s that helped her create the images of the town of Macomb that are stilled burned into the minds of people who read the book years ago. Even in seemingly close-knit communities, members can suffer from problems identifying or interacting with one another. But as Atticus Finch says in the book, we never really understand people until we view the world through their eyes.

It goes without saying that relating to others can be difficult sometimes, that is why empathy and emotional intelligence are such critical skills, especially for leaders. Many of us come from different cultural backgrounds, have different age demographics, different interests, or have a host of other things about us that make us singular, but we still have to be able to relate to one another on some functional level in order to live together. We do not have to be as starkly different as some of the characters and groups in To Kill A Mockingbird are in order to illustrate the point of the importance of empathy. Even within close-knit groups of people who may seem similar, albeit on the surface, people can still experience the seemingly insurmountable task of relating to and experiencing another's experiences.

This may lead some to think that life would be a lot easier if we were all the same, and this is something that some people have suggested as ways that human beings might progress in the future. Some scientists claim that they can eliminate suffering by modifying genes to remove birth defects, allergies, illnesses, dwarfism or other causes of short heights. What is next? Eliminating genes that cause people to be too tall or bad at music? One could argue that it is these differences among people that make life interesting and exciting. If people were all the same, then artists and poets would have no inspiration. It would be hard to pen a poem about a beautiful woman if all women looked exactly the same. Every poet has their own idea of the sort of person, or even the sort of object, that inspires them.

The point here is that differences should not be perceived as an obstacle that needs to be overcome by emotional intelligence. Studies suggest that good leaders use empathy to relate to people that have different skill backgrounds, hail from different parts of the world, or otherwise distinguishable from others the leaders typically work with. Does this mean that leaders should only hire certain types of people? No. Studies also show that diverse workforces lead to innovation and resilience as a diverse group is capable of coming up with a diverse set of ideas that may prove beneficial to a company. Therefore, if you are approaching the subject of emotional intelligence from the standpoint of improving leadership capabilities or another workplace skillset, keep in mind that being able to empathize with people makes you a better leader and ultimately benefits your organization.

In fact, empathy is regarded as so important to company dynamics that some organizations have begun to pen empathy manuals or guides to help their employees learn to be more empathetic. As we have established, emotional intelligence is not merely something that you are born with and that is it: the end of the story. Emotional intelligence can be learned. Team leaders can train for emotional intelligence and coach it with regular training initiatives. Although this may seem like devoting time toward something that provides minimal (albeit some) benefit to an organization, the potential benefits are actually so great that it is difficult to accurately measure them.

Studies show that 50% of managers are rated poorly by their employees. It is believed that much of this poor assessment of leadership by staff stems, at least in part, from a lack of emotional intelligence shown by leadership. There is a saying, People may not remember what you said to them, but they will remember how you made them feel. Leaders who are able to show active empathy engender the support, confidence, and respect of their employees and peers alike. Remember, empathy is not merely just sympathy—that is, demonstrating tolerance and compassion.

The key here is to have empathy: to truly feel what another is feeling. The mother who is dealing with a sick child and is distressed. The father who is working multiple jobs to make ends meet and still cannot keep his head above water. Being a leader means truly jumping into another's skin and relating to them. You do not want to be the manager who fires that aforementioned father for a minor infraction. This will not only adversely impact the individual who is fired, but it also impacts how your employees perceive you: as someone who lacks empathy for others.

We can drive the point home further by pointing out that others can generally tell when someone is being genuine with them or not. You may demonstrate being sympathetic for others through your words and gestures, which is important, but if you do not actually have empathy within yourself, then it will show. This exercise is not as difficult as it may seem to some people. This is not about putting on a show. Having empathy is as simple as thinking that just as you would want someone to relate to you when you are going through a difficult time, by the same token you should learn to relate to others when they are going through their own troubles.

Of course, part of the problem here is that life does not always dole out the hard times equally. Some people may have difficulty feeling empathy because they have not had many struggles in their own lives. People in the United States often do not feel sympathy for the homeless because they make assumptions about who homeless people are and why they are homeless. It can be difficult for people to really walk in another's shoes when they actually have not walked in their shoes. But if you remember that life can change in an instant and that your own circumstances may change, it may help you to see that others going through hard times really are not that different from you.

The adage goes that we should be compassionate to others because one day we may need someone to be compassionate to us. By showing empathy, we not only infuse our lives with positivity, but we help to encourage empathy in others.

Going back to the point of empathy as a critical leadership skill, by demonstrating empathic behaviors in their management capacity, a leader also sets the stage for their own employees demonstrating empathy when they go on to become managers. Some individuals reading this may be managers in their organizations. You may be thinking that an organization where everyone is super-sensitive and obsessed with emotions and feelings will be an organization where work is not being performed. Studies suggest that leaders showing empathy perform betters than leaders that do not. Workers will be more motivated to work for an employer that perceives them as a valued member of the team rather than just another warm body in the assembly line.

It may help future and present leaders to use the analogy of the leader as a king and his or her team as the subjects.

Subjects that are dissatisfied with the king or feel that the king is unconcerned with them rebel or they do not support the king when the king turns to them for support. Louis XIV of France famously said, "I am the state," and he may have meant that power in the kingdom was concentrated in his own person, but he also made the statement that the king was somehow intrinsically connected with the collective achievement of both the people and the kingdom.

This was illustrated all too well when, almost 80 years after the death of Louis XIV, the people of Paris stormed the Bastille and began the French Revolution, one of the most important events in world history. The French Revolution set the stage for the political and social changes that have created the world that we live in. If it were not for the French Revolution, men and women in the Western world might still be paying feudal dues to their lords and being excluded from any expression of political or personal power.

By failing to have empathy for their people, the kings of France became alienated from them, which caused the people to see the kings as being responsible for their sufferings (which they were, at least in part). There is a film called Jefferson In Paris that demonstrated how little empathy the wealthy elites of France had for the peasants that toiled the land and generated the wealth that the peasants spent. In this scene, a noble couple had a fancy dinner and it becomes warm in the dining room. They tell

69

the servants to smash the windows to let the air in because the windows were designed to not be opened. The windows that were smashed would be replaced. Whenever the couple entertained and the temperature grew to warm, the windows were smashed only to be replaced the next day. All of which was paid for by peasants who could not feed their children.

This is an extreme example of a society where there is no empathy, or at least where a segment of the population feels no empathy for the other. It is frightening to think that our own society moves in this similar direction, especially in a country like the United States that was intended to represent a set of rights designed to engender personal freedom and to resist tyrannical institutions. Leaving aside the discussion of whether or not the United States has succeeded or failed in this design, if we all took the time to have empathy for one another, we could create better work environments, better home environments, and improved relationships.

How to Improve Your Emotional Intelligence

In any competitive environment, you need to develop your emotional intelligence so that you succeed at what you do. Let us look at the top ways of increasing your emotional intelligence:

Learn to Respond instead of Reacting

When faced with a situation that threatens to become conflicting, you need to learn to respond rather than reacting to the conflict. When faced with a conflict, feelings of anger, as well as high levels of emotions, are too common. They push you to make impulsive decisions which will lead to bigger problems as well.

You need to understand that when faced with conflict, the solution you are looking for is a resolution to that conflict and nothing else.

You also ought to understand that conflict resolution is all about the two of you – when you fail to see sense in the argument, you will not see an end to the conflict.

Learn to Listen

Many conversations go south because one of the people that are involved in the conversation fails to listen to what the other person is saying.

Emotionally intelligent people have mastered the art of listening, and they wait for their turn before they speak. They make sure that they listen and then understand what is being said before they respond.

They also listen to the body language of the conversation, making sure that they read the various facial expressions, the gestures and body movements of the person before they make any assumptions.

When you learn to listen, you prevent any misunderstandings that might come up, and you also learn to respond the right way and show respect to the person you are speaking to.

Maintain a Positive Attitude

Anytime you approach someone with a negative attitude; you will not listen at all to what they have to say. This is because you have already made a judgment in your mind that the person is wrong or that they aren't up to par, and this will become a stumbling block when it comes to an understanding of them.

Emotionally intelligent people have learned how to be aware of those around them, and they reserve their attitude so that they don't let anything slip. They know what they need to do so that they can have a good day and enjoy an optimistic outlook toward other people.

Take Criticisms Well

A vital part of increasing your emotional intelligence is to tale criticisms well. Instead of always getting defensive or offended for small things, you need to take some time to understand where the criticism is coming from and then how it affects other people or their performance. They then take some time to resolve any issues that come up in a constructive manner.

They Empathize

People that are emotionally intelligent have the capacity to empathize with others. They know that empathy shows that they are strong, not weak. When you are empathetic, you get to relate to other people at a basic human level, and it opens a lot of doors for mutual respect and understanding between people that have differing opinions.

Emotion Intelligence and Empathy

Many empaths suppress their gifted abilities, which can come across in a number of physical, mental, and emotional symptoms. When an empath suppresses or blocks their abilities, they often suffer from an increase in aggression, addictive behaviors, poor health choices, negative self-talk, weakness, chronic pain, and more. These symptoms are due to the blocked energy you may be holding or due to the fact that you are going against what is in your very nature. While it is understandable why an empath would want to hide their ability, this is often because of a lack of understanding them. When an empath can fully understand just what they are capable of, this gift will no longer feel like a burden but something unique that they are willing to use and share with the world.

One of the first steps in helping to develop your empath gift is to first understand and accept that while you can feel other people's emotions and energies, they are not your responsibility. Yes, you may fully understand what they are going through, and you can provide them with ways to heal or overcome these things, but that is all you can do. It is up to the other person to accept the guidance you provide, and it is their choice alone as to whether or not they do. You may be feeling a great need to be persistent in helping people, but they are the ones that have to take action. You can only do so much, and once you become fully understanding of this, you will be more willing to embrace your gift. You won't be able to help everyone, but those you do help will take it with grace and gratitude.

On top of understanding that others will need to take responsibility for making the changes necessary to better their situation, you must also understand that you are responsible for your own emotions. As an empath, you have the ability to project more negative or more positive energy into the world, and the choice can ultimately be yours. You need to understand that you also have a tendency to play the victim and, at times, use your abilities as a way to escape from everything you are feeling. This is not an easy task for an empath as distinguishing your own emotions from others can be hard to identify. This is where having high emotional intelligence as an empath can be highly beneficial.

Increase Emotional Intelligence

It may seem as though empaths would have a rather high emotional intelligence naturally. Emotional intelligence refers to one's ability not only to understand their own emotions but also to understand the emotions of others. It also refers to one's ability to properly manage and emotions and process emotional cues of others so as to react appropriately to them. While empaths may be able to understand emotions on a deeper level, this does not always translate to their ability to properly manage or separate their emotions from others. In order for an empath to develop their abilities, they need to first increase their emotional intelligence. This will allow them to distinguish their own feelings from those of someone else, this will allow them to react and manage these emotions in an effective way. To increase emotional intelligence, one must focus on five key components of emotional intelligence.

1. Self-awareness. Without first developing your self-awareness, you will not be able to effectively develop the other components that will increase your emotional intelligence. Self-awareness for an empath is especially important as it relates to your ability to recognize your own emotions, how you handle your emotions, what triggers them, and how their emotions can impact those around them. Being able to fully understand your own emotions will

make it far easier to distinguish between your emotions and those you feel from others.

2. Self-regulation. Self-regulation is a crucial factor for increasing emotional intelligence. When you are able to self-regulate, you are able to respond appropriately to the emotions you are feeling. For an empath, this is a valuable skill to develop because it focuses on being able to regulate not only the effects your own emotions have on you but also the effects of others' emotions. One of the best techniques for self-regulation is to focus on your breathing. When you become overwhelmed by emotions, yours or others, it is best to turn your attention to your breath. Focus on keeping it steady and calm. This will allow you to let the emotions run their course and keep a clear mind. When the intensity of these emotions dissipates, you will be able to better recognize which were your own and which ones are from others. As an empath, this can be a helpful and quick way to remain calm when confronted with intense emotions from multiple people. Remember to keep your focus on your breath; when you notice you are putting too much attention to the emotions you are feeling, remind yourself to return to your breath.

Self-regulation is what can make the increase of the other areas of your emotional intelligence possible. It is through self-regulation that you can truly begin to understand the control you have over your own emotions, and this understanding as an empath will allow you to better control how you let other people's emotions affect you. If you do not develop your self-regulation, you will constantly feel overwhelmed and bombarded by emotions and react in unhealthy or unproductive ways.

3. Motivation. There are many factors that can motivate individuals; most empaths are motivated by the desire to help and heal others. In order to increase your motivational skills, you need to keep track of what you have accomplished even if it didn't turn out the way you anticipated. For an empath, this can be a list of ways you were able to comfort others or how many times you turned the negative energy you absorb into positive. Motivation can come in many forms, but you have first to be able to recognize and celebrate the things you accomplish. Empaths can be challenged by this when they are confronted with an overwhelming amount of negative energy. It is through this component that many empaths can learn to see how they have been able to overcome these negative situations and focus on the positive outcomes of the day.

4. Empathy. Empathy is a skill most empaths will not need to work on much since they naturally are highly empathic individuals. This doesn't mean there might not be room for improvement. Having empathy allows you to step into the other person's shoes, but it is also about being there to help the other person work through what they are feeling. This is

the desire for all empaths, but this is where things can get off-balance with the empathy component. Most empaths take empathy to the extreme, which is what will cause their energy levels to drop and is what causes empaths to shut off their gift abilities. Finding a balance between fully understanding how another feels and effective ways to help is a fine line. What can help an empath gain better balance is to practice loving-kindness. This is a simple process that allows you to send love and kindness to those who need it in your life or to those you are grateful for. This can be an effective practice that will help empaths release the negative energy they absorb from others and transform it into loving and positive vibes. This also helps you build up your compassion for others, which is a slightly different trait that empaths can develop.

5. Social skills. For an empath, developing healthy social skills can be overwhelming, but in working on this key factor of emotional intelligence, you will be able to put to use all the other skills you have been developing. When you develop your social skills, you will find that using your empath gift to help and heal others becomes much easier. Social skills refer to your ability to manage and maintain not only relationships with others but also the impact you have on them. How can you influence a more positive way and move them in a direction that is beneficial for both of you?

Increasing your emotional intelligence as an empath can greatly help in distinguishing your emotions from others, as well as give you a better idea of how you can use your abilities in the most beneficial way. But increasing your emotional intelligence, as with everything in life, requires having balance. If you focus too much on improving one area of emotional intelligence over another, you can lose sight of your goals, self, and confidence in your abilities.

Aside from increasing your emotional intelligence, empaths can also develop their gift through other practices and techniques.

How Being Empathic Can Help Your Physical and Mental Health

Being an empath is not something that you can turn on and off at will. It changes the way that you experience and perceive the world around you. This means that empaths do not necessarily experience the average day-to-day interactions in the same way that other people do. Empaths have a unique experience when it comes to work, family, and relationships. Over time, empaths also have different health as a result of their sensitivity to the world around them.

How Being an Empath Affects Work

Something that is different about work than many other settings is that empaths have less control over who they encounter in the work environment. There is a good chance that you will encounter unpleasant people or emotional vampires in the workplace. Even when you try to limit these encounters, interacting with these types of people can leave you feeling drained, unfocused, and unable to put your best foot forward at work. This is not to say that all workplace interactions are bad. In fact, with the right considerations, many empaths learn to love their area of work.

Even though there is a chance of negative interactions in the work environment, working can also be a positive experience. Most empaths prefer small businesses, self-employment, or doing virtual work without having to go into an office. When empaths do work with people, it may be important to ground themselves before and afterward to return to a positive state of mind. The average workday for an empath may include several mini-breaks, where you find somewhere to center your mind and release the emotional energies of the people around you.

In addition to changing the dynamic of your work environment, being an empath may also affect the job field that you go into. Some empaths embrace their desire for being alone and look for jobs where they can express their talents while choosing how much they interact with others. It is not uncommon for empaths to seek out self-employment, where they may work as writers or editors, actors, bloggers, artists, songwriters, or web designers. Outside the realm of creativity, empaths may work from home as virtual assistants or in a field where they excel, like accounting, law, plumbing, or electricity. This gives empaths the ability to set their own hours and take the jobs that they want to do. Working as a park ranger, as a horticulturist, or in the landscaping industry is another great idea since it allows you to connect to nature.

Empaths who are aware of their gift might seek out work in the help profession, such as working in the humanities like social work and therapy, healing as a doctor or nurse, or professions like hospice work, volunteering with non-profit organization, life coaching, massage therapy, natural/holistic specialist, and yoga instruction, to name a few. While these types of professionals can bring empaths in contact with negative energies, by being aware of your empathic nature and learning to release negative energies, you can easily fulfill your need to help people.

Something else to be aware of is that empaths do not respond well to stressful environments. You are not going to perform well under a boss who likes to put employees down or in an environment where you are paired up in groups to do work all the time. High-stress environments should be avoided for empaths to be successful. For example, even though working as a firefighter or EMT can be fulfilling, these types of careers are highly stressful and emotionally charged, so they may not be the best fit for the average empath.

Even though being an empath may limit the areas that you want to work in, being an empath does not limit your success. There are several benefits to being an empath in the workplace as well. For example, most empaths are natural-born conflict resolvers because they do not like disharmony. This can translate into great problem-solving capabilities in the workplace. Empaths are also great conversation starters, which can make initiating business relationships easier. Finally, the intuition that empaths experience can help guide them through the work environment and help them understand which work relationships they should focus the most of their energy on. By knowing how to concentrate your energy, you reduce the risk of wasting your time interacting with unpleasant energies for no reason.

How Being an Empath Affects Family

Some empaths have the gift of being born into a family that accepts their gift and understands their need to have downtime and space when they are overwhelmed. Others, however, grow up in an environment where they are considered sensitive, rather than empathic. Many empaths struggle as children and adolescents because they do not know they are an empath. Without this knowledge, they do not know how to control their gift or nurture themselves in the way that they need to.

Empaths fall into one spectrum or the other in familial relationships. They either isolate themselves, away from the emotions of others, or they learn to block everything out. Those that isolate themselves may be seen as quiet or shy. However, empaths may also be viewed as lazy because of their isolation, especially because empaths struggle with doing things that they are not comfortable with. On the other end of the spectrum are empaths who are considered moody. They may be misdiagnosed with bipolar disorder or another mental condition because of their constantly changing mental state.

Even once you are an adult, being in a family can take its toll. This is true whether you live at home with a relative or have created a family of your own. Empaths who decide to have children may be overwhelmed. Their selfless nature can cause them to give everything they have to their children, neglecting their own needs. As children age, this can become problematic. Empaths will struggle with administering boundaries and punishment because they want to make their children happy. Additionally, children do not have the mental capacity to respect space. Teaching them young and making it a habit to have alone time is critical to an empath maintaining their own health.

Familial relationships are different from friendships and romantic relationships because people do not get to choose their family. Some empaths flourish staying connected and close to their family as adults, while others may choose to estrange their family or limit contact. It is not uncommon for empaths to avoid familial gatherings, especially since most families have at least one person that is especially unpleasant to be around during the holidays. This might be the grandfather who is overly critical of what everyone is doing in life or the aunt who never stop rambling about her medical problems. If empaths do go to family gatherings, they often take their own vehicle, so they are not obligated to stay if they become overwhelmed. A family's acceptance of the empath's abilities may also influence whether they choose to maintain a strong bond with their family as an adult. Some families are naturally more accepting than others.

Something else to note is that empaths usually form strong bonds with their family (and people that they are close to, like close friends or romantic partners). This strong connection does not go away when that person is not in the same physical place as the empath. If you have ever felt a strong surge of emotion while you were alone or had a bad feeling, only to receive a call that a loved one had died or was hurt, you may have already experienced this deep connection. This allows the empath to know the well-being and emotional state of the people that they care about. With practice, some empaths can tune into a certain vibrational frequency and focus on the state of a certain person.

How Being an Empath Affects Relationships

Navigating traditional relationships can prove overwhelming for some empaths. The average relationship is built after spending time together, having new experiences, and developing a familiarity with someone. However, empaths may struggle with this togetherness in relationships, even those that they have developed. As empaths are deeply in tune with the emotional vibrations of the world around them, they may be over-sensitive in relationships and become upset with the way their partner is feeling without knowing why. Empaths may also be offended easily or quickly become overwhelmed with the closeness.

A common obstacle that empaths experience in relationships, even healthy ones, is finding the time to be alone and process feelings. This is especially true as the relationship progress and the couple decides to live together. Having a constant connection to someone else's emotions, and processing them as well as your own, can be overwhelming. This causes the average empath in a relationship to withdraw and feel anxious or overloaded. These feelings, accompanied by a lack of physical space, can quickly become overwhelming. As the other person picks up on the empath distancing themselves, they may question them about it or try to spend more time together, when the reality is that the empath needs to be left alone to recharge.

Even though relationships can be challenging for empaths, this does not mean that you are doomed to be forever alone. Empaths can have successful relationships when the traditional sense of a relationship, one where both partners are constantly spending time together, is redefined. Empaths must choose partners who understand their need for physical space to be happy in a relationship. This is especially true during times of conflict, when two people may nitpick and fight with each other instead of taking the time to be alone and calm down before coming back together to discuss the problem.

Some empaths have an innate need to heal others and they seek out relationships with people who are damaged in some way, such as emotional vampires. Seeking out these types of relationships is self-destructive, especially when the empath chooses to turn a blind eye to their partner's behaviors. People who want to find happiness in a partner must choose someone who is emotionally balanced and understanding. Even if the other person is not an empath themselves, they should be in tune with their empathic side and have compassion for others. The ability to compromise is another critical skill that empaths should look for in a partner. While your partner should respect boundaries when you are clear about your needs, your partner is going to have needs too. For example, imagine that your partner tends to seek physical comfort after a disagreement, while you need time to recover and find a place of peace before being physically affectionate. A good compromise might be that they give you 15 minutes to gather yourself and then you give them the physical affection they need to feel okay.

Something else to keep in mind when getting into a relationship is that empaths need their own space. If you decide to live with a romantic partner, it is important to set clear boundaries and have your own space. Empaths will suffocate if they do not have somewhere to retire when they are feeling overwhelmed. It is also important to be clear about your needs with your partner. Even though you are highly sensitive to the world around you, it does not mean that your partner understands the things you need. Remember that even though you need space, there will be times when it feels natural and comfortable to be physically connected to your partner. Finding the perfect balance will let the relationship thrive.

Another obstacle that empaths face in a relationship is sleeping arrangements. Sleeping next to each other at night is a major part of many relationships, as it promotes feelings of togetherness, relaxation, and safety. For empaths, sleeping together causes emotional energies to transfer between both partners. This can be stressful and make it hard for some empaths to get the rest that they need to from their sleeping hours. Once again, it becomes important to communicate your needs and then compromise. Be sure that you can rest the way you need to at bedtime and be sure that your needs are not making your partner feel lonely.

If you are worried about moving in with a partner or having them move into your space, give it a test run first. It can be damaging and stressful to move in together too soon, especially if you are still adapting to the togetherness of being in a relationship. Try spending a few days together and then work up to a week. Use this time to realize your needs and preferences and take note of how your partner is responding. Then, come back and discuss it with them to see how things could be improved.

How Being an Empath Affects Health

One thing that empaths frequently experience is stress and anxiety. It is mentally draining to constantly feel the emotions of others and the body's defenses become weaker afterward. Some common health problems that empaths deal with are lower back problems and digestive disorders. Western medicine may attribute the related problems to stress, but traditional Chinese medicine, Buddhism, and other Eastern cultures attribute the problems of the lower back and digestive tract to the position of the solar plexus. The solar plexus is one of the chakras. It is considered the 'emotional seat of the soul', which explains why empaths would have problems in this area. Empaths experience the emotional charge of others through the solar plexus chakra and the physical toll that it takes on the body causes harm to the digestive system, triggering a wide range of conditions that range from stomach ulcers to irritable bowel syndrome. In the lower back, the most problems are felt by empaths who are not in touch with their empathic nature. Those that shut out the way they are feeling and block out their empathic nature often struggle with lower back pain the most.

Chronic health problems are also common in empaths, which are a result of not knowing how to set healthy energy boundaries. These chronic problems come from tapping too deeply into energy stores and draining the body. In addition to chronic back pain and digestive conditions, some chronic conditions that affect empaths include hormonal problems like depression, anxiety, headaches, migraines, and fatigue. Additionally, as you tap into other people's experience, it lowers the function of your adrenal gland and immune response. This weakens your body to fight off sickness that you may encounter, so empaths may become sick more frequently than the average person.

Complications from being overweight can also harm empaths. While not all empaths are overweight, it is not uncommon for the body to store extra pounds even when the empath eats properly and exercises regularly. This is often caused by being an empath that is not in tune with their emotional side. The physical weight is meant to act as a barrier to the outside world, desensitizing the empath and helping them block out the world around them.

It is also common for empaths to take on the symptoms of the people that they care about. Some people may refer to this as a type of sympathy ailment, but it goes beyond sympathy because empaths physically experience the symptoms of the cold, back pain, and other ailments. While being an empath can take a toll on health, both physical and mental, taking care of yourself can help you have a longer, healthier life. You will find advice for keeping the mind and body of an empath healthy as you read.

Change Your Mindset

I believe that success and happiness are all about our mindsets. It affects everything in our lives, even how we react and handle the world around us. To achieve your goals, you need your mindset to level up with your aspirations.

The Path to Self-Improvement

Your self-talk has a direct connection with whether or not you have a positive or negative mindset. Consider changing your negative self-talk into a full-on empowerment speech. Who better to encourage you than yourself? It'll have the biggest impact. One of the ways you can do this is by using the positive affirmations I mentioned earlier.

Your mindset is also a reflection of how you see yourself. If you constantly believe, for example, that you're a slob or a bad worker, you will eventually train your brain into believing and following these thoughts. Through reading, you might be surprised at how quickly you pick up on the author's way of thinking. Look into some literature that will lead you in the right direction and try to avoid dark and heavy reading until you're in a better headspace. Reading is an excellent activity for an empath to take up due to their ability to see how others feel and think. You may find that books help you feel more positive, depending on their genres and titles. Go for self-motivating and happy books and take note of how much your mindset changes by journaling.

Using your environment to exercise your way of thinking is maybe one of the best options for an empath. We tend to forget that there is a lot more out there than little old us when trapped in a certain mindset. You might think you're stuck in the worst situation possible until you see someone else in an even worse predicament than yourself. Nature can be your getaway and "mind cleanser" when you really need it. There is nothing like beautiful scenery to readjust your way of thinking and make you appreciate the beauty of this world and life. As a bonus, sunshine is fantastic for a natural mood-booster. Once your head is clear again, you can carry on with your self-improvement journey. Sometimes all we need is a bit of a break from our own minds in order to get back on track. There's no better break than a walk in nature. You could even take that book along.

Surround yourself with people that have your desired mindset and try to celebrate your daily small achievements in life; it will lead you to accomplishing many more.

You Are Good Enough

Trust me, everyone on the planet has had a moment where they felt like they weren't good enough. Worse than that, I believe all of us have let the words and thoughts of others dictate how we feel about ourselves. No one can make you feel that way if you do not let them. Ultimately, you are in charge of your feelings and thoughts. Do not let anyone take that away from you.

A perfect example of what can make us feel like we're not good enough is the opinions of others and that little voice in our own head.

Shut down your inner critic. He's not doing you any good. You can talk back. The moment that little voice starts nagging at you about something that makes you feel inferior, shut it down. By shifting your focus onto something else or just simply saying "no," you are training yourself to recognize your self-worth. Make a list of what boosts your confidence on those days that you just aren't able to get rid of that voice. Perhaps you should consider saving or writing down messages that someone said that put a smile on your face. If they're truly worth it, stick them up somewhere you'll see them often, like the bathroom mirror.

It is so easy to compare ourselves to others on a daily basis as we always want to be the best that we can possibly be. The hard truth is that there is always going to be someone better than you. There will always be someone smarter, faster, or more attractive. You need to make peace with it or it will eat you up inside. You don't need to be better than everyone else. You only need to be you. Trust me, being you is a pretty great thing. Being the best you is what is important, not being better than someone else.

Social media is one of the things that is a major cause of people not feeling good enough about themselves. Many of us have at least one social media account and it is incredibly difficult to avoid, particularly since they are designed to be addictive. We so easily compare ourselves to a picture-perfect life online while completely ignoring the fact that we all have our flaws and rough days. Just because someone is more likely to share their fun and exciting days online doesn't mean there aren't bad ones they don't show you. Let go of the unrealistic idea that everything is perfect for anyone who isn't you.

Do things that make you happy and make you feel good. Compliment that stranger on their shoes if you really want to. If you make them feel good, you're bound to make yourself feel even better. I don't know about you, but I love making other people smile. Just be kinder to yourself and know that being human is about being flawed. It's not something to put yourself down over.

Stop Procrastinating

Oh procrastination, how much more would we get done without you in our lives.

I'm going to tell you, my humble reader, a secret. If you want to make changes in your life, it's up to you to do it. You need to put aside all those reasons not to because in truth, there really isn't a reason at all. Stop procrastinating. Make the changes.

Aim for your desired direction of change and go for it. Choose the fruit salad over those biscuits that are seductively whispering sweet nothings in your ear. Cut off that toxic person that causes nothing but upset in your life. These are some of the most important first steps into realizing your full self-worth. You know yourself better than anyone, even if it doesn't always feel like it. If you want to do something or your mind is telling you to do something, there is probably a good reason for it.

Of course this is not as easy as it sounds; it requires hard work and dedication. To start off, pick one personal change that seems most important to you and aim for it. Remember that even baby steps are better than standing still. Write down your progress to keep yourself motivated and to be able to reflect on how far you've come. Be patient. As with all good things in life, it will take time to make these changes, so don't get discouraged when things don't happen immediately. Nobody else will be able to take the first steps for you, but once you begin, you'll realize how much you're really worth it.

And believe me, you are worth it.

Take Control of Your Situation

It feels good to be in control at all times. Whenever you feel negative thoughts taking over your life, you will trash them and then give yourself some rules that you will follow.

Enjoy a Stress-Free Life

When your soul and mind are filled with positivity, you won't have any room for stress to destroy your peace. You can live a life free of stress.

How to Change Your Thoughts and Transform Your Life

The good thing about all this is that the mind can be controllable. Let us look at the various tips that you can use to change the way you feel or the way you do things.

Use Positive Affirmations

Well, you know too well that affirmations aren't always positive, they can also be negative.

The sad thing is that many people only use negative affirmations when talking to themselves or when they plan to do something. For instance, when faced with a huge task, many people will first make negative affirmations that will then become their truth.

Affirmations have an impact on the decisions that the brain makes, which is the reason why you need to have positive ones that will make you go for good things.

Positive affirmations work like mantras; they come with a spiritual and sacred force about them that will make you stronger. Avoid negative thoughts such as "I can't," "I might" and focus on affirmations such as "I should', "I can," and more.

Remember that the brain is always adapting to thought patterns that you pick up, and it then directs your organs to react the right way.

Know When to Stop

You might do something, but you won't do all the things all the time. If you make a mistake, you need to know the right time to stop when you make a mistake. Stop cursing yourself over what you would have done differently at any time.

This shouldn't mean you don't need to look into your past mistakes so that you can plan your future intelligently; instead, you need to know what to take up from your past and what not to take up.

Count Your Joys

Many times, we focus on our misgivings and then forget that we have had good times before.

They think of a situation that could be better by now and forget the ones that might have turned out worse than they already are.

When you learn to appreciate something, you make it possible to unlock the joy of life. It makes you see what you have to be enough and to be more than enough. You will be able to turn denial into acceptance, confusion into clarity, and chaos into order. It can even turn a stranger into that friend that you always wanted.

Instead of complaining over what you don't have, it would be better to enjoy and appreciate what you already got. If you have achieved some success so far, you need to aspire and enjoy what you have done so far instead of feeling sad that you haven't achieved what you dreamt about.

Savor the Thrill of Your Achievement

It is one thing for you to achieve your goals, and it is another thing for you to enjoy it when you have achieved it.

So, you need to aim for something, and then once you achieve what you aimed for, you enjoy it so that you go to the next.

Hold Your Head High

Many people always tend to feel low when they are faced s by demoralizing conditions. They feel low, and this shows in the way that they talk and walk. If you tell your brain that you are feeling low, then it will communicate to your organs, and they will act according to the communication – you will feel more miserable.

On the other hand, if you train your brain to read only the positive vibes even in trouble, you will be able to lift your spirits, and then your body will react the same way. This is the best way to beat depression when things are going wrong.

Seek Happiness in the Present Time

Don't associate your happiness with the future; rather, you need to be happy in the present. When you postpone your happiness to the unsure future, you will end up living in sorrow all the time. The time for you to be happy is now because yesterday is gone.

Master Your Emotions

You need to always be a master rather than a slave to your moods. You need to be a ruler of your happiness kingdom.

Try and make sure other circumstances and people don't determine your moods.

Many people tend to depend on material possessions to be happy, try, and get your happiness from within yourself regardless of the situation.

For instance, if you have been ditched by your girlfriend, don't allow the heart to be a slave to their emotions. If the person has decided to be happy without your presence, then you also can do the same.

Meditate Daily

Meditation helps you to connect with your inner self in ways that you cannot imagine. Try and find the best meditation approach that will help you to manage your inner feelings at all times.

Talk to a meditation expert and identify the best method that you can use to meditate on a daily basis. Get the right time to meditate, whether early in the morning or late at night so that you can meditate the right way.

Take Charge of Your Emotions

6 Steps to Controlling Your Emotions

To dodge the consume of carrying on during an enthusiastic upsurge, find a way to quiet your elevated soul and calm your uneasy personality. At the point when the minute has passed, you'll be thankful you had the option to be the ace of your feelings. Dr. Harra is a smash hit creator, analyst, and relationship master. Look at her new book: The Karma Queens' Guide to Relationships.

This post was distributed on the now-shut Huff Post Contributor stage. Givers control their own work and presented openly on our site. In the event that you have to signal this section as oppressive, send us an email. Feelings are the most present, squeezing and once in a while agonizing power in our lives. We are driven step by step by our feelings. We take risks since we're energized for new prospects. We cry since we've been harmed and we make penances since we love. Beyond question, our feelings direct our contemplations, expectations and activities with better authority than our discerning personalities. In any case, when we follow up on our feelings too rapidly, or we follow up on an inappropriate sorts of feelings, we regularly settle on choices that we later mourn.

Our emotions can adjust between perilous limits. Veer excessively far to one side and you're verging on rage. Steer an excessive amount to one side and you're in a condition of happiness. Similarly, as with numerous different parts of life, feelings are best met with a feeling of control and sensible point of view. It is not necessarily the case that we should prevent ourselves from beginning to look all starry eyed at or hopping for satisfaction after extraordinary news. These genuinely are the better things throughout everyday life. It is negative feelings that must be taken care of with outrageous consideration.

Negative feelings, similar to fierceness, jealousy or sharpness, will in general winding crazy, particularly following they've been activated. In time, these sorts of feelings can develop like weeds, gradually molding the psyche to work on unfavorable emotions and commanding day by day life. Ever met an individual who's reliably irate or threatening? They weren't brought into the world that way. Yet, they enabled certain feelings to mix inside them for such a long time that they became ingrained sentiments emerging very often.

So how might we abstain from working on an inappropriate kinds of sentiments and ace our feelings under the harshest of conditions?

Pursue my six stages to control your feelings and recover objectivity in any difficult circumstance:

Try not to respond immediately. Responding promptly to enthusiastic triggers can be an enormous misstep. It is ensured that you'll state or accomplish something you'll later lament. Before disproving the trigger with your enthusiastic contention, take a full breath and balance out the staggering motivation. Keep on breathing profoundly for five minutes, feeling as your muscles not tense and your pulse comes back to ordinary. As you become more quiet, certify to yourself this is just transitory.

Here are three different ways to oversee your mind-set:

1. Mark Your Emotions

Before you can change how you believe, you have to recognize what you're encountering at this moment. Is it true that you are anxious? Do you feel disillusioned? It is safe to say that you are pitiful?

Remember that outrage in some cases covers feelings that vibe helpless - like disgrace or humiliation. So give close consideration to what's truly going on within you.

Put a name your feelings. Remember you may feel an entire bundle of feelings on the double - like on edge, baffled, and eager. Naming how you feel can take a ton of the sting out of the feeling. It can likewise assist you with taking cautious note of how those sentiments are probably going to influence your choices.

2. Reframe Your Thoughts

Your feelings influence the manner in which you see occasions. In case you're feeling on edge and you get an email from the manager that says she needs to see you immediately, you may accept that you will get terminated. Assuming notwithstanding, you're feeling upbeat when you get that equivalent email, your first idea may be that you will be advanced or complimented on a vocation all around done.

Consider the passionate channel you're taking a gander at the world through. At that point, reframe your contemplations to build up an increasingly practical view. On the off chance that you discover yourself thinking, "This systems administration occasion will be a finished exercise in futility. Nobody is going to converse with me and I'm going to resemble a nitwit," remind yourself, "It's dependent upon me to get something out of the occasion. I'll acquaint myself with new individuals and show enthusiasm for finding out about them."

Some of the time, the most effortless approach to increase an alternate point of view is to make a stride back and ask yourself, "What might I say to a companion who had this issue?" Answering that question will remove a portion of the feeling from the condition so you can think all the more objectively. In the event that you wind up harping on negative things, you may need to change the direct in your mind. A brisk physical movement, such as taking a walk or wiping off your work area, can assist you with halting ruminating.

3. Participate in a Mood Booster

At the point when you're feeling awful, you're probably going to take part in exercises that keep you in that perspective. Disconnecting yourself, carelessly looking through your telephone, or grumbling to individuals around you are only a couple of the run of the mill "go-to awful temperament practices" you may enjoy. In any case, those things will keep you stuck. You need to make positive move in the event that you need to feel much improved.

Think about the things you do when you feel glad. Do those things when you're feeling awful and you'll begin to feel good.

Here are a couple of instances of mind-set sponsors:

- Call a companion to discuss something wonderful (not to keep grumbling).
- Take a walk.
- Ponder for a couple of moments.
- Tune in to inspiring music.
- Continue Practicing Your Emotional Regulation Skills

Dealing with your feelings is extreme on occasion. What's more, there will probably be a particular feeling - like indignation - that occasionally outwits you.

In any case, the additional time and consideration you spend on controlling your feelings, the rationally more grounded you'll turn into. You'll pick up trust in your capacity to deal with inconvenience while additionally realizing that you can settle on solid decisions that move your state of mind.

5 Steps to Building a Rock-Solid Self-Confidence

Building self-confidence is an ongoing process that needs determination and energy. Here are some steps to think about when you are trying to build yours:

Step 1: Step Out of Your Comfort Zone

If you are going to have unshakeable confidence, you have to be willing to step out of your comfort zone so that you can do things out of the ordinary. You have to stir up that urge burning within you to be extraordinary.

Perhaps you have a brilliant idea that your belief could benefit your company, but you do not know how to share that with your boss. Perhaps you have a crush that you never dared to approach.

The problem that comes with not acting on these desires is that you will stagnate right where you are. Truth is, when you fail to explore new experiences, you are letting fear take away your sunshine. You are simply digging deeper into your zone of comfort. The hole that you have been sitting in for several decades now.

Yes, it may be intimidating to make the first approach into the unknown, risking being embarrassed by failures. But if you think about it, it's just 'FEAR' – False Evidence Appearing Real. What is the worst that could happen? Often times, you are just overthinking. Stepping out of your comfort zone can be so daunting, but it is important if you wish to fulfill your life's purpose and have unshakeable confidence. This could be the way you can finally prove to yourself that you can achieve anything you set your mind to.

After all, what is the worst that can happen? You can share with your boss and steer the company to success, or the boss simply turns it down. You could ask that girl or boy out, and they could say either yes or no – You also get your answer without wasting too much time guessing. Either way, it is a win-win situation.

The secret to having solid confidence starts with you!

One thing that I will tell you for sure is that to get out of your comfort zone; you have to start by setting micro-goals that will all eventually add up to the bigger picture. Micro-goals simply refer to small pieces of the larger goal you have. When you break your bigger goals into chunks, accomplishing them becomes quite easy, and you will have so much fun while you're at it. This will also build up your momentum to keep pushing until you have reached your target.

So, we suppose that you have a business idea or strategy that you would like to share with your boss but haven't gotten the courage to do it. What you can do instead is break your major outcome into smaller goals that eventually yield similar outcomes. Take small steps to get started, no matter how small it is. Instead of taking the big leap and feeling overwhelmed, starting small will take the pressure off you. When you do this, you simply make things quite easy to digest and make follow-ups easy.

So you like that girl or boy and have no courage to tell them how. But he or she may not be single in the first place. So your micro goal should be to establish a rapport with them first before you dive into the deepest end of things. Even before you ask them out on a date, get to know who they are by just initiating a short conversation with her/him. Isn't that better? This does not sound like you are stalking them.

That said, you have to appreciate that when you set micro-goals, it allows you to step out of your comfort zone. As you achieve your micro-goals one after the other, you will realize that every small wins can help you get the confidence you need to move forward. Challenge yourself that you are going to do something out of the ordinary every day and see how that grows your confidence.

Step 2: Know Your Worth

Did you know that people with rock solid confidence are often very decisive? One thing that is pretty admirable with successful people is that they do not take too much time trying to make small decisions. They simply do not overanalyze things. The reason why they can make fast decisions is that they already know their big picture, the ultimate outcome.

But how can you define what you want?

The very first step is for you to define your values. According to Tony Robbins, an author, there are two major distinct values; end values and means values. These two types of values are linked to the emotional state you desire: happiness, sense of security, and fulfillment among others.

Means Values

These simply refer to ways in which you can trigger the emotion you desire. A very good example is money, which often serves as a mean, not an end. It is one thing that will offer you financial freedom, something that you want and hence is a means value.

Ends Values

This refers to emotions that you are looking for, like love, happiness, and a sense of security. They are simply the things that your means values offer. For instance, the money will give you security and financial stability.

In other words, the means value is the things that you think you desire for you to finally get the end values. The most important thing is for you to have clarity on what you value so that you can make informed decisions much faster. This, in turn, will give you a strong sense of identity, and that is where you draw everlasting confidence from. You have to be in control of your life and not the other way round.

One way you can do that is ensuring that you define your end values. You can start by dedicating at least an hour or two each week to write down what your end values are. To get there, start by stating what your values are that you'd like to hone to get to your dream life.

Some of the questions that might help you put things into perspective include:

- What are some of the things that matter most in your life?
- Are there things that you do not care about in your life?
- If you were to make a tough decision, what are some of the values that you will stand by and what are those that you will disregard?
- If you have or had kids, what are some of the values you will instill in them?

Step 3: Create your own happiness

Happiness is a choice, and also the best obstacles are self-generated constraints like thinking that you're unworthy of happiness.

If you do not feel worthy of joy, then you also don't believe you deserve the good things in life, the things that make you happy and that'll be precisely what keeps you from being happy.

You can be happier. It is dependent upon your selection of what you focus on. Thus, choose happiness.

Happiness is not something happens to you. It is a choice, but it takes effort. Don't wait for somebody else to make you happy because that may be an eternal wait. No external person or circumstance can make you happy.

Happiness is an inside emotion. External circumstances are responsible for just 10 percent of your happiness. The other 90% is how you behave in the face of those conditions and which attitude you adopt. The scientific recipe for happiness is external conditions 10%, genes 50 percent and intentional activities - that is where the learning and the exercises come in - 40%. Some people are born more happy than others, but if you're born unhappier and practice the exercises, you will end up happier than somebody who had been born more joyful and does not do them. What both equations have in common is that the minimal influence of outside conditions on our happiness.

We usually assume that our situation has a much greater impact on our happiness. The interesting thing is that happiness is often found when you quit searching for it. Enjoy each and every moment. Expect miracles and opportunities at each corner, and sooner or later you will run into them. Whatever you focus on, you may see more of. Pick to concentrate on opportunities, decide to focus on the good, and choose to focus on happiness. Make your own happiness.

Step 4: Be Ready To Embrace Change

Have you ever found yourself obsessing about the future or the past? This is something that many of us find ourselves doing. However, here is the thing; the person you were five years ago or will be five years from now is very different from who you are right now.

You will notice that five years ago, your taste, interests, and friends were different from what they are today and chances are that they will be different five years from now. The point is that it is critical when you embrace who you are today and know that you are an active evolution.

According to research conducted by Carol Dweck, it is clear that children do well at school once they adopt a growth mindset. In fact, with the growth mindset, they believe that they can do well in a certain subject. This is quite the opposite of what children with a fixed mindset experience because they believe that what they are and all that they have is permanent. Therefore, having the notion that you cannot grow only limits your confidence.

What you should do to embrace all that you are is stopping self-judgment. Most of the time, we are out there judging people by what they say, how they say it, what they wear, and their actions. In the same way, we judge ourselves in our heads comparing our past and present self.

For you to develop a strong sense of confidence, it is important that you start by beating the habit of self-judgment and negative criticism. Yes, this is something that can be difficult at first, but when you start to practice it, you realize how retrogressive that was.

You can start by choosing at least one or two days every week when you avoid making any judgment at all. If you have got nothing good to say, don't say it. If there is a negative thought that crosses your mind, you replace it with a positive one.

Gradually, your mind will start priming to a state of no judgment, and it will soon become your natural state of mind. This will not only help you embrace others but also accept yourself for who you truly are.

Step 5: Be Present

Sounds simple, right? It is important and necessary that you build your confidence. By being present, you are simply allowing your mind, body, and soul to be engaged in the task at hand.

Let us imagine speaking to someone that is not listening to what you are saying. This is something that has probably happened to a good number of us. How did you feel? On the other hand, imagine speaking to someone, and you feel like you were the only person in the room. Feels pretty special, huh?

The reason why you feel special is that they were present at that moment. They paid very close attention to what you were saying, feeling every emotion with you. They were engaged in the conversation at a deeper level. This way, you can retain information while still experiencing empathy.

To be present, you have to develop a mental double-check. This simply means that you should mentally check-in on yourself regularly. To do that, you have to develop a mental trigger or calendar when you ask yourself where your mind is. This is the time when you act as an observer of your mind.

Are you thinking of dinner reservations while in a meeting? Do you think that you are not good enough? To call yourself out of these negative thoughts means that you mentally check in on yourself every often. Once you have the answer to your question, take in a deep breath and bring back your focus on your most important things.

Chapter 2.   Relationships

Empath Friendships and Relationships

Empaths need to be very careful when it comes to being friends with people or with those they are in a relationship with. There are people out there who seek out empaths, thinking that they are weak and can be controlled. Remember the two friends who were at the casino? One of them refused to get out of her chair as she did not want to lose her slot machine; however, the other friend jumped up to help the elderly lady after she fell off her scooter. That friend showed no concern, and she explained that she knew other people were going to go help her anyway, which was true, including her empath friend, who ran to the woman's side. Friends come in all shapes and sizes, all character traits, as well as mental variations. These two friends, in particular, have been friends for over 20 years, so that instance did not make or break their friendship; however, they did discuss why they both reacted as they did. Having a friendship where you can openly talk about issues or something that was bothersome definitely makes it easier.

Being an empath in a friendship can be a good and bad thing. You may twist it to empaths having a difficult time finding friends due to manipulative people taking advantage of them, and that is true at times. However, here are some reasons why empaths make the best friends:

- Empaths know what you are thinking before you say it.
- Empaths have the ability to feel others' emotions as if they were theirs.
- They recognize toxic people, such as narcissists, right away.
- Empaths avoid egotistical people and will want you to as well.

Empaths know what you are thinking before you say it. If you are telling an empath a story, they will be able to tell if it is true or not. Most of the time, they will tell by looking at you. However, if you have been friends for many years and are talking on the phone, they will be able to tell any embellishments that you may make. The friend of the empath may not realize this as typically an empath will internalize it for future reference; however, if they do wait and the truth comes out, be prepared to hear about it. On the other side, when you do see your empath friend, all they have to do is look at you to know how you are feeling. You do not necessarily have to tell an empath anything at all; they can tell if something is off just by looking at you. You can try to tell them that everything is fine or that you are not doing anything wrong, but they just have that feeling that you are and will not let you get away with it. Empaths will instantly pick up on vibes, body language, and facial expressions to know how you feel. Half of the time, you do not even need to tell them something is wrong, and that in itself makes it easy to be a friend with an empath.

Empaths have the ability to feel others' emotions as if they were theirs. Empaths, can pick up on others' emotions very easily. This is beneficial in a friendship because the empath will not have to ask you repeatedly what is wrong; they will just sense it. Empaths are very easy to get along with because they tend not to ask you a lot of questions; they typically have an idea when you need your time and space, so they do not probe a lot. If they can feel the pain of those who are far away or on television when there is violence, just imagine how good of a friend they will be to those closest to them as they feel their pain.

They recognize toxic people, such as narcissists, right away. Empaths will pick out toxic people in a few seconds of seeing them. If you are talking to someone and the empath picks up bad vibes, telling you to stay away from that person, you need to stay away from that person. An empath will not tell you that if it is not to protect you from being hurt. An empath will know when someone is being dishonest. Most of the time, the empath can pick up on the intentions of someone, and they are telling you to protect you. This is their way to save you from being hurt in the future.

Empaths avoid egotistical people and will want you to as well. Egotistical people are one of the most annoying people on the planet. Empaths cannot stand when other people think they are better than everyone else. They will go to great lengths to avoid these types of people. It may even mean they isolate themselves for a while so they can avoid and recharge their energy. If you have an empath friend like this, just try to understand where they are coming from, that they need to isolate to protect themselves from energy drainers. In order to escape at times, empaths love to daydream and slip into their own peaceful world where there are zero toxic people to ruin their energy.

Empaths make great friends; they just need to find friends to balance them out. Like the two at the casino — one saved the slot machines, and one saved the elderly lady by picking her up off the floor.

Managing Your Relationships and Environment as an Empath

Empaths desire relationships with other human beings just like everyone else.

However, they differ from non-empaths on how they cultivate and nurture these relationships. More importantly, their level of sacrifice and commensurate benefit differs significantly from that of non-empaths. This makes it extremely important for empaths to manage their relationships in such a manner that matches sacrifices with benefits.

In this Part, we are going look at the workplace relationship as one of the most important relationships where empaths are likely going to be more disadvantaged on the cost-benefit scale.

More often than not, empaths find themselves more drained and draught in relationships and environments with strenuous social interactions. As we have seen before, while non-empaths are likely going to be charged up by vibrant social interactions, empaths are more likely to be discharged. Thus, it is important for empaths to learn how to survive in such socially strenuous environments... be it at work, social events, or intimate relationships.

Empaths, like other human beings, are greatly shaped up during their childhood. It is at this malleable stage that certain enduring characters are molded. However, it can become a big challenge when it comes to raising a child empath. There are likely going to be a lot of misunderstandings. And with these misunderstandings, there are likely going to be a lot of reactions from parents that may hurt, hinder, or inhibit the growth potential of an empath child and thus constrain the child's development. Many empaths suffer childhood trauma due to having been poorly mishandled by caregivers (especially parents) who did not understand their unique needs and treated them in a harsher or more hostile way in the belief that they were being 'abnormal' or 'too demanding of attention'.

Thus, managing relationships and environments is extremely important to the health and wellbeing of an empath – right from childhood to adulthood.

How to Manage Your Work Environment and Boost Your Productivity as an Empath

It is inevitable that empaths, once at their productive age, will experience the work environment. Their sensitivity won't be muted simply because of work. They will still carry with their nature, and personality as empaths at the workplace.

And just as empaths are frequently misunderstood at home and social environments, they too are misunderstood at the workplace. This calls for them to take greater responsibility towards managing their sensitivity such that it does not inhibit their productivity.

Naturally, empaths are more prone to procrastination than non-empaths, this is because they take their time thinking through before acting.

This procrastination can also have a negative impact on their punctuality and timekeeping. Sometimes, due to their mood swings, they may wake up some days with greater inertia than others. The higher the inertia, the less conscious it is to keep time. Lateness and absenteeism increase with inertia.

Empaths are extremely sensitive to their environment. They love the natural environment characterized by calmness and serenity. Clutters, especially from unnatural objects can drain their energy and leave them more lethargic and highly sensitive.

To cope and create a conducive work environment where empaths can be more productive, it simply means that they have to give importance to decluttering, punctuality, and avoiding procrastination.

Declutter

A cluttered environment is an energy-sapping environment to an empath. Clutter saps energy from the empath thus causing the empathy to feel tired, irritated, worn out and confused.

A cluttered work environment lowers the empath's productivity. This can cause the empath's career to be frustrated as the bosses will consider the empath as a low-energy, and underserving of greater responsibility which comes with higher pay.

At worst, a cluttered environment can cause a strain in the relationship between the empath and fellow workmates. This is because of the empath's level of irritability soars, which means that the empath will become easily angered with just minimal provocation.

To declutter, the empath has to practice decluttering the workspace as a habit. This habit involves:

Clearing the workstation and arranging things before the end of working hours – this will ensure that the empath will arrive the next day to a clean and organized work environment

Clearing any pile-up soonest possible – an empath must avoid procrastination. Thus, the empath should embark immediately on any new assignment and attend to any incoming mail or document.

Ensuring that, apart from the in-tray and out-tray, no documents are left scattered on the workstation

Filing off documents that are not of immediate attention

Tucking shoes and extra garment (such as a sweater, jacket, coat, etc) away from the workspace. While most offices have provision for shoe racks, few have provision for extra garments away from the workspace. It is good to vouch for a wardrobe so that extra garments can be kept aways for the workspace sight. If allowed, you can make a personal initiative of bringing a portable wardrobe to your workspace.

Keep time

Keeping time is extremely important to an empath. While some empaths are good timekeepers, some are not. Even those who are good timekeepers, they may experience periods of extremely low moods and dampened spirit such that they may end up arriving late.

Keeping time, just as decluttering is also an important habit.

The best time-keeping habit is to establish a routine.

Work routine

This will depend on your work schedule. While some schedules are flexible such that you have control over (if you are the self-employed or senior manager), others strictly tight such that you have no control over.

Whether your work routine is flexible or tight, it is important to consider the following:

- Do not skip your meals
- Engage in mobility exercises
- Have breaks to relax or refresh
- Evaluating day-to-day plan

To evaluate is to weigh the outcome against targets/expectations as you carry out your implementation. It is the key part of managing success.

In our case, we implemented a day-to-day plan to increase productivity. Under evaluation, you will have to review the result of your implementation against set goals.

In managing success, you need to:

Devise effective measurement standards – Without measurement standards, it is impossible for you to be able to determine performance. There are various established standards for each particular task. Your experience can also be used to create a reasonable benchmark to which you can use to measure performance. The standard should be challenging but achievable.

Develop an effective feedback reporting system – once you have devised effective measurement standards, the next thing is to have an effective feedback reporting system. This system is akin to the quality control section within the production department. Every performance needs to be measured against the standard and the outcome reported immediately for quick action.

Layout effective control mechanism – a control mechanism is that mechanism that helps to regulate performance such that any negative deviation is rectified.

Rewarding success /Reprimanding failure

A reward is a positive gain you get in making any given undertaking. In this case, when you achieve your target, you need to have some gain. Psychologists have discovered that reward triggers that 'feel good' part of the brain, which brings motivation to do more. Thus, rewarding yourself for your achieved target goes a long way in re-enforcing your motivation.

After evaluating the implementation of the day-by-day plan, the next thing is to reward yourself. Since this is part of structured productivity, this reward mechanism must also be structured.

The reward process encompasses the following steps:

- Establish reward criteria – A reward criterion is a standard of attainment, which you have set such that achievement of that standard is rewarded. For example, if the target per day were jogging 3 miles a day, reward criteria would be, for every 3 miles of jogging achieved, you get to reward yourself with a good treat at the dining table.
- Create the most impacting reward mechanism – a reward mechanism should be such it furthers your endeavor. For example, it is your desire while jogging to be fit and healthy. If you choose to take soda and junk foods at the dining table, this works against your endeavor – to stay fit and healthy. Thus, the food at the dining table should be such to help you boost your health. Such food should be a balanced diet of the natural whole meal.
- Endow the reward – this is the actual giving of the reward. Having a great treat at the dining table is the actual endowment of this reward.

In case you have experienced your very own cases of indiscipline such that they prevented you from successfully implementing your strategy, then, you need to reprimand yourself. This reprimand could take the form of:

- Denying yourself the undue indulgences - For example, if your target was jogging and you ended up in a bar. The next logical thing is to deny yourself from drinking at the bar.
- Sacrificing other activities that are not important so that you can allocate more time to implementing your strategy - Definitely taking alcohol at the bar is not as important as jogging. You may need to sacrifice this alcoholism for the sake of your jogging endeavor.
- Keeping off a wrong company that deviates your attention from your goals - If it is due to your friend's undue influence that you ended up in the bar despite your plan to avoid it, then, you would probably need to avoid your friend at such times you need to go jogging. That is if your friend is unwilling to go jogging with you.
- Sacrificing resources from not-so-important ventures into implementing your strategy - Spending money at the bar drinking simply means that you still have money that has not been allocated to priory areas. Commit that money to priority areas and you will not have much left to indulge it in alcohol.

Avoid procrastination

To overcome procrastination, it is extremely important that you first isolate the disease from its symptoms. When you treat the disease, the symptoms will naturally die. However, when you focus on treating the symptoms, you will get temporary relief while the disease remains uncured.

The following are key steps to overcoming procrastination:

- Know what to do
- Device action plan
- Sharpen your resolve (tools and techniques)
- Work on your mindset
- Work on your habit

Know what to do

Knowledge is power. In the first section, we started off by embarking on knowledge of what procrastination is.

Let's explore knowing what to do in order to overcome procrastination. The first action is drawing the action plan itself.

The second important thing to do is to sharpen your resolve. It is a lack of determination and self-discipline that denies you focus on your goal. Thus, to be able to discipline yourself to focus on your goal, you must sharpen your resolve.

You must have realized that sharpening your resolve is mind-driven. Thus, you must work on your mind in order to succeed in sharpening your resolve. Your mind is the ground in which the tree of procrastination has its deep roots and derives its rich nutrients.

As we have seen in our first Section, procrastination is a habit. Like all other bad habits, procrastination begins in the mind. That's also the very place it must begin to be fought.

Sharpen your resolve

Sharpening your resolve requires you to regain your lost Willpower. Willpower is the innate ability to overcome inherent inertia. The greatest reason why procrastination happens is inertia.

Due to all other reasons, as we have discussed and shall continue to discuss, inertia brings that lazy reluctance to take action. You want to stand up but something seems to hook you onto the seat; you want to wake up but something seems to pin you down on the bed; you want to walk out but something seems to glue you onto the sofa.

You want to leave chatting on social media but something still nags and seems to shout 'wait for my next post!'; You seem to be arrested into a perpetual vicious cycle of waiting; You snap out from one cycle of waiting into the next awaiting cycle of waiting.

Your endless cycle of waiting cranks your willpower stamina making it not hit on when expected.

Willpower is that force that urges you to actualize your will. It keeps you focused on asserting your determined will regardless of the swaying from others, be it persuasive or coercive.

Key attributes of willpower are;

- Ability to postpone instant gratification
- Ability to overcome bursts of short-term emotional temptations in order to achieve long-term goals
- Ability to override destructive thoughts and impulses

Self-control

Lack of willpower is due to many mind problems. However, the following are the most prominent causes of lack of willpower which you must confront in order to sharpen your resolve to end procrastination;

Scarcity – perpetual scarcity makes it easy for people to lose their willpower. For example, those who wish to have a balanced diet may give up on their willpower if inadequate supplies of fruits and vegetables become perpetual.

Money troubles - studies found out that money troubles have a strong negative psychological effect on the poor. Money troubles impair their thought-process as they slowly adapt to conditions that require less willpower to overcome. For example, it is a bad habit to pick from dumpsites, but money troubles may cause the poor to do that not because they don't know it is a bad habit, but their willpower has been lowered by money troubles.

Constant decision-making – when people encounter many scenarios that require quick and constant decision-making, their mind gets worked-up and soon their willpower to continue making more decisions gets impaired.

Stress – Stress is a result of overworked mental energy. Willpower consumes energy. Thus, when you are stressed, there is less energy available to your willpower.

Empaths and Work

Depending on what type of job you have, the office environment can be an interesting dynamic between coworkers. There may be cliques, there may be those who keep to themselves, and there may be those who do not do what they are supposed to do. The workplace can be an odd collection of different types of personalities and work ethics.

Empaths may work a wide array of jobs, some more depleting than others. In order for an empath to feel fulfilled with both their individual and communal senses, they could potentially have a difficult time finding the right job for them. Here are some positions that would work best for an empath to use their gift:

131

- Nurse: Since empaths are caregivers, being a nurse would be a great fit for an empath. Empaths want to help, and using your gift to help comfort sick patients would fulfill your needs as well as the patients.

- Writer: Empaths can also have a way with words, and it can be quite therapeutic for them to get their feelings out and on paper. When an empath is able to get creative, they release the powerful emotions that they may have held inside. People would most likely relate to them as they have plenty of feelings and emotions to relay.

- Psychologist: A psychologist is also there to help those who have an illness of sorts, just on a mental scale. Since empaths can feel so deeply and understand what others are thinking, they are able to help those who have a mental illness on a better level.

- Artist: Many artists see things differently than the rest of us and have a unique collection of perspectives. Since an empath is more connected to their surroundings, they tend to be more creative than others when it comes to art and the emotion that goes into it. With that, their creativity will be second to none when it comes to being an artist.

- Veterinarian: Empaths care not only for people but also for all living things, including animals. This could be a very rewarding job for an empath, as they will be able to assist with the care of animals as well as their owners.

- Musician: As an empath, your feelings can pour out on paper, which, in turn, could make an absolutely amazing song. Many musicians pour their hearts and souls into their music, which makes their songs more relatable to others.

- Life coach: Empaths have lived through a lot of nonsense when they hit a certain point in their life, and with that, they want to help others either avoid trauma or help them heal trauma. You want the best for people, and you want to help them become better people. As an empath, you prefer that all people around you gain a level of success. You do not get jealous; you feel happy for them. This is an uplifting and rewarding position for an empath as you will be using your gift to the fullest and helping people be the best they can be.

- Teacher: As a teacher, your goal is to help kids get to where they dream to be. You will help them along the way and make a big impact in their life, and that, in return, will make your life more fulfilling. When a teacher is able to pick up on the quirks and emotions of their students, they can change their students' lives forever. They will not only understand the student, but they will also know how to offer the right amount

133

of motivation and support to assist them. There are many times that teachers make more of a difference for children than anyone else, and empaths are definitely up for that support system challenge.

- Guidance counselor: Being a guidance counselor is similar to being a mentor; you will be guiding a child or adult toward a better life. You will be able to figure out what people have in terms of character traits and personality, which will help find them with a list of positions that may fit them as a person so that they can lead a successful life. Since empaths tend to understand how others think and feel, it will be an easy task to figure out how to guide someone in the right direction.

- Social worker: Social workers have a difficult job, but they are around to help their clients through terrible situations. This type of position is great for an empath as they love to make a difference in other people's lives. When this position works out well and there are times it will not, the empath will be involved in the achievement of happiness for those around them as well as themselves. The only downfall would be that, when something does not end very well, an empath may deplete all energy and emotions due to an unhappy ending. Empaths who are very secure and have thick skin would be best for this type of position.

- Nonprofit organization volunteer: This could be many things, but all of which are set to help someone or another. For example, if someone has a child in an ice hockey organization that they have also played back in the day, they may love to sign up to help coach a team. There may also be board level positions that could provide a lot of fulfillment by helping educate the parents about the programs they offer at the organization. These types of organizations need workers that are empaths as they strive to make a difference. They need people who want to make a difference to fulfill their level of happiness as opposed to those who are money-driven. Volunteering is more fulfilling as it will let you help without expecting anything in return, and that is typically where empaths thrive.

- Self-employed: Since an empath may battle ups and downs, with bouts of isolation, being self-employed would help them as they could make their own schedule. Being self-employed, they are on their own to make decisions; empaths would thrive in this type of environment. There is no need to risk having toxic people around them as they would be in control of their environment. This is the perfect work for empaths who have waves of needing isolation or do not have enough energy to deal with coworkers.

- Lawyer: This job is not typically where an empath would excel at. It seems that there are more snakes as lawyers than those who want to look for others' best interests. Because empaths do love to help, can be assertive, and can look out for the best interest of their clients, a position like this is great for them.

While this list is not all-inclusive and some of the positions may not seem like they would be a good fit for an empath, many do utilize their strengths.

How to Manage Your Work Environment and Boost Your Productivity as an Empath

You may have heard the expression "nice guys finish last". In my experience, those with higher empathy are far more effective in the workplace than those with lower empathy. Different companies tend to reward and promote differently, and sometimes sheer cantankerousness is the only dimension that matters, but in general the modern team-oriented workforce requires employees and managers who can get along with others. Deadline pressures and high stakes can make some people forget the value of empathy in the workplace, but that doesn't mean it isn't an attribute worth cultivating. Empathy can also be good for business, especially in industries offering premium services with a personal touch.

Being an empathetic manager doesn't require sacrificing productivity. It's possible to be both person-focused and task-focused. In fact, as employees feel valued, their contributions may increase. Attending to their emotional needs and ensuring vacation and rest are part of the equation can lead to increases in overall productivity. Accountability is an essential part of the equation, too. With good accountability, employees know exactly what is expected of them and can be rewarded for meeting or exceeding expectations. They can also know in advance what the consequences of poor performance will be, so there are no surprises.

As a manager in a technology setting, I once had an employee who was ineffective in his work. Instead of holding him accountable, I focused on becoming his friend. His work continued to be poor. It affected our relationship and created resentment, leading to an unfortunate confrontation.

After learning from this experience, I had another employee who did not show up for work and didn't contact me to say he would be out of the office. This happened three days in a row. It was an offense that could have resulted in immediate termination, but I decided to give him another chance. I clearly explained the consequences of a repeat occurrence. When it happened again, I let him go. I'll admit it was hard for me to do, but I owed a duty to the company and the consequences had been clearly explained. Accountability and integrity both required me to act decisively, but I did not act out of hate or malice. I simply did what I said I would do. He told me later that he had a drinking problem and being fired was a wakeup call. He got into a treatment program after that, and I hope and pray he found the help he needed.

I've always enjoyed watching outtakes. Those moments when even actors in serious dramas find themselves laughing intrigue me. I've often wondered what would happen if a director or producer decided to lecture those actors and actresses about wasting time and money instead of using the breakups as material for a gag reel.

It seems the work of acting requires a certain amount of artistic freedom, and repressing such jovial behavior would likely limit a person's ability to get into character and deliver a quality performance. If that's the case on the big screen, why do other industries insist on belittling employees? The best work cultures I've seen treat people like people, not dollar signs. Policies are procedures are in place, but they are not oppressive and camaraderie among employees is valued.

Good working relationships with co-workers can be one of the more fulfilling aspects of the workplace. It can be difficult, though, to balance the various demands of a job with making investments in quality working relationships. It can also be difficult when boundaries are crossed between work and personal life.

Avoiding gossip and negative talk about co-workers, especially those in management positions, and the company itself can lead to greater workplace fulfillment. Everyone has strengths and weaknesses. There's a time to address problems in the workplace, sometimes directly with the person, or with the person's manager, and there is a time to walk away from the drama.

One challenge I've experienced is overly talkative co-workers. I work in an office setting, and friendly people sometimes stop to visit with me for long periods of time. I love talking with people, but it can keep me from being productive. Sometimes, however, I'll find myself needing to politely end the conversation, which can be difficult with some co-workers. It's important to establish appropriate boundaries so resentment doesn't build.

When an employee leaves a company, it can be tempting to take the departure personally. After seven years of hard work for a grocery store, my accountant friend gave her 2 weeks notice and was told to leave immediately, because they didn't want to see her disloyal face there anymore.

As a manager, when I saw employees leaving, I was happy they had found something better. Though at times it left a hole to fill, growth and change is only natural. When employees leave, celebrate them, thank them, and honor their contribution. The ability to transcend ego is an essential management skill. Empathy and leadership go hand in hand.

Those who work in customer service are fully aware of the difficulties that can arise when a customer is angry. Showing empathy in such situations can be extremely difficult, especially when customers are being completely unreasonable. Here are some techniques that can help in these situations. These techniques can be used in other situations as well, such as when a spouse or child is upset.

- Make sure the customer is heard
- Acknowledge the customer's concerns and repeat them back
- Find out what the customer feels would be a fair resolution to the problem
- If the customer is asking for something that cannot be offered, negotiate with the customer to determine a compromise

These steps may not always diffuse the conflict or resolve the issue, but they're much more effective than responding with anger, which will simply make the problem worse.

On the other side of the equation, as you work with customer service personnel, try to remember there's a human being on the other end of the phone or screen.

Companies can, at times, be extremely frustrating. They often have blanket policies in fine print and, being imperfect institutions, may fail to deliver on their promises. Lawyers and judges make good livings prosecuting contractual violations, and there is a time and place for litigation. However, there is also a time and place to cut losses. Some things simply aren't worth sacrificing peace of mind.

Everyone has a breaking point. What we do when we reach ours goes a long way towards defining our character. When we are angry at a company or policy or circumstance, we may mistakenly direct our anger at the messenger. This serves no one. Before making that angry call, take a moment to reflect on how you might act if your best friend worked at that company and happened to answer.

How to Connect with Others?

Intentional change always begins with awareness. The empath's world can be boggling, and life becomes much less so when the conditions are understood. Children sometimes become upset when unable to describe what is happening on the inside. Once they have words to convey their agitation, however, they quickly calm down, because what was once vague is now real.

Empaths live in a world they often can't describe. They doubt its validity, as well as their perceptions. Sensitives benefit greatly from observation, and understanding why they have been feeling what they have been feeling. Once that is established, the chaos is no longer chaos, but something with structure and patterns. Now there is something with rules, and this can be understood and mastered.

Learning about how subtle energy works gives you the theoretical knowledge to interact on multiple levels, without losing balance. Energetic tools and techniques give you practical skills to maneuver the environment effectively, and manipulate the subtle world the same way anyone would influence the material plane.

Acceptance is central. Without it, little progress can be made. This means accepting yourself and the whole situation. Reversing the self-neglect and choosing to see yourself as worthy can take some time. Fear of being egotistical often gets in the way of self-love, but it's the ego that makes one question one's own worthiness. The difference between self-loathing and a healthy regard for oneself is night and day. It is the difference between feeling tortured and being at peace. Choose peace.

What being a sensitive means for an empath in years to come can often provoke anxiety and fear. This can be a miserable experience, where the mind dreams up a variety of potential worrisome situations that are rarely based in reality. Relax. It's a journey. Start at the beginning and let the rest unfold.

Attend to what needs to be addressed now, and learn to be ok with uncertainty. Life is unpredictable already, so why does having empathic traits make this any different? People often run from themselves, but where is there to run to? It's like a hamster on a wheel.

A note of warning: People who ignore their gifts do not tend to fare well. Doing so is trying to escape a connection to something greater than yourself, and every individual always knows — on some level — that this is what they are choosing. It amounts to no more than burying one's head in the sand. Empaths who repress or ignore their experiences remain imbalanced, and are never truly happy.

Campbell claimed that myths from around the world relating a sort of hero's quest always have the same fundamental steps. It begins with the hero living a normal life, and leaving home when he feels urged to do. This nudge from the universe is "The Call to Adventure".

The hero then abandons the known world upon the answer of The Call, to undertake a mission in the uncharted territory of unknown and unexplored realms. On the journey, the hero faces tests, meets helpers, and — if successful — undergoes a personal transformation in which there is a newfound awareness and appreciation of the richness within.

The journey usually ends with the hero — now remarkably wiser from the ordeal — returning home, often to share their discoveries with humanity. This metaphor applies to any human who makes the bold decision to blaze their own path through the wilderness, in the attempt to find themselves and what life is really about.

Most people never receive The Call (at least in this lifetime), and for those who do, there is a choice to make whether or not to embark on it in the first place. The thing is, there's no journey (and no prize) if the hero refuses to answer The Call to Adventure. This potential hero has chosen the safe path, and will live the rest of their life with the sense that they missed out on their destiny.

Being an empath can be likened to receiving The Call. The choice of exploring a dimension to life that goes beyond the physical world is completely in your hands.

If you choose to embrace your abilities, being proactive is incredibly important. So much of the suffering empaths endure is due to reacting to circumstances. The situation "hits them", throws them off balance, and the empath strains to make the discomfort go away. It's a vicious cycle.

You may be so discouraged and exhausted that you struggle to find the strength to try to solve the problem. You may have become miserably content with managing symptoms, opposed to getting to the root of the problem. This is only putting on a band-aid, and becoming proactive will put the empathy back in control. You will benefit greatly from looking at your life and identifying the dynamics of difficult as well as positive situations.

Taking special precautions and working with multiple techniques may be necessary to successfully navigate the fields of energy. When you know of a difficult situation or person is in the near future, it is important to take whatever steps you need to neutralize the situation, or even turn it into a positive exchange.

Creating balance is the most complete way to thrive. This is embracing yourself as a whole being and operating on a physical, emotional, and spiritual level. People are multidimensional, and optimal functioning is experiencing wellness in all areas of life. Health is good, work is satisfying, relationships are positive, finances are stable, and a connection to divinity is strong. One feels content and purposeful. Balance is relative to the individual and situation, and what balances one will not always work for another.

Take some time to evaluate current circumstances and decide what is balanced and what requires attention. If you are interested in using something more scientific, plenty of avenues are waiting. Experimenting with an assortment of techniques is not a bad thing, but trying to reinvent the wheel is usually a mistake.

There are already a multitude of systems that teach how to balance the system. Whether it is Traditional Chinese

Medicine, Ayurveda, philosophies behind martial arts, naturopathy, contemplative prayer, shamanism, crystal healing, reflexology, reiki, or mindfulness doesn't really matter. All of these modalities come with theory, guidelines, tools, and a progression of steps to balance the body.

The experimentation involves figuring out which paths bring results. Be careful about trying to utilize too many different schools of thought, however. Many techniques complement one another, but each path utilizes different theories that drives the philosophy as a whole.

For example, tai chi teaches a completely different posture than yoga. Both methods work, and both techniques can be used, but it is impossible to follow one completely without contradicting the teachings of another. Another Zen parable describes trying to master two different disciplines as a hunter who chases two rabbits, and catches neither.

Many empaths naturally gravitate towards the helping professions or volunteering, and this can be a perfect way to use your heightened empathy and compassion in a constructive way. Once a sensitive finds a balancing point, the empathy loses its capacity for self-destruction. Instead, it is like sharing one's light with the world.

Sensitive souls may be particularly suited to specific situations like working with the homeless, drug addicts, refugees, the terminally ill, or those displaced by natural disasters. Providing physical aid, comfort, and emotional support are wonderful ways to heal others and yourself. Animals may be more suited to certain empath's preferences, and environmental preservation could be perfect for another.

Empaths may provide spiritual guidance or direct their psychic sensitivities into such activities as astrology or intuitive readings. Engaging in important work is not always so obvious. The gift of sensitivity can be directed towards fellow human beings in any situation or calling. Working at a bank or gas station and treating every customer as a light-filled being is equally valuable. Consciously raising a family and teaching kin the value of empathy can be most suitable. The key is finding a situation that matches your talents and interests. Feeling content is a sign that this has been achieved.

Loving-kindness meditations, also known as "Metta", come from the Buddhist tradition, and are designed to develop compassion. Cultivating a sense of love and reverence for all in the universe — with no desire to have this returned — is the goal. Loving-kindness is first directed at the self, because loving others is near impossible without self-love. The practices will help you further develop your gifts, as they continue to open your heart and prevent burnout.

Here is an example of how to do Loving-kindness meditation:

Find a comfortable seat and take a few minutes to relax and become still.

Focus on the heart center.

Say, either mentally or out loud, "I am filled with loving-kindness". Picture yourself with a heart overflowing with love and generosity.

Continue to repeat your affirmation and hold this imagery. Use any other words or visualizations that help support the sense of compassion. This should last fifteen to twenty minutes.

Practice regularly for a few weeks until you begin to feel its effects. Once a sense of loving-kindness for the self is established, move on to directing this energy towards others. The first five or ten minutes of the meditation remain directed at the self, but the rest will then be spent focusing on someone who summons forth feelings of love.

After practicing this for a few weeks, switch the focus from a loved one to someone neutral, possibly a stranger. This is a little more difficult. The most challenging step is sending loving-kindness towards someone who sparks feelings of hatred and animosity. With time, attitudes towards those who have brought harm into one's life will soften, and eventually be replaced with compassion and forgiveness.

Remember: What happens to one happens to all. So, the greatest gift anyone can offer the world is their own wellness. The universe simultaneously carries individual and collective vibrations. A person's frequency is on a spectrum of positive and negative energy, and an individual's experience fluctuates as life circumstances change.

The strength of most people's light is medium, with some people casting weaker rays and other people casting stronger. This means that those with stronger vibrations are affecting the whole more significantly than those with feebler ones. The vibration can be anywhere on the spectrum of positivity and negativity, so someone with a strong vibration may be spreading good or bad energy.

There are a handful of souls in the world, most unknown, who shine forth such pure radiance that it counteracts most of the world's negativity, and prevents mankind from plunging into darkness. Likewise, there exists incredibly malicious people who are harmful, and spread their hatred through mankind as a whole. With this concept in mind, flourishing as an empath is much weightier than one's own comfort.

Whether or not you choose to publicly use your precious gifts is a personal decision, but — with proper balancing — honing your empathic traits and tendencies can only bring about good. Being compassionate in daily life is like infecting the world with joy. What may seem meager is not meager, not at all. Like a single lit candle, the smallest acts of kindness can vanquish the dark.

How to Manage Social Fear and Anxiety

Anxiety disorders are very common today, and it is estimated, according to data from several investigations, that 20% of the population will experience an anxiety crisis throughout their lives. One of the most known anxieties disorders are fears, among which we can highlight social fear. But what is social fear? What can we do to overcome it?

Fear is an emotion that has played a fundamental role in the survival of human beings. And also this is fundamental in animals and in humans for survival. It mainly serves to guide us about the dangers that can threaten us at any given time, whether they are perceived in the external world or in the internal world. Activate in our body the escape or fight responses, as it is more convenient.

It is very easy to see this in animals, for example, in a dog, when he is eating with great appetite and hears a noise unknown to him, he stops, raises his head, sniffs, looks, that is, is oriented to see if the stimulus indicates that he has to bark because there is someone, or run away to hide if he is very scared. In this orientation, the nervous system in a state of alert serves to make those decisions. If, when he orients himself, he rules out that there is a danger to him, he will continue to eat quietly.

The fear in the human being is a kind of alarm that goes on to warn us that something can put us at risk, to ourselves, to someone from our close environment or maybe we can simply be at risk, our esteem, our image or our feeling of security.

The fear reaction originates in the oldest part of our brain, which is characterized by rapid activation, from 0 to 100, instantly. For example, if when crossing a street, we see that a car is coming, the fright activates our nervous system, first making us jump backwards, then giving us the sensation of shock and finally we may think he could have killed me. We see there, as fear activates an immediate response to danger, even before we are aware of it, that is, we can think about it.

Fear becomes a problem when it is activated in us so often or for such a long time, that it really stops discriminating risks and dangers, feeling scared more or less constantly, for example in new situations, which do not represent in themselves a danger, but that they live in a threatening way.

And fear also becomes a problem when it arises associated with a stimulus, object or circumstance every time it appears or comes in contact with it, and that nevertheless does not carry in itself anything threatening or represent a real danger, but causes that the person constantly dodges them so as not to feel the discomfort that fear produces. This situation is what we call fear.

It is like living in a permanent state of alert or alarm, which, being constantly on, not only warns about the dangers but also stops discriminating and therefore serves as an orientation or for rapid reactions in survival.

It thus becomes a very limiting problem that causes loss of freedom, excessive worry, anxiety, among other difficulties that have to do primarily with adaptation to the environment, ourselves and others.

Fear is an irrational fear associated with certain external stimuli (fear of flying, dogs, insects, heights, blood, needles) or certain internal stimuli (fear of intimacy, contact social, to speak in public).

Its symptoms are varied and range from panic terror, with tachycardia, sweating, psychomotor agitation to paralysis, freezing, uncontrollable tremors.

Psychologically, these symptoms have to do with not feeling able to face something, with feeling overcome and not seeing oneself in a position to face any object or situation, with a sense of risk of life or death and, above all, with the conviction of not being able to successfully cross certain circumstances related to what causes the fear, which leads the person to avoid everything that could mean an approach to the object or phobic situation.

How to Overcome Social Fear?

Learn to Manage Anxiety

Searching for our own ways to manage Anxiety will help us. For example, playing sports, meditating, or learning relaxation techniques... The less anxiety we experience, the less we will have to deal with at the most difficult times.

Seek Professional Help

If you feel that you cannot go it alone or that you need external support, do not hesitate to seek professional help. Research has shown that cognitive-behavioural therapy, along with the development of social skills and techniques to control Anxiety, work to overcome social fear.

As we see, social fear is a limiting problem that impoverishes our relationships, but one that we can progressively overcome if we strive. Above all, we need to try.

Gain an In-Depth Understanding of Other People's Emotions

We've already established that they're drawn to healing and bear the type of personality that wants the world to be a better place, but how do they go about making it one? Sure, compassion is a huge part of empathy, but what else can they do? I'd be happy to tell you.

The good that an empath wishes to do—or, rather, is capable of doing—is quite dependent on what type of empath they are. Naturally, pardon the pun, the environmental/geomantic empath has more of a pull to fix the earth. This is the same for the plant/flora empath. When an empath homes their gifts, they can use them to maintain balance and restore harmony into the world. They have their own unique ways of doing this.

Empaths are fantastic listeners. They genuinely care about and enjoy learning about others, mostly because they can feel the emotions of the other person. There's a sort of rush you feel when someone tells you their stories as it can feel as though you were actually there. When someone needs support, an empath can perceive that and provide it accordingly. The empath can sense things like fear or danger, and if they've strengthened their gifts or are attuned to them, they can use the skills and adaptations they've developed to remove themselves and others from such a situation. They don't talk about themselves much, but if they do, it reveals that they have a great deal of trust in the person they're sharing with. Often, however, people seem to trust them quickly. This is because they relate to others in their own unique way.

It is because of this relatability that people feel a pull toward empaths. It doesn't matter if the empath is aware of their empathic abilities; people will still be drawn to them. People are willing to pour their hearts and souls out to empaths who are complete strangers without necessarily intending to do so. It happens on a subconscious level.

Needless to say, sometimes the empath needs that release too. That's why it's imperative that they find some of their own kind or they keep those special friends close. They're exceptional people.

Another way empaths use their abilities to bring good into the world is the ability to solve problems. Since they enjoy learning as much as they do, they study many things, and this means they are constantly sharpening their minds. Sometimes this is a subconscious action. The empath brings new meaning to the saying: "Where there is a will, there is a way."

Though it helps others, you should be wary of the fact that people will often want to offload their problems onto you. These people might not even know you. If you don't keep your guard up and strengthen your energy, these problems can convert into being your problems. Make sure that you keep the two separate. You don't want to be dragged on. Be honest with yourself and others. If a situation feels like it is going to bring negativity your way, it is okay to take a step back and tell the other person that you can't handle it. This is an act of self-preservation.

I know that sometimes it might feel like you are thrown into scenarios aimlessly and in them, you drink up the emotions of others, but you are stronger than you think. Empaths have to be strong to be able to carry both their own feelings and the feelings of others. Consider yourself a type of energy warrior. You absorb all this energy and transform it into something valuable. You have the ability to shift the negative to positive. Purify the world. If anyone can do it, an empath can.

Remember how I said compassion is one of the best ways for an empath to avoid emotional distress? Some empaths find that they need to be in a constant state of compassion in order not to suffer adverse effects from outside influences. Others try to be as open as they can be, allowing each feeling and sensation to pass through without much notice, and in doing so, they release all judgment and try to be as honest and carefree as possible. Then there are the empaths who believe in crystal healing in order to transfer and create energetic healing. The empath who heals the world in whatever manner they need to is the empath who has a great sense of inner peace and balance because they know that they are following their calling in life.

If you've already found what you're meant to be doing—say, for instance, mine is releasing my creativity into the world in any manner I deem appropriate—then you know what I mean by feeling a sense of balance. If you're still looking, don't give up. Follow your intuition and it won't lead you astray. Bear in mind that you may fail a few times. You may think that you've found that thing you're meant to be doing only to realize that it was nothing more than a step toward where you're meant to be. Keep searching even when you hit this wall. You are on the journey you are following for a reason. That reason will reveal itself to you soon. An empath's gut is usually right.

Detach Yourself from The Past

The past can be a great thing to learn from, but most often, it is a place many become stuck in. You can learn to let go of the past and accept that what has been done is done. You can begin to move on from the attachments you have with it. As an empath, you want to learn to stay in the present moment more. While it is fine to take a lesson from the past, you want to leave the emotions, energies, and negative thought patterns.

How to Detect and Handle Energy Vampires

Another problem Empaths are called to face and tackle is the toxic people they may come across and drain their energy, often without their knowledge. There is a term for those toxic people and they are called "Energy Vampires" or "Emotional Vampires". Those people are called like this because they feed on an Empath's emotions and energy, so they target them specifically. When around these people, Empaths will feel in pain, drained, tired, anxious, sad, and scared. This term is mainly used for sociopaths and narcissists, but it can also include other categories of people who tend to drain Empaths emotionally. There are certain signs that warn you about the presence of such a person and it will be wise for you to watch out.

To start with, an "Emotional Vampire" will drain your energy to the extent that you will not be able to look after yourself. For example, after some time you may feel your body freeze, sweat may start forming on your body, and your intuition starts sending signals that something is wrong about the situation. You may also have a small pain on certain parts of your body since you will get a sense of being helpless. This happens because this person will completely ignore your feelings and they will lack empathy when it comes to you and his or her surroundings. Their aim is to exhaust you so that you will yield and stroke their ego. In other words, they will make you tell them exactly what they want to hear, which goes against everything an Empath stands for.

Another sign of being in the presence of this type of person is when you are no longer with them; you will still feel the negative effect they had on you. For example, your thoughts may be filled with every cruel word they said or cruel thing they did to you and others. You will get emotionally exhausted by trying to understand why they act this way and find some reason behind their way of thinking. Prolonged exposure to these people may get you to question your own beliefs and make you doubt yourself, your choices, and your gifts.

If you are away from them for long periods of time or even a few days and you start feeling energetic again and every doubt you ever had for yourself vanishes, then you need to consider erasing them from your life altogether. Being away from toxic people will help you refill your energy levels and be away from their negative emotions and way of acting towards others. It will feel as if a weight has been lifted off your shoulders and your happier self will reemerge. However, all of this will fall apart once you meet them again.

With toxic people, a simple dialogue over a problem or a situation that should have reached an easy and simple conclusion will leave you drained and confused. Such conversations may include matters of honor, fairness, moral code, or decency. These people will argue with you on things most people accept as right and will refuse to acknowledge that they should give others respect unless it suits them. They will defend their wrong and toxic behavior to you and are insensitive to the pain they cause you over their inability to act with kindness not only to you, but also to everyone.

From the above signs, it is fairly easy to conclude that these people never care about returning the kindness you show them back. They keep you close because they want you to cater to their every need, even though they blatantly overlook your needs. For as long as you give in to their every demand, they will keep you close. Whenever you converse with them, they will only talk about themselves and how amazing or sad they are. They will surely decide on matters that will affect you without asking you first and without caring how much you will be affected by them. By doing those things, they think they control you and that is what makes them think they are superior.

Even though they keep you close because you tend to their every need, remember that they also do that because it makes them feel superior. So, they will not hesitate to damage you and your reputation since they see you as an object and not as a person with emotions. If you succeed in something they haven't, they will get jealous, they will need to make your success their own, and they will stop at nothing to do this. They will start brushing off your success as something unimportant before they strike with everything they have. They will not hesitate to do so at the thought of losing you because, according to them, you will forgive them if they fake the remorse they will not be feeling afterward.

The above is only a general description of the signs you need to watch out for that will show you the importance of staying away from these people. To be more specific, there are certain types of people that will hurt Empaths and fall into the term "Emotional Vampires".

Fake people can harm Empaths because they don't even know who they are. They are called fake because they change personalities like people change clothes in order to fit into a group. Empaths are able to sense this type of person and they should not try to change him or her. It will take a lot of work that will emotionally drain you and you may never succeed. Though you can support them, if these people are not ready to accept themselves, there is nothing else that can be done about them. For example, people who pretend to be tough, but in reality they are bullies. Empaths should keep close and help a person who is genuinely tough because life had treated him in a way that he or she should build up defenses against the world. People who fake toughness by being rude to someone to make them feel in control are a red flag for Empaths since they detest anyone who is rude and cruel.

People who have huge egos are toxic not only to Empaths but to everyone. They don't have any ounce of empathy for other people and the only thing they care about is themselves and how they will have a nice time. Obviously, they think they are better than others and an Empath will never coexist with a person like that. The truth of the matter is that this type does not trust other people and even though they brag about their successes, their confidence is low. Also, manipulative people are extremely toxic for Empaths. Even though they will realize their nature immediately, manipulative people are attracted to Empaths because they are kind and manipulators think they are easy to control.

People who complain about everything in their life can drain the energy of an Empath in a flash. Their negativity effect Empaths too much and when they finish a conversation with them, they are emotionally exhausted. They are not necessarily bad, but they will never be responsible for their actions and never actually try to better their lives. Even when the Empath tries to make them happy and solve their problems, they are never satisfied and happy with any solution presented to them. Eventually, the Empath will realize that no matter the positive thoughts he or she sends to the complainer, they will never see the bright side in anything. The right thing to do is to cut all ties because this negativity will exhaust you, regardless of the number of times you recharge your energy.

Needy people are also bad for an Empath's state of mind and are filled with negativity. They may appear nice and sad and the Empath will feel the need to take care of them and relieve their pain. However, before the Empath even realizes it, this person will have leached upon him or her and even try to imitate their way of thinking and style of life. They may even stalk you and whenever you are unable to relieve their pain, they may get aggressive with you. Even if they don't reach these extremes, they will certainly blame you for their pain and praise you for every happy moment they may get. In conclusion, they will never take upon themselves any achievement or problem that will present itself in the future, starting from the moment they met you.

How to Protect from Energy Vampires

If you are in the presence of people like we described above, you need to understand that to maintain a calm state of mind you need to untangle yourself from them, if possible. Empaths refuse to accept that not all people are good and will want to fix everyone who has a mistaken view of life and treat others with no respect for their feelings. However, this will backfire and will only harm you. If you can't cut them off completely, there are things you can do to protect yourself.

To start with, you need to accept that Emotional Vampires are real and are extremely dangerous to Empaths. Empaths have the tendency to stay in a friendship or romantic relationship that is toxic because they start coming up with excuses for Emotional Vampires. Sometimes, they refuse to believe that there are people so close to them that choose to be with an Empath for selfish reasons. But this is true and you need to know what you are up against in order to protect yourself and deal with the situation accordingly.

Always listen to your instincts. At first, your instincts will tell you how wrong it is to be in the presence of Emotional Vampires, but if you choose to ignore it and stay with them, those people may make you question your abilities. If you are in this state, you should start writing down everything your instincts tell you about someone. Write down when a person lies or causes problems due to his or her hurtful behavior. Do this thing for everyone you meet even if you don't associate yourself with them. This way, you will eventually learn to identify them without the help of a notebook since you will be able to recognize the clear signs that you are dealing with an Emotional Vampire.

When things get too overwhelming because of Emotional Vampires you could always ask for help from a true friend of yours. Someone you trust and resort to whenever you start to doubt everything. Arrange a meeting with him or her and pour out your problems. Then, you will either get a piece of extremely helpful advice from your friend or you will listen to yourself talking about your problems out loud and the solution to your problems will dawn on you.

Energy vampires will always try to keep you under their control. They want your energy, your soothing words, and the calmness you project. They will manipulate you or be frustrated with you whenever you try to place some distance between the two of you. It doesn't matter; you are entitled to please yourself first and not everyone else for a change.

But don't do this once a year; Energy Vampires do it often, most especially. You have a right to be happy and when someone is angry because you need some alone time, they can stop thinking about themselves and let you have a relaxing time.

It is apparent that one of the most effective ways to protect yourself from an Energy Vampire is to cut down the times you see and talk to this person. Whenever he or she asks to go out with you or starts long conversations, you can refuse. As an Empath, you have to stop saying yes all the time, particularly to toxic people. You may think you can help them, but you will rarely succeed in nurturing empathy for these people. Practice saying no and if you find that too difficult try to give them vague answers that will later turn into negative ones.

Protect yourself by limiting the time you spend with things that can drain you of energy. You could spend less time on social media, watching the news or limit the time you spend in your relationships if you feel drained. These measures are important for all people and Empaths should adhere to them by the book due to their sensitivity. For example, if your friend goes through a tough time, you can go out with them, but stay for as long as you still feel alright. Don't stay too long as to get exhausted by trying to make them feel better. Your partners, friends, and family exist to make you feel better, not constantly drain you of your energy. Even though

165

we all have gone through difficult times, if you realize that someone is draining you more times than you can count, then the time has come for you to set some boundaries. Take some hours out of your day and dedicate them to yourself, to do something that relaxes you and pleases you.

Empaths and Narcissists

Should empaths and narcissists get together? That would be an emphatic no! But somehow they often seem to, so the question then is why? Some say that empaths are in direct opposition to narcissists. This would seem difficult to prove but let's take a look at the differences and why they do get together.

It would seem that people with narcissistic personalities have little or no empathy and people with empathetic personalities are sensitive to extremes and cannot help tuning in to other people's feelings and senses. Narcissists flourish when given attention and admiration and empaths consume people's feelings like a sponge. This does indeed make for a toxic union!

Narcissists engage people with whom they will achieve the most mileage with in terms of what they want. Sad to say, but for this reason, they have been known to actually prowl for empaths. The narcissist will often view the empath as a very loving person however empaths fall for narcissists because they are quite well versed in misrepresenting themselves. At first, they use the façade that they are nice and loving people, and then when questioned about their behavior, they often turn nasty.

Empaths have their own set of unfathomable problems. They continue to believe that they can bring home little birds with broken wings, and get them all fixed up so in the end, they will be rewarded for their healing and compassionate behavior, and for being so wonderful, and then the "little bird" will fly away and be happy forevermore. Of course, this sounds more like Aesop's Fables than real life but this is how they operate. They do this over and over again and more often than not, still do not understand why everyone is not just like them, with an overabundance of caring and love. It is always their wish to heal with that love and in nearly always does not work in the slightest.

Empathy isn't about instinctive behavior and narcissists are not about giving unto others. Just unto themselves and generally this plan is indeed, etched in stone. Empaths believe that "mindfulness" is all that they need to get through any situation and narcissists believe that those expressing mindfulness are an easy target.

Some experts suggest that empathy comes from not only emotional needs but also administrative control to coordinate the entire experience. While both are held up by similarly specified and acting neural patterns, research has shown that the deception of copycat behavior is part of human nature and may often be seen as occurring on an unconscious level.

So we often fall into inadvertent copying of the facial expressions of others with whom we are involved in one way or another, and this can include speech patterns, demeanor and disposition, as well as the copying of bodily motion and mannerisms. Doctors in neurology have even agreed that when you see someone in pain, you may actually become somewhat triggered in the same area of your own physiology.

How to Protect from Narcissists

Each type of vampire requires a unique kind of handling. However, there are general rules of thumb that cuts across.

The following are the general rules of thumb when it comes to handling any type of energy vampire:

- Don't lose your self-esteem – most energy vampires suffer from low self-esteem. Don't let their negative self-image about themselves become your self-image. What they paint of you is of their very own tainted lens. Don't see yourself from their tainted lens. Rather, see your self from your very own crystal – clear lens. To achieve this you need to cultivate a higher sense of self-awareness.

- Boost your level of self-awareness – to remain you, even in the extreme provocation, extreme criticism, blame games, etc, you've got to have a higher sense of self-awareness. Self-awareness enables you to look inwards and seek your true identity, true feelings, and true self-image rather than becoming prey to other people's identity of you, other people's feelings of you, and other people's image of you. To achieve a higher sense of self-awareness, you need to practice mindfulness meditation, reflection, and introspection.
- Rise above them – just as an eagle soars high to disable a ground prey, an empath has to soar high to disable energy vampires. When you remain grounded to their level, these bearish vampires will seize you and devour you. Rising high above their territory makes you more powerful and unreachable. How do you rise above? Rising above means being too high to be infected by their low self-esteem. It is about being too high for their energy-sucking proboscis to reach you. If it is criticism, rising high could including keeping off them and if you can't keep off them, disable them.
- Cultivate a thick skin – cultivating a thick skin means that you become impenetrable such that the vampires' energy-sucking proboscis cannot pierce through. Criticism, negative talks, gossips, insults,

etc., cannot affect you. These are their piercing intrusions. When you develop a thick skin, instead of the vampires gaining more energy from you, they lose more in a failed attempt to suck from you and thus either die off or keep off.

- Exercise your power of NO! – one great weakness of most empaths is their inability to say NO! even when their powerful intuition tells them enough is enough. They still create a room, create more space for tolerance. They tolerate until they reach a level where the only coping mechanism is addiction and codependency.

Conclusion

Empaths are all around. We are all together in this and can show each other the magic and love behind being someone with such a powerful gift. When you are ready to let go of how other people affect your state of being, you can become a person who has a true gift of knowing and sensing what is going on all around you. You can discover more about your empathic skills and abilities, the more you know about how much you can be affected by others in your life.

You may have a lot of work to do to prevent all of the negativity in your life. As you read these pages, you may have had a lot of red flags regarding your relationships at home and at work, or with situations and experiences that occur regularly. You may also have learned that you can approach your life in a new way and choose the methods outlined in this book to help guide you toward living fully and happily as an Empath.

This book is all about you. When you stand up for yourself and let go of the things, people and places in your life that shift you out of your true self, then you give yourself the freedom to be a light of love in this World. Empathy is something we all need to practice, but when you are an Empath, you don't have a choice: it is a part of who you are all day, every day.

As you move forward, you will now have all of the tools that you need to transform your experience as an Empath. You can overcome any of your fears, hurts, and anxieties, knowing that many, or most of them could be coming from someone, or somewhere else. You can use your gift to help others, ensuring that you create healthy boundaries with your energy so that you can stay grounded and positive. You will have the time and energy to live the life you truly want because you are not constantly brought down by the energy vampires in your life.

Practice the strategies daily until they are a part of your regular routine. Use them as a jumping off point to create your own energy protection rituals. These guidelines are meant to be a starting place to help you move forward and adopt the way of life for yourself as an Empath. You are not like everyone else and so you have to take care of yourself in a different way.

Let this book be a guide on your journey towards embracing a life of empathy. You have a gift and it is yours to share, with the right people, in the right places, at the right times for you. Enjoy your empathic abilities and continue to strengthen them as you practice these guidelines and strategies. You will continue to understand your gift more and more if you approach it with healthy boundaries and self-love. May your empathic bring light and love to the world.

HOW TO TALK TO ANYONE

learn how to improve communication skills and talk to women, men, in public, at work at anytime and anywhere with confidence, increase your self-esteem, manage shyness

MIND CHANGE ACADEMY

Table of Contents

Introduction

Hello there!

How've you been? Exhausted?

It's understandable. Failing to effectively get your point across in communication, particularly in the relationships we have to deal with daily such as family, friends or even co-workers can make you feel drained.

After all, if you have to explain yourself twenty million times, who wouldn't be annoyed, right? Do you hear that little voice inside your head, the one that keeps agreeing with everything you just read—quite the antagonizer isn't it?

It feels an awful lot like you're mad at the people around you, doesn't it? It's as if their misunderstanding and failing to fall in line is a reflection on who they are as people.

Well, be that as it may, have you ever wondered if there is something you could fix in terms of how you are communicating?

Think about it—have you been having trouble communicating? Have you ever felt like what you are saying and what you mean aren't really the same, and you haven't been coming across well?

Yes?

Have you ever wondered why?

The lack of dynamic communication at work and home is extremely damaging to both careers and healthy family life. This is because feeling frustrated or unheard when dealing with people you engage with daily is basically the textbook build up to a mental breakdown. As human beings, we need to know that what we do matters, and we need to feel respected and appreciated. And the only way to ensure that, is by working on our communication skills, so we are better equipped to understand and deal with one another.

So, how are you supposed to do all of that? Look no further, here at Effective Communication—5 Essential Tips and Exercises to Improve How You Communicate in This Divided World, Even If It Is About Politics, Race or Gender!—we have you covered!

With modern day communication becoming more and more difficult, with so many divisive issues such as race and religious freedom being pushed to the forefront, it's understandable that people with different views would have a tough time finding common ground from where they can respectfully disagree. But it's not impossible!

And we are here to walk you through exactly how to do this!

Ready?

It's okay; you don't have to be—for now, just listen.

When you are communicating, or when you are being communicated with, there are five key concepts that will determine how effective this communication is going to be. They are often called the five Core Concepts of Communication and are listening, delivery, empathy, honesty, and winning. Every single one of these topics has the unique ability to help change minds and attitudes when properly applied.

You know what that means, right?

It means no more fights at the dinner table or pulling your hair out over what your boss has been saying. Once you've gone through this book and actively applied each of these five techniques, you'll be ready to take on the world—literally!

So, what do you say?

Are you ready now?

Awesome! Keep scrolling; we got you!

Chapter 1.   The Basics of Communication

Meaning, Concept and Process of Communication

Effective communication is generally a business term, and it's something that is generally used to ensure that a complete, coherent form of communication is being undertaken, and in such a manner that the person you are communicating with understands the message conveyed in the way in which the communicator intended it to be understood.

Pretty easy, right?

What you just did is the single most complicated thing mankind has ever done. In fact, only the human race is capable of full communication, to the extent of ensuring that the message we deliver is "conveyed in the manner in which the communicator intended it to be understood."

Generally, we turn to the seven C's of communication. Correctness, whereby you ensure that the information you are delivering is correct and accurate. Clarity makes sure you aren't complicating things, remember to stay focused and stick to one issue. The best way to do that is to ensure you are Concise, cover what needs to be covered without embellishment, don't create too much build up just get in there, and get to the point. Having said that, it is equally important that you keep an eye out to ensure that the message being sent is Complete. And then in quick succession, you have Consideration, Concreteness, and Courtesy. Your concreteness comes from the authenticity of what you are saying, and to finish off, there is a courtesy which is the polish on top that keeps the audience happy and willing to listen.

But all of this is about the message we are dealing with— how we deliver this message is a whole other issue.

So, let's get straight to it, shall we?

Mindset and Approach

We all share an internal desire to relate to the world around us. Imagine for a moment, if you could no longer communicate and nobody was able to understand anything that you're trying to tell them. Life would be an unending series of frustrations on your part, mostly. Remove this ability and suddenly life becomes a struggle when nobody can understand your needs and vice versa.

Before you can begin successfully improving your ability to communicate with the people around you, there's something that you need to do first. Your ability to interact with others is going to stem from the experiences you have had in the past, and since experience can be the most effective teacher or all, the experiences of the past are going to impact your communicative ability moving forward. If you can't understand yourself at the most basic level, you can't expect others around you to understand who you are and what you need either.

Effective communication begins with you, and the first place to start is through developing a level of self-awareness about yourself. The ability to reflect on your internal experiences and make sense out of it allows you to accurately process your emotions. This will enable you to determine just how much far your thoughts and emotions are influencing your communication process and the way they affect your nonverbal cues. If you were trying to have a professional conversation but you were in a bad mood over something that happened earlier, having those feelings still coursing through your system is going to negatively impact the conversation you're now trying to have. Your tone might sound harsher than you think, or the annoyance and stress you're feeling might be reflected on in the slight frown between your brows or the downward curve of your mouth. Little signals will be picked up on by the receiving party. Understanding yourself better with the right level of self-awareness might have made you realize that perhaps you were not in the right frame of mind for an effective conversation, and you could have then made the necessary arrangements to postpone it to a better time, or you could have given yourself time to prepare beforehand.

For an effective conversation to take place, emotions must be regulated, and you cannot regulate your emotions without self-awareness. Why is it so important for emotions to be regulated during the communication process? Because our emotions influence our speech and thought process. When you're feeling particularly angry, those emotions might make you perceive the message you're receiving in a different way. What was meant as an innocent remark suddenly gets taken out of context and an argument ensues? A situation that could have easily been avoided if you understood yourself to know that perhaps you were letting your emotions cloud your judgment. An awareness that could have led you to react very differently and produced an entirely different outcome.

To a certain extent, being able to communicate effectively involves emotional intelligence. The five core skills that make up emotional intelligence - empathy, social skills, self-awareness, self-regulation, and motivation - are also the core skills that make you a whiz at conversing with just about anyone. Self-awareness and self-regulation give you the skills you need to be able to assess your own emotions, capabilities and then regulate the appropriate action to achieve the most desirable outcome. Empathy and social skills help you connect beyond more than just the surface with the person you're talking to. To be able to put yourself in their shoes, see what they see, feel what they feel, that gives you the valuable insight you need to tailor your messages accordingly. Last but not least, motivation gives you the determination and the drive that you need to stay focused on the bigger picture, to stay focused on why you're having this conversation and what message it is you're trying to deliver.

Without emotional intelligence, making the necessary connection you need with your audience in order to be able to engage them effectively becomes increasingly more difficult. Self-awareness is such a vital part of the communication process and here's an example of why. There will be some people who, despite your best efforts, will prove to be almost impossible to communicate effectively with. You might have family members with whom you can't see eye-to-eye with, no matter how hard you try. You may have colleagues at work with whom you're constantly butting heads with, even though you're trying to best communicate with them to the best of your abilities. As challenging as these people might be, you still have to interact with them, it's unavoidable. Self-awareness can be a big help in this instance.

When you know what your strengths are, you can use them to your advantage in the moments when you need to communicate with these challenging individuals. Knowing your own strengths and weaknesses is crucial because once you know the warning signs within yourself, you can then mitigate the potential for arguments to ensue.

The Self-Communication Principle (Intrapersonal Communication)

Before you begin any kind of important speech, you need to be confident about the content you're going to deliver. This process is called intrapersonal communication, and it involves having a conversation with yourself. Most people don't realize it, but we already have internal dialogues with ourselves all the time. Whether you're doing it consciously or not, the scenarios you play in your mind, the conversations you imagine yourself having, that's all part of the intrapersonal communication that's going on.

The internal monologues we run in our minds are just as important as the external conversations that take place. Communicating with ourselves is an important tool that helps build both our self-perception and self-esteem. The self-talk you have with yourself affects your emotional and mental wellbeing more than you realize. The next time an internal dialogue is happening, tune in and pay close attention to what you are telling yourself. Is the self-communication that's taking place positive? Or does it slant more towards the negative? The latter, of course, is going to drain you of your motivation and your energy levels, robbing you of your self-esteem and confidence in the process if you're constantly focused on your flaws and all the things you can't do. Positive self-talk, on the other hand, can have the complete opposite effect, empowering you and boosting your confidence and self-esteem levels, making you feel like you can conquer any obstacle that comes your way.

Visualization is a strong part of the self-communication principle. Athletes, motivational speakers, and successful individuals rely on visualization to mentally prepare themselves for the performance ahead. Athletes visualize themselves giving their best performance before they head into the game. Motivational speakers imagine themselves in front of a crowd, inspiring the crowd to live their best lives. Successful people visualize themselves achieving their goals. You are now going to apply this same visualization technique by picturing in your mind the way you want a conversation to go before you have it.

Type of Person: Visual, Kinesthetic and Hearing

While communicating, we use words and phrases such as, "It is clear to me," "I feel it," or "It sounds great." All of these expressions have a similar meaning. However, they represent a different sense. The first is the sense of sight, the second - feeling, the third - hearing.

When most people speak, they predominantly use one of them. When at the particular moment they are more visual in their talking, you will find words like: "clear," "simple," "I can see," "a perspective." In the case of a person using more of a sense of feeling, there may be words like: "I feel," "hard," "hold," "smoothly," "touch," etc.

When it comes to sensory perceptions, there are three main types you can gather from a person, depending on the way the person uses language to communicate with others:

- Visual – People whose sensory perception is visual would tend to use "seeing" phrases such as "my vision is clear," "I see what you mean," "your future is bright," and words such as "view," "imagine," "color," "hazy," "clear," "foresee," "appear," or "outlook." They also tend to describe things in terms of "seeing" such as "small," "light," "brown," "rectangular," etc.

- Hearing – People whose sensory perception is auditory would tend to use "hearing" phrases such as "I hear you," "she scratched the floor," "his voice was sharp," "I am listening to you," and words such as "listen," "talk," "discuss," "hear," "sound," "call," etc. They also tend to describe form in terms of "hearing" such as "loud," "noisy," "beeping," "ticking," etc.

- Kinesthetic – People whose sensory perception is kinesthetic tend to use "feeling" phrases such as "I feel that is the best way to do it," "My feelings do not support this," "She was warmly welcoming," "I feel that," "I can't grasp that" or "I fear that," and words such as "touch," "feel," "afraid," "fear," "warm," "cool," "rough," "smooth," "wet," etc.

Pay attention to these details and learn to adjust your style of speaking accordingly. First, you can practice creating longer sentences having a characteristic of each type of sensory perception above, so it becomes easy and natural for you to use them during real conversations. Pick one of those rapport-building techniques and use it in your next conversation. Then try another one and test how it works for you.

Every time focus on just one element, teaching your brain exactly what it should catch in the other person's speaking. Thanks to this, you will learn the ability step-by-step and will soon be able to use it automatically. Then, being able to adjust yourself through all of these ways at once, you will become a significantly better communicator.

I will also tell you about different, often repeating, verbal patterns and models of thinking and how to recognize them and utilize this knowledge.

It is important that you remember to be vigilant and careful when you talk and listen to people. Besides the fact that I promised myself to carefully listen to other people's words a long time ago, I would often find myself in a situation when at some point I forgot to pay attention to the linguistic structure and turned the "autopilot" on instead, losing track of my goal in the conversation.

With time, however, I developed the ability to be present and attentive to what the other person was saying. I started noticing the beliefs and values, experiences, specific words and phrases relating to the senses very easily. Remember, it's just another skill that you can learn.

This knowledge gives you great opportunities. Use it effectively and start to use it in your life as soon as you can.

The Levels of Communication Verbal & Non-Verbal

Verbal Communication

Speech is what most people think about when the word communication is mentioned.

We use our speech so much in communicating with other people that we have tens of thousands of words for different things.

The English alphabet alone has twenty-six different letters representing particular sounds used in English speech. In other cultures, like Chinese and Japanese, their "alphabet" is more syllabic with hundreds of symbols representing particular things. In some African dialects, there's even a tongue click represented in English as an exclamation mark.

Given the complexity of speech and all of its components, it's our most powerful and versatile communication tool. Let's discuss each of these components, then move on to the nonverbal elements of communication.

Language

The first component I want to discuss is language because one thing can have different terms used to describe it among the thousands of different languages and dialects in the world.

If you're someone who wants to communicate effectively with someone, you first have to make sure that you speak the same language.

If you only know English like most Americans, then you're okay if you're only ever around people who speak English. However, when you're suddenly in a situation where you're to talk to someone who doesn't know English, then you're automatically placed at a huge disadvantage.

In my job as a company representative, I get exposed to people who speak different languages, but the most common language I encounter is Latin American Spanish.

I never understood Spanish back when I was young, and growing up in California, there were a lot of kids who spoke both Spanish and English, and their parents sometimes only spoke Spanish.

I remember hanging out with at my friend's house after school one time, and his grandma approached me telling me something in Spanish, and I couldn't make out what she was telling me, so I called my friend over. He then translated for me, telling me that his grandma was asking if I was hungry and wanted some tamales. I said I wasn't hungry, but I would love to try their tamales, which my friend translated back to his grandma.

If I knew how to speak Spanish, I wouldn't have been confused about what his grandma was saying, and I wouldn't have needed to call him over to translate for me.

It was when I realized that I needed to learn Spanish because I didn't want to be confused like that again. I started hanging out at that friend's house more often and gradually picked up on their language.

Until now, I can understand Spanish very well, although my accent is still funny according to that same friend, who I still hang out with a lot and go on hikes with monthly.

If you're in an area with people who speak a different language, it would be to your advantage to learn to speak their language.

That way you don't miss out on anything and also sometimes it's fun to listen to people talk when they think that you don't understand them.

Also, learning to speak a different language makes you smarter and helps you avoid little mishaps that happen because of things getting lost in translation.

Your Vocabulary

How many words do you know? It's kind of hard to count because each of us knows hundreds of different words we use in conversations.

How about your spelling? Are you a good speller, or do you often find yourself being confused about how something is spelled? Do you use "night," or do you spell it "nite?" Do you know the difference between "you're" and "your," or do you use "your" interchangeably?

The way you spell matters a lot only if you do a lot of writing, but if you're only talking most of the time, then you might not have to worry too much, although you might still want to improve on your spelling.

Essentially, your vocabulary is the number of words you know. It matters because the type of conversations you hold and the level of intelligence you display largely depends on the type of words you use in talking to someone.

For example, if you're not a big gamer and you start talking to someone who is into gaming a lot, you'll start hearing things like "fps" and a lot of gaming jargon that I myself do not understand.

I have a friend who is heavy into games, and aside from simply playing, he makes it a hobby to find bugs in the games that he can exploit to perform things that aren't even supposed to be possible in the game officially.

When I talk to him, sometimes I don't get the things he's trying to tell me, and I always find myself asking for clarification. Eventually, he got annoyed by my clarification requests that he learned to dumb things down for me.

The kind of words you use in speaking to someone can really define you in their heads.

When I took a marketing class, we were taught to use simple words that a ten-year-old can clearly understand because most people don't use complicated words in everyday speech. If you start using deep words, then a lot of what you're trying to say in your marketing campaigns could simply fly over people's heads.

So basically, we were taught to keep our words light and easy to understand. That's essentially what you should do as well. You have to keep your words at a level where the person you're talking to is not getting confused.

Grammar

Grammar refers to the way your words are organized. You can be the most eloquent person out there knowing so many complicated words. You can also know every possible language out there. But, if your grammar is terrible, then your message won't be sent as clearly as you want it.

Now, most adults develop grammar naturally. The way most people normally speak in their native tongue is the correct grammar. The problem usually arises when you speak a different language.

For example, in English, you say, "I understand Japanese," but in Japanese, the grammar structure is "Watashi-wa Nihongo-ga Wakarimas" or in literal English, "I Japanese understand." If you're a native English speaker and you speak Japanese to a Japanese person, you might speak it in a way that follows the English grammar structure instead of their native grammar structure.

If you want to communicate effectively, you have to understand the grammar rules very well, and you have to structure your words and sentences in a way that doesn't muddle the message you're trying to relay.

Your Tone

Now that we're done with the actual words themselves let's go to the other stuff about the way you speak that gives context to what you're saying because really, there's a lot more to what you're saying aside from the words you use and one big part of it is the tone of your voice when you are speaking.

Here's how important your tone is. As an example, I want you to imagine the following:

Your mother yelling your first name.

Your lover gently speaking your first name.

Your friend casually calling you by the first name.

In each case, the same word is used, which is your first name. But, each is said in a different tone, and each case means a different thing than the others.

That's how effective tone is when you use it. The mere tone of your voice can be a message in itself. It indicates your mood and your intent.

Even if you use the nicest words you can find in your entire vocabulary and use the best, most eloquent grammar; it's still not going to come across as something good if your tone indicates hostility because you're yelling and the way you speak is pointed.

At the same time, even if you use the most hostile, offensive words you have and even threaten violence, the effect won't be as intimidating if you say it in monotone. I was actually going to say, "if you use a soft tone," but sometimes, violent threats can sound even scarier if spoken in a soft voice.

Your tone can easily change the context of your statements, so you have to understand how your tone of voice works and what the appropriate tone is for every message you want to send.

Your Speed

Aside from the tone of your voice, other indicators also exist, such as the speed of your speech.

Of course, there are times when you have to control the speed of your speech like when you're speaking to someone who is hard of hearing. In that case, you normally have to speak a little slower for the other person to be able to hear each word you are saying properly.

When you're in a hurry then, of course, you have to speak a little quicker than usual, so you can finish delivering the message in the short time you have to deliver it.

For the most part, however, when you don't consciously control the speed of your speech, it usually indicates your energy.

When you speak very fast, to the listener, it could indicate high energy. It's when you're excited or agitated. On the other hand, when you speak very slowly, then the listener might take it as a lack of enthusiasm on your part.

Sometimes, people even associate slow speech with a low level of intelligence because somehow, it seems like it takes someone who speaks slow, a little more time to process their own words.

So the speed you use when talking to people is also very important, and you need to be aware of it and control it as much as you can.

Your Volume

Your volume can say a lot, too, about the nature of the message you're trying to tell someone.

If you've ever whispered to someone's ear, then you know that you probably had to speak it softly to avoid being overheard by others. On the other hand, when you're watching a game, you're probably yelling loudly at the players because you want them to hear your frustration and tell them what they should be doing.

So basically, the volume of your voice could indicate how much you want to be heard.

I remember an uncle of mine who has hearing problems. He always yells his words because well, he can't hear himself speak, and he forgets that other people can hear fine, so when he can't hear himself, he thinks other people can't hear him as well. So, he speaks loudly to hear himself speak and assure himself that the people he is speaking to can hear him as well.

Other than wanting to be heard, your volume can also indicate your confidence levels.

Usually, a shy person speaks softly because they're afraid of being heard and humiliated. On the other hand, a person who is self-assured may speak a little louder because they want to be clearly heard.

Nonverbal Communication

Now that you know the components of verbal communication and why each of them should matter to you, we'll discuss the components of nonverbal communication because communication is not just about what you are saying. It's also about what you are doing because everything you do sends a message, and as someone who wants to project charisma, you need to be aware of these as well and be able to master and control nonverbal communication as well.

Before we proceed to discuss the components of nonverbal communication, let me tell you the story of a man named Jeremiah Denton.

Back in the Vietnam war, he was captured and forced to go on a propaganda video in 1966.

While the video was being shot, he pretended to be irritated with the lighting used during filming and blinked while talking during the video. As it turned out, his blinking was a message in morse code saying "torture."

Since then, every video being sent out by kidnap victims, figures like terrorists and criminals, and politicians are thoroughly analyzed for hidden messages before anything else is done with them, like broadcasting on TV, for example.

Also, if you've ever seen the show Lie To Me, the premise is how they analyze nonverbal cues, which then becomes clues to solving crimes or resolving conflicts in the episodes. It's a TV show, but it doesn't mean that the concept of reading nonverbal cues is all fiction. It's actually being actively practiced.

As I said, your nonverbal cues also send a message, and you need to be a master of it as well and not just be reliant on verbal communication.

Proxemics

In simple terms, proxemics is the study of how you use space in social interactions. Basically, what it means is that the distance between you and another person and where you are relative to the things around you and the people you interact with have meanings.

I know it can still be a bit confusing, but I'm sure it will be a bit clearer once I go into further detail.

First, have you heard of the term "personal space?"

If you haven't or if you've heard it used but didn't fully understand what it means, then let me explain.

According to experts, particularly Edward T. Hall, in his book The Hidden Dimension, we have four different zones determined by our preferred distance when it comes to other people. I'm going to discuss it next, starting from the outer zone, down to the innermost zone.

First is the public zone, which is the outermost zone, and it's said to be between twelve to twenty-five feet or more.

In this zone, there's no physical or even eye contact. Think about when you shop at the department store. You try to keep a distance from the other shoppers as much as possible, right? It's because you don't know them, and you're probably not even remotely interested in them.

The second zone is called the social zone, and it's anywhere from four to twelve feet away from you.

Again, think of shopping at the department store. Imagine meeting an acquaintance, maybe someone who you've seen at work a few times, and you want to say "Hi." Or, maybe you saw someone you found interesting or is standing at a product you're curious about, and you want to ask for their opinion about the product. You get close to them, but not too close, right?

You just get close enough for them to hear you talk to them, but you keep a safe distance where they can't just reach you without you noticing or being able to react.

The third zone is called the personal zone, which is about eighteen inches to four feet from you.

This is the zone where you keep your friends and other people you're comfortable with, like certain family members. It's close enough to talk and to shake hands.

When you see a friend the department store, you approach them and even pat them in the back or shoulder for them to notice you if you were coming from behind.

The fourth zone is called the intimate zone, and it's from eighteen inches to direct contact.

It's usually where you keep the people you really care about and are really comfortable with, like your really close friends, significant other, or your children.

When you see them in the department store, you're comfortable enough to hug them or kiss them.

So, basically, the amount of distance you place between you and another person could be interpreted as your level of comfort and intimacy with them.

When you stand too far from a person, then they might take it as you not being comfortable around them.

In addition to the different zones, there's also your eye level in relation to another person, or how high you are positioned from the other person.

For example, you might get intimidated by someone who is far taller than you or when you're sitting, and they're standing in front of you while talking to you.

Usually, a higher position indicates power over the person in a lower position. If you've seen the Star Wars prequels or at least have seen the meme where Obi-Wan Kenobi tells Anakin Skywalker that he has the higher ground and presumes that he has a greater advantage, it's like that.

That's why politicians and other people giving speeches are usually positioned higher using a stage or a podium. Someone giving a speech on a stage is going to be taken more seriously than someone who gives a speech on the ground floor. Of course, there are practicality issues that have to be considered, so it's not always true.

However, according to studies done in the medical field, in particular, doctor-patient relationships are significantly better when the doctor levels with the patient by stooping or sitting down than when they stand up and tower over a patient lying down in a hospital bed.

Introduction to Emotional Intelligence

Goleman has made popular the concept of emotional intelligence that defines as the ability to understand and manage our emotions and those of those around us, in the most convenient and satisfactory way.

He believes that emotional intelligence is based on the ability to communicate effectively with ourselves and with others and that these skills are not something innate but learned, so we can always improve them.

When talking about emotions, it refers to attitudes (that is, beliefs loaded with emotions that predispose us to act in a manner consistent with them), and automatic reactions (not voluntary or conscious) with emotional content.

According to Goleman, people with emotional intelligence have the following characteristics:

- They understand their own and others' emotions, desires and needs, and act wisely based on them.
- They properly manage their feelings and those of others and tolerate tensions well.
- They are independent, self-confident, sociable, outgoing, cheerful and balanced.
- Their emotional life is rich and appropriate, and when they fall into an adverse mood, they know how to get out of it easily, without getting caught in their negative emotions.
- They tend to maintain an optimistic view of things and feel comfortable with themselves, with their peers and with the kind of life they lead.

- They express their feelings properly, without surrendering to emotional outbursts that they would later have to regret.

Goleman differentiates between intrapersonal and interpersonal emotional intelligence. The first is very similar to self-esteem, while the second is closely related to HH SS, as we will see in the next two sections.

Intrapersonal Emotional Intelligence

Goleman describes intrapersonal emotional intelligence in a manner similar to what we understand by self-esteem, although focusing on feelings. He believes that an important aspect of intrapersonal emotional intelligence is the ability to communicate effectively with ourselves; that is, to perceive, organize and remember our experiences, thoughts, and feelings in the ways that are best for us.

This intrapersonal communication is essential to control our emotions, adapt them to the moment or the situation, stop being slaves of them, and be better able to face optimally any setback, without altering ourselves more conveniently.

This emotional self-control does not consist in repressing emotions, but in keeping them in balance, since each emotion has its own function and its adaptive value, provided that it does not become excessive or does not "overflow."

Emotional balance is the desirable alternative to two undesirable opposing attitudes, consisting of 1) repressing or denying our emotions - which would make us inhibited - or, 2) letting ourselves be carried away by emotional excesses such as a self-destructive crush or extreme anger.

The search for emotional well-being is a constant effort in the life of any person, although many times we are not aware of it. Thus, for example, many of the daily activities, such as watching television, going out with friends, etc., are aimed at reducing our negative emotions and increasing positive emotions.

Interpersonal Emotional Intelligence

Goleman believes that interpersonal emotional intelligence is the ability to relate effectively to our emotions and those of others, in the field of interpersonal relationships. It includes being able to:

- Adequately express our emotions verbally and nonverbally, taking into account their impact on other people's emotions.
- Help others experience positive emotions and reduce the negative ones (e.g., anger).
- Get interpersonal relationships to help us achieve our goals, realize our desires and experience as many positive emotions as possible.

- Reduce the negative emotions that interpersonal conflicts can cause us.

For Goleman, a key factor in interpersonal emotional intelligence is empathy, which he defines as the ability to understand the feelings of others and put ourselves in the place of the other. Given its importance in the HH SS, we dedicate the following section to it.

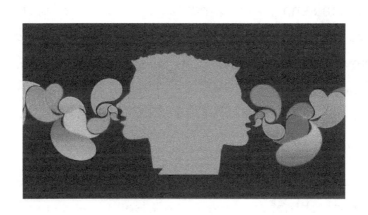

Chapter 2.   Effective Oral Communication

The First Rule of Conversation: Listen

A good speaker is someone who is also an excellent listener. Effective communication is as much about developing your listening skills as your speaking skills.

Don't interrupt when a person is speaking. Interrupting a person can send a wrong message. It tells the other person that you are more important than them or that what they are saying is not as exciting as what you are saying. It can also convey you don't care about what the other thinks or feels, or that you don't have time to hear their opinion/take on a matter.

Isn't it amazing how some people turn a regular conversation into a contest that must be won? It isn't always about saying the best lines or having the last word. Some people don't believe in cooperating or collaborating but view everything as a competition. Instead of listening to other people, they will be thinking about what to say or framing their sentences when the other person is talking. They look to reply not to understand.

If you don't understand a thing, ask the speaker to go over it again. However, don't interrupt immediately. Wait for the speaker to pause. Once the speaker pauses, you can say something such as, "Wait a second, please. I didn't get what you just said about..." Offer acknowledgments to show you are keenly listening to the person. It can be anything from verbal nods to "hm" and "ah." The idea is to offer the speaker some clue that you are not just listening to him or her but also absorbing what they are saying.

One of the best acknowledgment tips is to reflect on the speaker's emotions or feelings by paraphrasing or validating what they said. "It must have been a terrible situation for you" or "You must be so happy!" or "I understand you are disturbed" are typical examples of acknowledging the speaker's feelings. Paraphrasing also works well. So what you are trying to say is......." This tells the speaker that you have been listening to them all along.

Keep an open mind and listen to the other person without succumbing to the temptation of judging and criticizing them. Sometimes, we feel an irresistible urge to throw in our two cents or give our opinion/suggestion about something as a person is peaking. At times what they say is even alarming! However, get out of the habit of mentally rating or judging what they are saying and just listen to them. Sometimes, all people want when they are speaking is a listening ear. They've probably already figured out what they want to do.

Unless the person is actively seeking your opinion or suggestions, avoid sharing it. Listen without making conclusions. Language is only a representation of the person's feelings and thoughts. You really don't know what is happening in a person's mind. Listen to them carefully to figure it out. Again, avoid being a sentence grabber. This is especially true when you are communicating with a person you know intimately. The urge to finish what they started saying is high. The speaker is led by his own train of thoughts, and you really don't know where it is headed. The person wants you to hear them not speak for them or throw in your two cents.

Empathy is crucial when it comes to being a good listener. Try and feel the emotions of a person while they are speaking, and express the same through facial expressions. For example, if the person is expressing sadness, your facial expressions should convey to him or her that you feel their sadness. This makes you come across as a concerned, empathetic and effective speaker.

Empathy is the cornerstone of active listening. Place yourself in the other person's shoes and feel the emotions and feelings the other person is undergoing at that moment. It paves the way for better communication. When the speaker realizes you are keenly listening to them and feeling their emotions, they are likelier to share more.

As a listener, you must be attentive yet relaxed. You don't have to keep staring at the person while he or she is talking.

Look away occasionally, and then get back to the speaker. Stay attentive though. Nothing irks a speaker more than an inattentive listener! Be mentally present and give full attention to what the speaker is saying. Screen out disturbances like electronic gadgets and background noises. Again, the biggest distractions unknowingly come from within us. We are likelier to be distracted by our own thoughts, biases, and feelings.

Ask questions only to get a better understanding of what the person is trying to say and do not interrupt the flow of what the speaker is trying to communicate. Let's take an example. Say a co-worker Jill is telling you about a recent all girls trip she took to Europe. She's talking animatedly and excitedly about all the things she enjoyed there. In the course of her conversation, she mentions the name of a common friend Rose who was also with her on the trip. You jump in faster than you can say "Jill" and ask about Rose. "Oh, I haven't heard anything about her for a while, though last I heard was she was divorcing her abusive husband." Then the conversation shifts towards poor Rose, her unfortunate custody battle, the well-being of her children, domestic violence and family laws and more. Now, everything regarding Europe and Jill's holiday fades into oblivion.

Typically, this happens all the time. A person starts on one note, and the listener in his or zest for asking questions veers the topic in an entirely different direction. If as a speaker you notice that you've taken the subject elsewhere, take responsibility of bringing the conversation to the original topic by saying something along the lines of "It was nice to hear about Rose, tell me more about your fun adventures in Europe though."

Conversation Start - Breaking The Ice

The sound of silence. Sometimes silence is golden. Other times it is awkward. For those that are not naturally blessed with the gift of gab, starting a conversation can be quite a task. The struggle can be evident which can make the person on the other end feel uncomfortable, not to mention the awkward feeling we get.

Once you master the art of small talk, you will never have to worry again. You don't have to dread a dinner party, a first date, or any other potentially awkward event that might put you on the spot, grasping for words to say, and wracking your brain to find something of value to talk about. Talk about nothing! It worked for Seinfeld and it will work for you too.

What is Small Talk?

Small talk is like a snack. It is...just a little piece. It can serve a number of purposes. It might be all you have, just like when you are hiking and you need a protein bar for nourishment. You may have a snack to enjoy while relaxing.

A snack can tide you over until a full meal; and it can be a teaser before the main course, similar to an appetizer.

Small talk is when you speak about non-controversial, seemingly unimportant, or trivial matters such as the weather or a sports game you watched on television. Basically, it's talking about nothing. Don't underestimate it, though. "Seinfeld" was a television show about nothing that ran nine straight seasons and was hailed by TV Guide as the World's Best Television Show EVER! Millions tuned in to watch it every week. I know. I was one of them. Almost two decades later, a significant number of people still watch the reruns. I do that too. I actually have many of them memorized. So why do I and so many other people love the show? Personally, I love the fact that I can just enjoy the characters talking about nothing. It requires no concentration, no analysis, no judgements to make or any other kind of thinking. I just get to listen to them talk.

"Hey, Joe! How's the weather?" You might ask your friend. "Fine," he might answer. "You know Texas in July. It's a scorcher but it's not been too bad."

Now, that's small talk. It's a leisure chat about nothing.

When you call your friend in Texas after a tornado and have a talk about the weather, that's quite the contrary. "Hey, Joe! How's the weather?" You might ask. "Oh man," he might reply. "A category 5 touched down right across the street from me. My neighbors are missing and our home is unlivable. We are homeless, Jim. Can we come stay with you for about six months while the insurance fights over our claim?"

Now THAT is...not small talk.

As mentioned before, small talk is a lot like a snack. It can be dished out for different purposes, just as a food snack is. It can tide you over to get to the meat of your conversation. It can serve as the main dish if that suits your purpose. You can small talk for pleasure and you can use small talk to whet your listener's appetite while waiting for the main dish.

Here's How It Is Done

- There are endless approaches to begin your small talk. Here are some of my favorite ways:
- Ask a question. What's even better is to ask a question about the person you are talking to or about something you know interest him.
- Take a look around the room. Something will spark an idea in you. Lay the subject out on the table, providing it isn't about your boss' wife flirting with the Personnel Manager or something inappropriate or controversial. If you see a smart phone and are talking to a tech geek, get his opinion on the latest model that is out.
- Brainstorm. This is done much like the above except, rather than going with what you see, it will be what

you think. A bear comes to mind. The person next to you used to live in the mountains of Colorado. Ask if he or she has ever seen a bear there. It's great if you can ease into the small talk by maybe mentioning a bear. "I saw on the news that a camper was attacked by a bear last week. Did you ever encounter one when you lived in Colorado?"

- In the event that the person you are wishing to talk to jumps the gun and asks you a question, feel free to answer with a question. A good way to do so is: "So tell me about your vacation this summer..." You can turn it to focus back on him or her by, "Speaking of vacations, I hear you took a fabulous cruise..." Don't worry. People are rarely offended by getting to talk about themselves. In fact, you will soon learn that it's quite the contrary.

How to Ask Excellent Questions - Avoid Yes/No Question

Why do we have conversations in the first place? Often, it's because we need to gain insight into a particular situation, or because we want to understand what someone else is thinking.

Asking the right questions is a skill that will make all the difference in every area of your life. Being able to answer questions shows that you are educated and knowledgeable, but knowing how to ask them is the mark of good judgment and a willingness to learn.

Social Questions – Striking Up Rapport & Moving Beyond Small Talk

As you know, people who talk only about themselves are seen as rude and boring. Asking questions is the best way of switching the spotlight onto your conversation partner. A good question will encourage the other person to open up, thus creating a sense of rapport and intimacy between you.

If you've ever overheard a conversation between two people that was based on thoughtful questions, you'll know that they can soon turn complete strangers into two individuals on the fast track to friendship.

They can also help you deepen a relationship with someone you already know, but have yet to really understand or connect with on any meaningful level. So, once you're past the small talk stage, how can you use questions to get to know someone better and pave the way for exciting conversations?

Share something about yourself before asking a personal question: There are a few useful findings from the world of psychology that I draw on when helping my clients ask better questions. First up, we have the principle of social reciprocity. This basically means that when someone does something nice for us, we feel compelled to do something for them in return.

Robert Cialdini, one of the most famous psychologists in the world, covers this nicely in his book, The Psychology of Persuasion. People who are willing to talk about personal experiences and opinions are usually perceived as more likeable than those who stick to impersonal or generic topics. Finally, when we tell someone else about ourselves, we are more likely to feel kindly towards them.

Before you ask any personal questions, start off by disclosing something interesting about your feelings or life experiences. This creates an atmosphere of trust, and also encourages your conversation partner to share something of their own.

If someone tells you something personal about themselves or their life, respond in kind. If you aren't prepared to answer a question, don't ask it of someone else. Answering in advance will also put someone at ease.

For example, "I'd love to travel the world one day. What's your biggest dream?" is better than, "What is your ultimate dream?" Show that you are willing to be vulnerable, and they are more likely to trust you.

Questions That Build Intimacy: Arthur Aron's Closeness-Generating Procedure

In 1997, a psychologist called Arthur Aron carried out a study that was to become a landmark in the social sciences. He put pairs of strangers together, and then gave them a set of questions printed on slips of paper.

Half the pairs were given a set of personal questions, and the other half were given a set of small talk-style questions instead. Strangers who asked one another the "closeness-generating" questions felt a greater sense of connection and comfort with their partners.

The moral of the story? Whenever possible, ask deep questions that go beyond facts and figures. To give you an idea of the difference between these categories, here are some examples taken directly from Aron's paper:

"Small talk" questions:

- How did you celebrate last Halloween?
- Where are you from?
- Where did you go to high school?
- "Closeness-generating" questions:
- Would you like to be famous? In what way?
- What is the greatest accomplishment of your life?
- What, if anything, is too serious to be joked about?

You'll have noticed that the closeness-generating questions require "deep" answers, and are personal in nature. You will have to use your judgment when deciding when to move from small talk to heavy hitting questions.

Wait until you are in a state of strong rapport with the other person, and then you can gradually move from relatively "tame" questions to the deeper topics. Always be prepared to move the conversation to more trivial subjects if they show any signs of discomfort.

Use the "Parroting" technique to encourage further disclosure: The parroting technique helps shy people open up. All you have to do is take the final two or three words of their answer, and turn them into a question. It's an easy, unobtrusive prompt that can yield more satisfactory answers.

Parroting is also less formal than asking a question in its entirety. It might take a couple of rounds, but I'd estimate my success rate with this technique is around ninety-five per cent.

For example:

- You: "Have you ever thought about what it would be like to be famous?"
- Them: "Yes. I'm not sure I'd really like it. All those photographers."
- You: "The photographers?"
- Them: "The paparazzi would come after me!"

- You: "Come after you?"
- Them: "Yes. Did you see that story about the movie star who…"

Listen for clues: If you pay close attention to the innocent (or not so innocent) comments someone makes; you will notice that they will make reference to the same topic(s) on multiple occasions. This gives you a valuable starting point for meaningful questions that tap into their deepest passions. I'll show you how this can work in practice.

I recently met a new contact for a business lunch. As we sat down, she brushed a spot of dried mud from her skirt. "Oh, look at that!" she said, "That's my dog's fault. He's always jumping up at me when I try to leave the house." The conversation then turned to my contact's business, and their latest products.

She talked about their range of remote webcams and viewing apps. "Of course, they're great for parents who want to check on kids and babysitters," she said. "And dog owners like them too!" I started to get the message – this woman was crazy about dogs. When someone is truly passionate about something, it usually pops up in conversation, even if the original topic is totally unrelated.

The meeting was proceeding well, but it lacked that special spark that makes for a truly outstanding conversation. Over dessert, I casually mentioned that I was looking forward to visiting my sister soon. "It's always great to spend time on her farm," I said. "You know, to get away from it all. And she has these adorable dogs! You mentioned you had a dog...? "I didn't need to say much more.

That was all the permission she needed. When the time came for us to part ways, she insisted that we meet up in the near future, and that I was "such good conversation." Of course, all I'd done was ask a simple but well-chosen question. This trick can build rapport in seconds.

Frame your question as something worthy of excitement: Before you even ask a question, take the opportunity to influence the way in which the other person will perceive it. If you say, "Now, here's a good question...," your listener is more likely to assume that whatever you ask is going to be interesting than if you say, "I know this is an obvious question, but...."

Ask meaningful "we" questions: If you can combine a "we" question with an issue that is important to your conversation partner, you're on to a winner. Note that both parts of the equation need to be in place. A trivial "we" question, such as, "Do you think we'll have to stay five extra minutes again at the end of this meeting?" is a nice piece of small talk, but isn't going to build a high level of rapport or encourage personal disclosure.

However, questions like, "So, do you think we'll be bought out by the end of the year?" or "Do you think we should all give more money to charity?" invite someone to think of you as members of the same team, and disclose their personal opinions at the same time. This will boost rapport and lead to interesting discussions.

How To Ask Questions When You Need Factual Answers

Of course, some questions serve one purpose only – to elicit factual information. You'll use these in business settings, and when you need to hone in on objective facts as opposed to how someone is feeling. Before you ask the question, make sure you know what you want to achieve.

For example, you might be looking to gain an in-depth understanding of how a department in your organization works, or you may be keen to learn precisely how a particular medical procedure is carried out. Keep your objective at the forefront of your mind, as this will guide you during the conversation.

Make Sure You're Asking The Right Person

The person with the most knowledge on a topic isn't always in the best position to answer your question. We all know people who have a great grasp of a subject, but are not very good at communicating information. Ideally, you need to ask someone who has relevant background knowledge, the ability to express themselves, and the confidence required to assert their opinions.

Obviously, you won't always have access to someone who perfectly fits that description, but these three criteria can help you narrow down your options. This is particularly relevant if your question is technical, or requires input from someone with a high level of expertise.

If you are approaching someone you don't know in the hope that they will help you answer an important question, do a little background research first. Consider where this person is from, their level of education, their interests, and even (if the information is available) their personality type.

Social media can be a great tool here! If you have a mutual friend, ask them for advice if possible. For example, you could ask, "I'm going to have a meeting with X, to ask them about Y. Any tips to help me have a productive conversation with them?"

Don't Waste Anyone's Time

Before asking a question, make sure that you've exhausted all the obvious avenues first. It only takes a few seconds to use Google, after all. Even when your own research doesn't turn up the answers you need, you should still be willing to show that you've made the effort.

For example, "I've looked through the relevant chapter in the textbook and I've been doing some research online, but I just can't understand this topic. Can you explain it?" will get a more sympathetic response than, "I just don't get this. Can you explain it to me?"

My friend Jack is a computer science professor. He once told me that his weakest students are those who don't understand how to use their initiative. They tend to email him every time they hit a stumbling block, rather than making the effort to use the many online resources available to them. Jack doesn't mind helping his students out (he loves passing on his knowledge!), but fielding the same basic questions day after day really annoys him. He is much more likely to respond positively to a student who has made a genuine effort to help themselves before coming to him.

If you get the impression that someone thinks you have wasted their time, ask them what you could do to help yourself in the future. This gives them the chance to pass on links to books, websites and other resources that will allow you to come up with answers independently.

When it comes to actually formulating your question, bear in mind the following points:

Start with the basics if you need clarification: If you aren't sure what a piece of jargon means, ask! It's better to risk mild embarrassment than it is to stay quiet and make a costly mistake later.

Ask only one question at a time: No one likes to be on the receiving end of a barrage of questions, and combining multiple questions into one long rambling sentence is a sure way of annoying or confusing someone. Establish the questions you need answering, and think of the most logical order in which to ask them.

If possible, write them as a list on a piece of paper or as a note on your phone. This might seem a bit strange if you are talking to a friend or relative (as opposed to a boss or professor), but it's a useful tool that will keep you on track. If you are asking several important questions, it's a good idea to take notes or record the conversation for review at a later date.

If it's a complex question, let them know from the outset: Let the other person know if you need to ask them an especially difficult question. Give them the opportunity to clear their mind so that they focus their full attention on what you are about to say.

Know when to interrupt: Generally, it's rude to interrupt someone if they are speaking, and the rule still applies if you have just asked them a question. However, there are times when interrupting is the most sensible course of action.

For example, if someone answers your question but then begins to venture far away from the topic at hand, a simple, "I'm sorry to interrupt, but I just want to clarify something" can work to get the conversation back on track. This trick also works if the other person didn't quite understand your question, and gave you an unexpected answer that doesn't make sense.

Don't get nervous if they pause for thought: If the other person stops talking for a moment, or waits several seconds before launching into their answer, don't take it as a sign that you asked the wrong sort of question. When someone pauses to gather their thoughts, they are paying you the compliment of treating your question as a matter worthy of serious consideration. Give them the space they need. Do not jump in and start talking just for the sake of filling the silence.

Do not lead someone down a particular path: If you want to know what someone really thinks, avoid asking them a leading question. Leading questions are those that encourage someone to answer in a particular way. For example, look at the following pairs of questions:

- Leading question: "What problems are you facing on this project?"
- Non-leading question: "Could you tell me how this project is going?"

- Leading question: "Wouldn't it be a good idea to donate more money to this charity?"
- Non-leading question: "What are your thoughts on the amount of money we currently donate to this charity?"

In the first example, the leading question assumes that the other person is facing some problems, which will encourage them to dwell on the negative aspects of their experience. The alternative allows for answers that focus on good news too, which would result in a more balanced assessment of the situation.

In the second example, the leading question suggests that donating more money to the charity is obviously a good idea, thus encouraging the respondent to agree. The non-leading question is open-ended, allowing the other person the chance to voice their true opinions on the size of the donation.

Try another approach if the first doesn't work: We all have our own quirks and preferences when it comes to asking and answering questions. For example, some people dislike direct questions, and interpret them as a kind of conversational assault. Don't be discouraged if you hit a wall. Think of a different way of phrasing the question.

Humor can also be a powerful tool in getting answers. A simple joke such as, "C'mon, the suspense is killing me here!" can lighten the mood, help your target relax, and therefore increase the likelihood that they will give you the answer you need.

Using Questions To Change Someone's Mind

Questions don't just work as a means of eliciting information. They can also be used to change someone's mind, or at least get them to consider alternative points of view. When trying to convince someone to change their mind, most people try to lay out a logical argument, or make a passionate plea as to why their view is right and the other person's opinion is wrong.

But when you take a minute to think about it, you'll realize that this doesn't often work. As soon as someone works out that you are on a mission to change their mind, the metaphorical shutters go down.

You'll have better luck if you ask well-chosen, open-ended questions that let a person challenge their own assumptions. We tend to approve of an idea or suggestion if we thought of it first – or at least, if we think we thought of it first. Therefore, encouraging someone to question their own worldview will often yield better results than trying to railroad them into accepting your opinion as fact.

Asking a chain of well-chosen questions gets someone to look at their own views from another angle, which might trigger fresh insights. This is pretty much what the best therapists do. They don't tell their clients what to think. Instead, they use the fine art of asking questions to help the client come to their own conclusions. When a therapist wants to suggest that a client looks at their situation in a new light, they only do so once the latter has had the chance to air their thoughts.

You can use the following questions to establish what someone thinks about a certain issue:

- "Could you tell me what you think about that?"
- "How do you feel about this particular issue?"
- "I'm really interested in your opinion. Would you mind telling me what you think?"

Once you have a good understanding of what they believe, you can encourage them to evaluate their beliefs using the following questions:

- "How did you arrive at that conclusion?"
- "When people argue with you on this issue, what points do they try to make?"
- "Are there any facts your theory can't explain?"
- "What evidence, if any, would change your mind?"
- "Do you have any friends who hold opposing beliefs?"

Listening carefully to their answers without interjecting will make them feel as though you are truly interested in what they have to say. In turn, they will be more likely to entertain your own views as well as evaluating their own opinions.

Only once they are in a receptive state of mind should you then put forward your own perspective on the matter. Obviously, there is no guarantee that they will take your views on board, but at the very least, you'll have enjoyed a respectful exchange of opinions.

Asking For A Favor – "Can" Versus "Will"

What about asking someone to grant you a favor? Appeal to someone's sense of pride, and your chances of success increase. All you have to do is substitute "can" for "would" or "will."

"Would you please help me find the conference center?" is less effective than, "Can you please help me find the conference center?" When you ask someone whether they can do something, they immediately start to take assess their own capabilities.

Internally, they will arrive at either a "Yes," a "No," or a "Maybe." Their answer is more likely to reflect their capabilities, not their desire to help you. "Can I or can't I?" is easier to answer than, "Will I help this person or not?"

Asking the right questions is a key conversation skill. The next time you succeed in getting a helpful answer out of someone, reflect on how you asked your question, and file that strategy away for future use. Remember that what works with one person may not work so well with another, so be prepared to tailor you approach as necessary.

How to Stop Fearing Judgment

The most meaningful thing you can perform to get over social anxiety is facing the social events that you are afraid of, rather than avoiding the activities. Avoidance keeps social anxiety going. When you prevent a nerve-wracking event, it may assist you feel okay temporarily; avoidance prevents you from getting very comfortable in social events and understanding how to cope in the long term. The more you keep away from the feared social event, the more worrying it gets.

It prevents you from performing things that you would love to do or achieve particular objectives. For instance, the fear of speaking up may prevent you from sharing your opinions at work.

While it seems not possible to get over a feared social anxiety event, you can overcome it by taking it one step at a time. What is crucial is, to begin with, an event that you can deal with and slowly work your way up to hard situations, developing your coping skills and self-confidence as you move up the anxiety ladder.

To work your way up the social anxiety ladder:

- Do not attempt to face your significant fear instantly. It is not a perfect idea to move quickly or take on too much. This might backfire and enhance your anxiety level.
- Being patient. Getting over social anxiety takes practice and time. It's a slow step by step progress.
- Apply the techniques you have learned to stay calm, for example, concentrating on your challenging negative thoughts and breathing.

Using Empathy in Conversation

How can you signal that you are ready and willing to take an empathetic stance? If you sense that someone wants to open up to you, here's how you can take steps towards understanding someone else's position.

Don't speak badly of others. Keep your tone nonjudgmental. Other peoples' actions and behaviors tend to come up in all kinds of conversation. Everyone gossips from time to time.

However, if you want someone to feel comfortable in opening up to you, you need to fight the urge to talk badly of others. Who is going to feel safe talking to you if you repeatedly demonstrate a willingness to stab other people in the back?

No one feels safe opening up to someone judgmental, because they worry that they'll also be judged! Obviously, you should also abstain from passing judgment on what your conversation partner is telling you.

You should also refrain from giving unsolicited advice. Assume that if they want you to make a suggestion, they'll ask for it.

Show that you are taking an expansive listening position. Remember, an expansive listening position is one in which you happily and patiently follow the listener's train of thought, without judgment.

If you show even the merest hint of impatience, the other person will shut down. They will assume that you would rather get the conversation over and done with. This isn't going to encourage them to trust you.

Ask them directly but gently whether there's something on their mind. If your conversation partner seems a little distracted, and their body language is tense, ask them whether there's anything they would like to talk about. Don't be aggressive about it. Just give them the chance to speak if they would like to do so.

Of course, if they tell you that something is bothering them but they would rather not discuss it, you should show empathy by telling them that you understand, and if they change their mind they can still come and talk to you.

Give them time to "empty the tank." When was the last time someone truly listened to you, without leaping in with an interruption or judgment? We all know that sometimes, we just want to tell someone exactly what we are thinking and feeling.

If we are lucky, they will have empathy for our position, and go out of their way to give us as much space as we need. If you find yourself occupying the role of listener, allow the other person to say all the things they need to say.

When you interrupt someone, you are signaling to them that your personal thoughts are more important than their right to speak. This isn't the message you want to send.

Try to show Unconditional Positive Regard (UPR). The humanistic therapist Carl Rogers used a concept called Unconditional Positive Regard when talking with his clients. He believed that everyone has all the resources they need to sort out their own problems, but sometimes they need the right kind of environment in which to work out the best solution.

This is a really helpful framework if you are trying to take an empathetic stance. Just as Rogers did, make a decision to accept the other person just as they are, regardless of their speech or actions.

This doesn't mean that you have to agree with what they have done, and it doesn't mean you should let them act in a threatening or inappropriate way. Think of UPR as a tool you can use to leave your personal biases to one side, and approach the conversation from a receptive point of view.

When you work from the assumption that the other person is at heart a good, rational individual with the capacity for change, you likely to show them true acceptance and react in an empathetic manner.

What To Say When You're Told Something Shocking

Empathy is one of the greatest gifts one person can give another, but it should come with a warning label. When you create a safe space for someone, there's every chance that they will share their deepest personal secrets with you.

This won't always make for easy listening. Some of these secrets will be sad, but relatively "normal." Experiences that most of us can relate to, such as feeling hopeless after losing a job, or feeling deeply depressed after breaking up a with partner, fall into this category.

On other occasions, you might find that your conversation partner tells you something that shocks you. No matter how prepared you think you are, or how much life experience you have accumulated, sometimes it only takes a few seconds for a conversation to take a surprising turn.

You might not be able to contain your outrage or sadness. As long as you don't make your own emotions the center of the conversation, it's fine to let the other person know how you feel.

You are not a robot. A simple statement such as, "To me, that sounds terrible," or "I can't help feeling sad for you" will leave them in no doubt that you care, but at the same time draws a firm line between their feelings and your own.

Always aim for honesty. If they ask you how their revelation makes you feel, let them know. Be authentic and open with your emotions, because this in turn will allow the other person to feel safe in telling you what is going on in their mind and heart.

If you can't help but react strongly to something you are told, make sure that you tell the other person that they aren't to blame. Tell them that you are honored that they chose to open up to you, and emphasize that your feelings are yours alone to deal with.

Sometimes, the best answer is actually no answer at all. Remember, people do not always open up because they want or need someone to tell them what to do. Often, they open up because they feel the need to be heard.

A simple gesture can also do well in place of words. A light touch on their arm, a slow nod of the head, or even a hug (if you already have a close relationship with the person) can provide a lot of comfort.

Improve Communication Skills

The most successful people who eventually go on to become leaders and managers in the workplace are the ones who can make great impressions on everyone they work with because of how well they communicate. Of course, being able to do the job well does play a part of it as well, but when you can meaningfully and effectively communicate with the people you work with, you are already halfway towards success.

At work, we are required to communicate a lot more than we normally would in our everyday lives. We're communicating with clients, with colleagues, with managers, with bosses, through emails, over the phone and even during meetings and presentations. Here is what you can do to improve your communication skills at the workplace:

- Improve Your Body Language – Body language is applicable in the workplace too, perhaps even more so because this is where it really matters. At work, the way you carry yourself and communicate is just as important as how well you get the job done. Remember how our nonverbal cues can speak volumes even when we don't say a word? So, while at work, always adopt confident body language whenever you step into your workplace. Do not

69

slouch, do not fold or cross your arms, do not frown or look sullen. Always be positive, and project a warm and welcoming manner, smile and make eye contact with the people you pass by.

- Avoid Over-Communicating – Avoid being long-winded and beating around the bush when you have discussions and conversations at work. You may think you are trying to be as effective as possible by communicating every little detail, even what is seemingly unnecessary, but avoid doing that because there is such a thing as over-communicating. Even in presentations, droning on for too long puts you at risk of losing the attention span of your audience. The best way to communicate effectively is to be brief, concise and only communicate what is necessary and relevant to the situation or discussion at hand.

- Seek Feedback – The best way to know if you are effective in what you do, or if what you are doing is working, is to seek feedback honest feedback from your colleagues. Regularly seeking feedback will help you discover what areas you should be working on to improve, and often it is others who can shed better perspective on the things that we may overlook.

- Engage with Your Audience – If you are tasked with presenting at a meeting, this is a great way for you to put into practice your effective communication skills.

Now, business presentations are not the most riveting topic, and attention spans will drift eventually, so what do effective communicators do? They engage with their audience. Being effective in your communication requires that you can deliver the points you want to say to an audience that is paying attention. During the meeting or presentation, ask questions and encourage your audience to respond and share their points of view.

- Watching Your Tone of Voice – At the workplace, you need to always ensure that your tone is professional yet friendly and welcoming at the same time. Sometimes it may be necessary to be assertive to stand firm on a point, but still, try and maintain a professional tone when you do that to avoid coming off as aggressive. Effective communication at work requires that you be able to master being confident, direct, professional yet calm and cooperative at the same time.

- Checking Your Grammar – This step is applicable for emails and written communication at the workplace. The most effective communicators are ones who can write flawlessly with no mistakes because they put in the extra effort to check and proofread everything that they type or write before they hit the send button. Check it twice, check it thrice, check it as many times as you need to ensure everything is completely on point before it gets sent. You will impress everyone with your perfect grammar and punctuation, and the ones who read your emails will be able to understand what you are trying to say just as if you were standing there in front of them talking to them.

- Speaking with Clarity – Good communication means being able to be easily understood by everyone you speak to. One of the easiest ways to do that is to simply improve your speech clarity. Pronounce and enunciate your words properly, don't rush through your sentences, don't mumble, don't mutter and avoid using those conversation fillers that were talked about earlier (avoid the um's and ah's). Practice being able to put forth the messages that you want to say is as few and concise words as possible, this will help you speak with clarity because you already know exactly what needs to be said. Preparing your talking points ahead of time is another great way to boost speech clarity and keep the conversation fillers to a minimum. It also helps avoid excessive and unnecessary talking about irrelevant points, because you want your receiver to be clear about the message, not walk away from the discussion still feeling more confused about it.

- Practice Friendliness – Would you enjoy speaking to someone who is unfriendly and stand-offish at the office? The obvious answer would be no. Nobody would want to engage in a conversation because they would be put off by the person's very demeanor even before they have said a word. To become an effective communicator at work, you need to start adopting a friendly and approachable persona which will encourage your co-workers to want to approach you and have a conversation with you. A friendly approach is even more important when you are having a face-to-face discussion, especially if you are in a managerial position because your colleagues aren't going to want to open up to you if they feel intimidated even before the discussion has properly begun.

- Be Confident – Being confident is an important part of becoming an effective communicator overall. When you interact with others around you at the workplace, the moment you show you are confident you will find it much easier to hold effective conversations with your colleagues and team members that will result in things getting done. Why? Because they are drawn towards your confident approach. Confident people are not thwarted by challenges, they rise to meet them, and this is what people at work want to follow.

Somebody who knows what they are doing and is doing it with confidence.

- Say No to Distractions – Meeting rooms exist in the workplace for a reason, and its time to make full use of them. The best way to have a meaningful conversation with the people you work with is to keep the distractions to a minimum. In an environment like work where so many people are working in close proximity with one another, phones can be constantly ringing off the hook, people will be on the move walking up and down, and several conversations could be going on at once. Not exactly the most conducive environment to hold a discussion, much less an effective conversation. Keep the distractions to a minimum, go into a meeting room and close the door, put the phones away and then when both parties are ready, begin your conversation.

- Keep Your Points Consistent – To be able to deliver messages effectively means you need to be able to remain on point and consistent with what you are saying. It helps if you stick to the facts and the focus of the discussion at hand, write down and prepare your talking points before you hold the conversation. Your points should flow smoothly, and nothing should contradict each other because you could end up confusing the receiver of your message and they become unsure about what it is you are trying to say. Your key points of your message are also at risk of being lost when you contradict yourself far too much. Plan and prepare ahead, make some notes and have them ready if you need to refer to them to help you stay on course. This is how you practice becoming a more effective communicator.

- Remain as Transparent as Possible – There is nothing that is disliked more at the workplace than a lack of transparency. If you are in a leadership position especially, transparency is important in your efforts to become a more effective communicator overall. Never try to hide information, or leave out bits and pieces of information when working with your colleagues on a project or working in a team. It makes it difficult for everyone involved to communicate well if they don't have all the necessary information on hand to work with. If you are the one that is in charge of a team project, communicate clearly with your peers on what the deadlines and the goals of the project are, and ensure that everyone is clear on what needs to be done before moving forward.

Persuasive Communication

By definition, persuasion is the act of making an effort to convince someone to do something or change their beliefs in favor of some that you think are worthwhile. Empathy cannot lead you to persuasion because it causes you to see that the other person is right in his own right. However, if you fully understand where a person is coming from, you can strategize and come up with a way to persuade him or her to change his or her mind. This is why persuasion is said to be an art.

You see, art is any activity that a person uses to express the emotions buried inside. It conveys complex messages that words wouldn't carry. It, however, can be intellectually challenging, complex, and coherent. That said, the product of your art must be an original piece. It, therefore, demands a great deal of skill and patience.

The art of persuasion does not check all boxes in the definition of art because people take various approaches to persuasion. Some will persuade without even showing an ounce of emotion while others are all about the emotional appeal. In addition, you cannot talk of persuasion as an art in the sense that other art forms like music and paintings are. It is also easy to persuade without intending to be unique in any way. However, persuasion does indeed contain other qualities that qualify it to be an art: it is complex, intellectually challenging, it conveys a complex message, it can be quite original, and it highlights your point of view.

You may wonder what the point of persuading is. Why should you waste your precious time and energy persuading others?

Isn't it also a form of manipulation? The truth is that you need to learn how to persuade others to achieve any success in life. Every seller has had to persuade a customer to buy his or her products. Every teacher has had to persuade parents that he can do a good job. Every married person has had to persuade his or her partner to marry him or her. Every employee has had to persuade the employer to hire him. Every successful politician has had to persuade voters to vote for him.

As you can see, almost every success in life demands that you convince others that you have the capacity to fit and fulfill the mandates of the position you intend to fill. Persuasion seems to run in the bedrock of every human endeavor.

The Basics of Persuasion

The following are the principles of persuasion. govern the ability to convince people to share your ideologies and points of view:

Scarcity

People are more drawn to people, products, or opportunities that are exclusive or limited in edition. When people perceive an impending shortage, they tend to demand scarce resources, and if they can be bought, they buy them in excess.

Companies take advantage of this tendency and suggest shortages in their supply (only five pieces remaining), limiting the time an offer is available (available for three days only), or suggesting scarcity in the frequency with which an offer is made (annual sale). Customers, driven by the fear of missing out, respond by making purchases, most of which are unplanned and impulsive.

In life, everything is measured by its relative value. If someone thinks something is valuable, I will be driven to accord the same value to the item. We often want to own things because others have them. As such, if you want something to be considered valuable, you must make it scarce, and that includes yourself too. In communication, if you want people to value your words, talk less.

Reciprocity

Whenever you do good to someone, there is a natural nagging and drive to reciprocate the gesture. This behavior is ingrained in human DNA so that we can help each other survive. Interestingly, you also could tip the reciprocity scale to favor you disproportionately by giving some small gestures that show your consideration to others, and when you ask for some help or a favor, the others will happily offer it.

Authority

It is impossible to persuade anyone to do something when you do not appear to have expertise or knowledge in that field. No one wants to be led to the shaky ground of trial and error. A persuader must radiate special skills and expertise. Experts are more likely to be trusted. They radiate authority in their fields. Therefore, when you intend to persuade a person to take a particular stand, ensure that your knowledge and familiarity with that subject or field is beyond reproach. When you do this, you will build your reputation as an expert or personality in that particular field.

Liking

One of the impossible tasks is to convince an enemy to do anything. It is an exercise in futility. No one trusts or likes dealing with someone they consider unpleasant. What if you are dealing with strangers, how do you get them to like you? It's very simple. You only need to appear open, kind, attentive, sympathetic, and empathetic. Also, let people know that they are highly regarded and appreciated. Appreciation is demonstrated through acts such as giving presents, inviting the people to special events, offering 'inside' information, and by making regular phone calls. People also appreciate feeling that you understand them and their interests. If you have the chance, give valuable ideas or suggestions, and you will have them eating from the palm of your hand.

Consistency and Commitment

Consistency assures a person that he or she will get the results he or she expects or got in a previous similar engagement. Before people commit themselves to you, they want to see signs that you are committed too, and consistent in your giving results. The best thing is to give these signs of commitment and consistency step by step, and the other party will slowly buy into your ideas.

For example, when dealing with a customer that wants to buy a dress, create the consistency that convinces the customer that you are best suited to sell the dress. You could say, "Yes, we have the dress in red, yes we have a changing room where you can try on your dress, yes, we can also deliver the dress to you, yes, we have an in-house seamstress who will make your preferred alterations for free, yes, you can carry your dress home today." Ensure that all the customer's concerns can be addressed, and when you are done, the customer will have no choice but to stick with you.

Suppose a friend or coworker calls asking if he or she can come over to share some personal information, show that you are committed to listening to what the friend has to say, and to doing all you can to help. Say, "Yes, I am available to speak to you now (or in a little while), I promise that our conversation will be confidential, you are free to speak to me about anything, I will help you as much as I can, you have my complete attention." When you say this, the individual will likely feel safe and will want to speak about the issue of concern. After the conversation, assure the individual that you will be available to talk when called upon to do so.

Social Proof and Consensus

People are the ultimate advertising tools; when someone thinks of you or the items you are selling to be good, be sure that he or she will make that known to other people the person comes into contact with. What's more, human beings tend to be more convincing than other ad methods. For example, a customer is more likely to read customer reviews and to believe them, over and above ads on various media platforms. Therefore, as you market yourself and your products or services, always refer to those who would have something positive to say, such as references in your resume or happy customer reviews. Their opinions will be more convincing than anything you would say to market yourself.

How to Persuade Someone of Your Opinion

Having understood what persuasion is and the principles that govern it, let's now see how to go about it. The first thing you ought to keep in mind is that you can persuade anyone, naturally, without even trying much. The following steps and techniques will teach you how to influence, from a marketing and a personal perspective, but these techniques are viable in any interpersonal engagement you are involved in, from making new friends, convincing an employer to hire you, networking, and relating with friends. They include:

Take Up Mirroring To Help Create A Subconscious Agreement With The Other Party

Mirroring is presumed to be one of the easiest and quickest ways to create accord between two parties. It refers to the acts of copying someone's volume, speed of speech, tone and body language in a bid to reflect that person's behavior to him or her, just like a mirror would reflect.

Research shows that mirroring a person's behavior produces more considerable social influence over the person being mimicked. The study found that individuals who mirrored had more success persuading the other party, and were regarded with more positivity than those who did not mirror.

The reason mirroring works so well is because behaving like the other person is behaving tends to put the individual at ease, which increases the possibilities of building a rapport with them. It breaks through any form of subconscious resistance the person may have and encourages the individual to trust you.

Typically, people mirror others subconsciously, but when you are learning how to do it for persuasion, you must do it consciously, until when it comes to you on autopilot so that it now is a natural part of your interactions. The easiest way to start is to try to match the other party's conversation tempo and stance. However, you do not just jump into it immediately. One cardinal rule of thumb is to wait it out, about 5 to 10 seconds before you start mirroring the other party's stance so that your attempts are not too noticeable. Remember that your mission here is to gain trust, not to arouse suspicion.

Be careful that mirroring sometimes backfires, especially when you mirror negativity such as raising your voice when another raises his or taking up negative postures like crossing your legs or your arms. Turning your body away from the individual also communicates negativity. Be careful not to do any of them.

Be Surrounded by Other Influential Persons

The law of averages states that the result of any particular situation is the average of all possible outcomes. Jim Rohn brought a new perspective to this law saying that a person is the average of five people he or she hands out with most of the time. He said this in reference to the fact that while we interact with hundreds or thousands of people in daily life, only a few of those have an impact on us. Their influence is very significant, to the point that they influence how we speak, how we think, how we talk, and how we react to situations, among others.

Whenever you keep the company of people you aspire to be like, you will naturally begin to emulate them, and will eventually have risen to their level. Therefore, when you want to learn how to persuade and influence other people, you have to keep the company of some influential people so that you be in a position to absorb their mannerisms, reasoning, general outlook on life and their knowledge because these are the factors that have contributed towards their success.

We all have the privilege of choosing our friends, the people we spend our time with, and it is better that you select people that are going to make you a better person, and make it easier for you to reach the goals you intend to achieve in life, one of which is to become an influential person.

Encourage the Other Party To Talk About Himself

People like speaking their minds. Science confirms that about 30 t0 40 percent of the words we speak are solely about ourselves. We love expressing our viewpoints, talking about our experiences, achievements, and others. Some are even comfortable talking about the struggles they are going through because it gives them some form of relief and eases the stress in their minds. When scientists studied the brain as people spoke about themselves, and scans showed some activity in parts of the brain that are primarily linked to value and motivation. It is this same brain area that is linked with a person talking about himself, and other thrills such as drug use, sex, and money.

Start with some small talk, then proceed with some meaningful questions. As the person speaks, keenly listen to the answer given, and where possible turn the answer around into a follow-up question to let the speaker know that you are enjoying their talk. This encouragement causes the other party to go deeper and reveal information he or she did not intend to give.

As the individual continues speaking, you will have a broader look into who they are, what they believe, and you will also figure out the areas of common ground so that it becomes easier to make a personal connection with them. The more you listen, the higher chance you stand to influence the person.

Take Advantage of the Pauses and Moments of Silence

As we mentioned before, silence is uncomfortable for many people. It makes them feel prompted to speak to fill it. An influential person must be fully aware of the effect that silence has on people, and use it to his or her advantage. Use silence to make the other party disclose some more information, give clues, or even make a mistake that could be to your advantage.

On the other hand, when you indicate that you are not afraid of silence so that you are unhurried and more deliberate in your speech and your actions, you elicit a feeling of confidence and control. Therefore, even in uncomfortable situations, be patient in your discourse, and you will appear confident.

Another advantage of the silence and the pauses is that they allow you to process the information you get better. You also get the time to consider the best approach for communicating some thoughts, so that you present your ideas in a humane, empathetic way that will help deepen the connection you have with others.

How to Improve Persuasive Communication

Sometimes persuasive communication does not work because:

- The person receiving the information does not trust the communicator
- They believe there is some hidden truth
- There is conflicting information about a particular situation
- If the information is not helpful

In order to improve your persuasive communication skills:

Know Your Audience

When using persuasive communication, it is important to understand your audience or the individual person you are communicating with. Persuasive communication becomes effective if it addresses the audience's needs or if the audience feels that, they can relate to the communicator in some way. One of the challenges here is because the audience has the power of choice, and the communicator is trying to influence them to make a particular choice.

Capture Their Attention

To capture the audience's attention, you need to be credible, influential, and authoritative. People pay close attention to authoritative figures or industrial leaders because they feel that they have something they can share with them and therefore have to be keen on what they are saying. This is why a good number of companies use celebrities to market their brands. Another way to capture the audience's attention is to use facts and figures, people are more inclined to listen when you have proof in comparison to just telling them to believe you.

Use Of Body Language

When communicating verbally, body language influences your ability to persuade as much as your words. When you fidget a lot, it comes out as if you are not certain of the information you are trying to covey or when you cross your arms, you come out as aggressive or hostile. Avoiding eye contact also shows that you are hiding something. In order to be more persuasive, you need to relax, avoid crossing your arms, use gestures and always maintain eye contact.

Tailor Your Message

Ideally, people have a chance of persuading other people more when communicating with them face-to-face. One of the advantages of this is that if an audience has follow-up questions, they can get immediate responses. In order to improve persuasive communication, it is important to tailor the message to the audience. You cannot use jargon when communicating with kids, instead, use simple language.

Communicate Their Benefits

In order to improve your persuasive communication skills, you need to convince your audience how what you are proposing will benefit them. If you are trying to get people to buy a particular brand, tell them the benefits they get over other brands.

Ensure Your Message Is Understood

When persuading either an audience or individual, it is important to ensure they understand your message before you get to the persuading part. Clarify or rephrase what you are trying to say for other people to understand it before you can persuade them.

Do It Repetitively

Another way to improve your persuasive skills is to do it repetitively. People rarely get on-board the first time around but when they hear it again and again even from other people, they get interested. This is the reason ads on media play several times a day. However, be careful not to oversell.

Be Honest And Truthful

It is important for the audience to build trust with the persuader before they can be persuaded. Always ensure that whatever you are selling truly does what you say. Sell something legit.

Everyone uses persuasive communication in his or her day-to-day life, therefore following the tips outlined above will enable you to hone up on your persuasive skills.

The Definition of a Rapport and the Process of Creating It

Rapport is the process of developing a connection with someone else. It forms the basis for meaningful and harmonious relationships between people. People can build rapport either instantly or over time. You develop a rapport with someone when:

- You both have positive thoughts and feelings about each other
- You are both friendly and show care and concern
- You both share a common understanding

A number of things like body language, eye contact and tempo can be beneficial in building rapport.

Chapter 3.   Body Language

Body Language in Communication

Non-verbal form of contact is a tremendously difficult yet vital part of general communication abilities. Conversely, individuals are frequently unconscious of their non-verbal actions. Researchers connect big significance to the individuals' ability for verbal communication. However, people have a corresponding path of nonverbal contact, which might disclose more than our cautiously selected language. Most of the nonverbal gestures and understanding of pointers is involuntary and carried out beyond our awareness and power. On the other hand, using our nonverbal signals we unsuspectingly convey plenty of messages regarding our physical and mental states. The signs we bring out, the pose in which we embrace our hands, the expressions we put on our bodies and the nonverbal persona of our talking contribute to how other people perceive us.

A fundamental responsiveness of nonverbal contact approaches, above what is stated might assist in developing communication with other people. The familiarity of these secret languages might be employed to support individuals to speak about their worry and may result in a superior understanding, which is the function of interaction. When we speak regarding body language, we consider the delicate signals we give and get to from others nonverbally. Several individuals wish to understand how to interpret body language. Body language might be clustered into a few categories:

Facial expressions

Scholars revealed seven widespread micro-expressions or small facial signals every person portrays if they feel a powerful feeling. People are attracted to observing the face to know if somebody has concealed feelings. The small signals shown on our faces are a vital element of nonverbal communication.

Body Proxemics

This is an expression of how a human body shifts in air. We are continuously observing how somebody is making progress, making gestures, leaning, shifting forward or backwards. Body activities notify people a lot regarding inclination and anxiety. Movements are involved in body language signals.

Ornaments

Outfit, necklaces, hairstyles, are all added to the nonverbal indicators. Not only do specific paints and fashions send indicators to other people, how we interrelate with our ornaments is as well important. Is somebody an adorer of his or her phone? Do they continuously touch their necklace? We must notice these vital body language signals.

Interpretation of body language

Reading body language might sound like a difficult task; however, mastering the art of interpreting them is vital. There are two methods of understanding body language in other people. Decoding is the capability of reading people's prompts. It entails how people read concealed feelings, information, and traits from an individual nonverbal signal. Encoding is the skill of sending signals to other persons. Encoding plays a key role in controlling your individual trademark. The first feeling you provide and the way you make someone think when you meet them for the first time.

Significance of nonverbal cues in interactions

Emphasizing what is stated verbally.

For instance, individuals might nod energetically when meaning yes to emphasize that they concur with the other individual. A gesticulation of the shoulders and a gloomy face when stating, "I am okay, thank you" might mean that matters are not all right at all.

Convey information about their emotional state.

Someone's facial appearance, his or her pitch of tone, and his or her body language might notify somebody precisely what you are undergoing, even when he or she has barely uttered a sentence.

Strengthen the link between persons

When you have observed partners discussing, you might have detected that they have a tendency of mirroring one another's nonverbal signals. They place their arms in parallel poses, they laugh uniformly, and they look at each other frequently. These activities strengthen their affair; consequently, building on their relationship, and assist them to feel coupled.

Offer response to the other individual.

Laughing and nodding inform somebody that you are paying attention and that you concur with what they are putting across. Body shifting and hand signs might point out that you desire to talk. These slight signs provide information quietly but unmistakably.

Normalize the course of interaction

There are several signs that people use to inform others that he or she has completed or wish to talk. A resounding nod and strong closure of the lips show that someone has no intention of speaking anymore. Maintaining eye contact with the person in charge of a conference and nodding faintly shall show that you desire to talk.

Features of Body Language

There are types of body language. This is because we cannot classify the different styles in the same category. Different body languages can be distinguished. So, which body language styles can be differentiated? Generally, the body language is divided into two columns. That includes; Body parts and the Intent

So what kinds in each class can be observed?

Let us start with the body parts and the language they communicate.

- The Head - The placement of the head and its movement, back and forth, right to left, side to side, including the shake of hair.
- Face - This includes facial expressions. You should note that the face has many muscles ranging from 54 and 98 whose work is to move different areas of the face. The movements of the face depict the state of your mind.
- Eyebrows - The eyebrows can express themselves through moving up and down, as well as giving a frown
- Eyes - The eyes can be rolled, move up down, right, and left, blink as well as the dilatation

- The Nose - The expression of the nose can be by the flaring of the nostrils and the formation of wrinkles at the top
- The Lips - There are many roles played by the lips, that include snarling, smiling, kissing, opened, closed, tight, and puckering
- The Tongue - The tongue can roll in and out, go up and down, touch while kissing, and also the licking of lips
- The Jaw - The jaw opens and closes, it can be clinched and also the lower jaw can be moved right and left
- Your Body Posture - This describes the way you place your body, legs, and arms connected, and also concerning other people
- The Body Proximity - This looks at how far your body is to other people
- Shoulder Movements - They move up and down, get hunched, and hang
- The Arm - These go up down, straight and crossed

Legs and the feet-these can have an expression in many different ways. They can be straight, crossed, legs placed one over the other, the feet can face the next person you are in a conversation with, they can face away from each other, the feet can be dangling the shoes

The hand and the fingers-the way that your hands and fingers move is powerful in reading other people's gestures.

The hands can move up and down, they can do some hidden language that only people of the same group can understand.

How one reacts to handling and placing of objects-this is not regarded as a body part but it technically plays a role in reading a body language. This may predict anger, happiness and much more.

This includes willingly making body movements otherwise known as gestures. These are the movements that you intended to make for example shaking of hands, blinking your eyes, moving, and shaking your body in a sexy way maybe to lure someone and much more. There are also involuntary movements-this are movements that you have no control over. This can be sweating, laughter, crying and much more. Facial Expression

The expression facial (also, facies, face), with the eyes, is one of the most important means to express emotions and moods.

Through knowledge and observation of facial expressions (that is, the moving face and not as a static object) we can get a better understanding of what others communicate to us.

We also make judgments about people's personality and other traits based on what we see in their faces. For example, people with attractive features are often attributed certain qualities that they may or may not actually possess.

The face and first impressions

In a first meeting between two people, the first five minutes are usually the most critical period. The impressions formed in this short space of time will tend to persist in the future, and even be reinforced by subsequent behavior, which is not usually interpreted objectively, but according to those first impressions.

Since the face is one of the first features we notice in a person, it can clearly play a vital role in the process of establishing relationships with others.

In these few minutes we form opinions about your character, personality, intelligence, temperament, ability to work, about your personal habits, even about your convenience as a friend or lover.

Talking to the face

Together with the eyes, the face is our best means to communicate without words. We use it (and the judgments of others will depend on the clues they get) to indicate how pleasant we are as people, to express our current state of mind, to show the attention we pay to others, and so on. However, facial expressions can be used to reinforce the impact of verbal messages, such as when a mother scolds her child: the expression on her face will show if she is really angry, if only a little...

The main function of the face in body language is the expression of emotions; although other parts of the body also contribute to the use we make of body language, so we should not believe that a message is clear and exclusively transmitted by a single part of the body.

The range of expressions is very wide, but there are a limited number of emotions that most of us can recognize with some reliability.

Paul Ekman and Wallace Friesen, have discovered that there are 6 main facial expressions:

The smiles

The smiles can be light, normal, and large. They are usually used as a gesture of greeting, to express varying degrees of pleasure, joy, joy, happiness. Even blind-born children smile when they like something. They are characterized by being beautiful and cheerful. Smiles can also be used to mask other emotions:

- Smile to hide the hardships.
- Smile as a submission response.
- Smile to make stressful situations more bearable.
- Smile to attract the smile of others.
- Smile to relax the tension.

- Smile to hide fear.
- Sadness, disappointment and depression

They are distinguished by lack of expression and by features such as: downward inclination of the corners of the mouth, low gaze and general decay of the factions. Normally these emotions are accompanied by a low volume of the voice or a slower way of speaking.

Although in most cases they are not very well distinguished from each other, there are other bodily factors that give us the assurance of knowing which emotion is being carried out as:

- Sadness
- Eyebrows slightly tilted towards the ears forming a semiarch.
- Shoulders regularly decayed.
- Inclination of the commissures at 45% of their normal range.
- Hands together and face down.
- Disappointment
- Eyebrows not fully inclined.
- Looking back, and down, usually to the left.
- Shoulders slightly down and with the hands at the sides of the body.
- Depression
- Normally inclined eyebrows.

- Tilt of the commissures slightly descending.
- Shoulders totally down.
- Legs and thighs parallel to each other.

But we must remember that each emotion is different according to each individual. Not everyone demonstrates the same factions.

Dislike / contempt

They express themselves with shrinkage of the eyes and puckering of the mouth. The nose is usually wrinkled and the head turned sideways to avoid having to look at the cause of such a reaction. It is the only facial expression that occurs in only part of the face, that is, in the middle of it. One end of the upper lip is lifted while the opposite side is in its original position.

Anger

The anger is often characterized by: gaze into the cause of the offense, closed mouth and teeth tightly clenched, eyes and eyebrows slightly inclined to express anger. Closed hands pressing and containing the feeling can also be seen in a situation of anger.

The fear

The fear is not a unique form of expression that reveals its presence. It can be revealed through very wide eyes, through the open mouth or by a general tremor that affects the face and the rest of the body.

The interest

It is often detected by what is called "bird head", that is, the head tilts a certain angle towards the subject of interest. Other features are: eyes more open than normal and mouth slightly open.

Another aspect to consider is the extent to which the complements in nonverbal messages are involved. Because the complements change our appearance, we must take into account their effects on the perception that others have of us. From this it can be deduced that we do not always transmit the nonverbal messages we try to send. The more aware we are of these difficulties of body language, without words, the better we can use it.

Other information about the face

Facial expressions, in addition to expressing emotions, also serve as a means of expressing personality, attitudes towards others, sexual attraction and attractiveness, the desire to communicate or initiate an interaction and the degree of expressiveness during communication.

Differences have been found in the way men and women use facial expressions to communicate. Women tend to laugh and smile more often than men, which does not have to be due to greater sociability or joy, it may be because they find the situation slightly uncomfortable.

The expression of the face is constantly changing during communication. Among the changes we can mention the so-called "micro momentary" facial expressions, as its name indicates its duration is a fraction of a second and usually reflect the true feelings of a person.

Posture

Expectedly, posture and body orientation should be interpreted in the context of the entire body language to develop the full meaning being communicated. Starting with an open posture, it is used to denote friendliness. In this open position, the feet are spread wide and the palms of the hands are facing outward. Individuals with open posture are deemed more persuasive compared to those with other postures. To realize an open posture, one should stand up or sit straight with the head raised and keep the abdomen and chest exposed. When the open posture is combined with a relaxed facial expression and good eye contact it makes one look approachable and composed. Maintain the body facing forward toward the other person during a conversation.

There is also the closed posture where one crosses the arms across the chest or crosses the legs away from someone or sits in a hunched forward position as well as showing the backs of the hands and clenching the fists are indicative of a closed posture. The closed posture gives the impression that one is bored, hostile or detached. In this posture, one is acting cautious and appears ready to defend themselves against any accusation or threat.

For the confident posture, it helps communicate that one is not feeling anxious, nervous or stressed. The confident posture is attained by pulling oneself to full height, holding the head high and keeping the gaze at eye level. Then pull your shoulders back and keep the arms as well as legs to relax by the sides. The posture is likely to be used by speakers in a formal context such as when making a presentation, during cross-examination and during project presentation.

Equally important there is postural echoing and is used as a flirting technique by attracting someone in the guardian. It is attained by observing and mimicking the style of the person and the pace of movement. When the individual leans against the wall, replicate the same. By adjusting your postures against the others to attain a match you are communicating that you are trying to flirt with the individual. The postural echoing can also be used as a prank game to someone you are familiar with and often engage in casual talk.

Maintaining a straight posture communicates confidence and formality. Part of the confidence of this posture is that it maximizes blood flow and exerts less pressure on the muscle and joints which enhances the composure of an individual. The straight posture helps evoke desirable mood and emotion which makes an individual feel energized and alert. A straight posture is highly preferred informal conversations such as during meetings, presentation or when giving a speech.

Correspondingly being in a slumped position and hunched back is a poor posture and makes one be seen as lazy, sad or poor. A slumped position implies a strain to the body which makes the individual feel less alert and casual about the ongoing conversation. On the other hand, leaning forward and maintaining eye contact suggests that one is listening keenly. During a speech, if the audience leans forward in an upright position then it indicates that they are eager and receptive to the message.

Furthermore, if one slants one of the shoulders when participating in a conversation then it suggests that the individual is tired or unwell. Leaning on one side acutely while standing or sitting indicates that you are feeling exhausted or fed up with the conversation and are eagerly waiting for the end or for a break. Think of how you or others reacted when a class dragged on to almost break time. There is a high likelihood that the audience slanted one of their shoulders to the left or right direction. In this state, the mind of the individual deviates from things that one will do next. In case of a tea break, the mind of the students will deviate from what one will do during or after the tea break.

By the same measure standing on one foot indicates that one is feeling unease or tired. When one stands on one foot then it suggests that the person is trying to cope with uncomforting. The source of uneasiness could be emotional or physiological. For instance, you probably juggled your body from one foot to help ease the need to go for a short call or pass wind. In most cases, one finds himself or herself standing on one foot when an uncomfortable issue is mentioned. It is a way to disrupt the sustained concentration that may enhance the disturbing feeling.

If one cups their head or face with their hands and rests the head on the thighs then the individual is feeling ashamed or exhausted. When the speaker mentions something that makes you feel embarrassed then one is likely to cup their face or head and rest the face on the thighs. It is a literal way of hiding from shame. Children are likely to manifest this posture though while standing. When standing this posture may make one look like he or she is praying.

Additionally, if one holds their arms akimbo while standing then the individual is showing a negative attitude or disapproval of the message. The posture is created by holding the waist with both hands while standing up straight and facing the target person. The hands should simultaneously grip on the flanks, the part near the kidneys. In most cases, the arms-akimbo posture is accompanied by disapproval or sarcastic face to denote attitude, disdain or disapproval.

When one stretches both of their shoulders and arms and rests them on chairs on either side then the individual is feeling tired and casual. The posture is akin to a static flap of wings where one stretches their shoulder and arms like wings and rests them on chairs on either side. It is one of the postures that loudly communicates that you are bored, feeling casual and that you are not about the consequences of your action. The posture is also invasive of the privacy and space of other individuals and may disrupt their concentration.

If one bends while touching both of their knees, then the individual is feeling exhausted and less formal with the audience. The posture may also indicate extreme exhaustion and need to rest. For instance, most soccer players bend without kneeling while holding both of their knees, indicating exhaustion. Since in this posture one is facing down, the posture may be highly inappropriate in formal contexts and may make one appear queer.

When one leans their head and supports it with an open palm on the cheeks then it indicates that one is thinking deep and probably feeling sad, sorrowful or depressed. The posture is also used when one is watching something with a high probability of negative outcomes such as a movie or a game. The posture helps one focus deep on the issue akin to meditating.

Additionally, crossing your arms to touch shoulders or touch the biceps indicates that one is deliberately trying to focus on the issue being discussed. Through this posture, an individual will try to avoid distractions and think deeper about what is being presented. If you watch European soccer you will realize that coaches use this posture when trying to study the match, especially where their team is down. However, this posture should not be used in formal contexts as it suggests rudeness. The posture should be used among peers only.

Then there is the crossing of the legs from the thigh through the knee while seated on a chair especially on a reclining chair. In this posture, one is communicating that he or she is feeling relaxed and less formal. In most cases, this posture is exhibited when one is at home watching a movie or in the office alone past working hours. If this posture is replicated in a formal context then it suggests boredom or lack of concentration.

For the posture where one crosses the legs from the ankle to the soles of the feet while seated, it communicates that one is trying to focus in an informal context such as at home. For instance, if a wife or a child asks the father about something that he has to think through then the individual is likely to exhibit this posture. If this posture is replicated in a formal context then it suggests boredom or lack of concentration.

Eye Contact

Reading eye contact is important to understand the true status of an individual, even where verbal communication seeks to hide it. As advised, body language should be read as a group, we will focus on individual aspects of body language and make the reader understand how to read that particular type of body language.

Your pupils dilate when you are focused and interested in someone you are having a conversation with, or the object we are looking at or using. The pupils will contract when one is transiting from one topic to another. We have no control over the working of pupils. When one is speaking about a less interesting topic, the pupils will contract.

Effective eye contact is critical when communicating with a person. Eye contact implies that one looks but does not stare. Persistent eye contact will make the recipient feel intimidated or judged. In Western cultures, regular eye contact is desired, but it should not be overly persistent. If one offers constant eye contact, then it is seen as an attempt to intimidate or judge, which makes the recipient of the eye contact uncomfortable. There are studies that suggest that most children fall victim to attacks by pet dogs if they make too much eye contact, as this causes them to feel threatened and react defensively and instinctually.

Winking

In Western culture, winking is considered as a form of flirting which should be done to people we are in good terms with. This varies, though, as Asian cultures frown on winking as a facial expression.

Blinking

In most cases, blinking is instinctive; our affection for the person we are speaking to causes us to subconsciously blink faster. If the average rate of blinking is 6 to 10 times per minute, then it can indicate that one is drawn to the person they are speaking to.

Eye Direction

The direction of the eyes tells us about how an individual is feeling. When someone is thinking, they tend to look to their left as they are recalling or reminiscing. An individual that is thinking tends to look to their right when thinking creatively, but it can also be interpreted as a sign that one is lying. For left-handed people, the eye directions will be reversed.

Avoiding Eye Contact

When we do not make eye contact with someone we are speaking to for extended periods of time, we are most likely uncomfortable with the person or the conversation. We avoid looking someone in the eye if we feel ashamed to be communicating at them. When we feel dishonest about trying to deceive people, we avoid looking at them. While it is okay to blink or drop eye contact temporarily, people that consistently shun making eye contact are likely to be feeling uneasy with the message or the person they are communicating with. For emphasis, staring at someone will make them drop eye contact due to feeling intimidated. Evasive eye contact happens where one deliberately avoids making eye contact.

Crying

Human beings cry due to feeling uncontrollable pain or in an attempt to attract sympathy from others. Crying is considered an intense emotion associated with grief or sadness though it can also denote extreme happiness known as tears of joy. When an individual forces tears to manipulate a situation, this is referred to as "crocodile tears." Typically, though, if one cries, then the individual is likely experiencing intense negative emotion.

Additionally, when one is interested in what you are speaking, he or she will make eye contact often. This is not entirely eye contact, though. Rather, the eye contact on the eyes of the other person is for the duration of 2-3 minutes, and then it switches to the lips or nose, and then returns to the eyes. For a brief moment, the person initiating eye contact will look down then back up to the eyes. Looking up and to the right demonstrates dismissal and boredom. Dilation of the pupil may indicate that someone is interested or that the room is brighter.

In some instances, sustained eye contact may be a signal that you want to speak to the person or that you are interested in the person sexually. At one point, you have noticed a hard stare from a man towards a particular woman to the point the woman notices and asks the man what is all that for. In this case, eye contact is not being used to intimidate but to single out the target person. You probably have seen a woman ask why is that man staring at me then she proceeds to mind her business but on taking another look at the direction of the man the stare is still there. In this manner, eye contact is used to single out an individual and make them aware that one is having sexual feelings towards the person.

However, people are aware of the impact of body language and will seek to portray the expected body language. For instance, an individual that is lying is likely to make deliberate eye contact frequently to sound believable. At one point, you knew you were lying but went ahead to make eye contact. You probably have watched movies where one of the spouses is lying but makes believable eye contact with others. The reason for this faked body language is because the person is aware of the link between making eye contact and speaking the truth.

Like verbal language, body language and in particular eye contact can be highly contextual. For instance, an individual may wink to indicate that he or she agrees with the quality of the product being presented or that he or she agrees with the plan. Eye contact in these settings can be used as a coded language for a group of people. At one point, one of your classmates may have used a wink to indicate that the teacher is coming or to indicate that the secret you have been guarding is now out.

Gestures

Hand gestures, in general, are rather accidental. They are important in telling us a lot about another person who utilizes his or her hands when talking, though. Also, in the case of arm movement, there are guidelines for constructive body language.

Leave Your Arms in An Open Position

The first step is to always have an outstretched hand. Open hands imply transparency and approval. Open palms mean honesty and integrity as well. There's also a way to read the open palms, though. If the hands are open when speaking or facing down, this means the individual's attitude is somewhat dominant. This is particularly noticeable in the case of handshakes. Nevertheless, it is a non-threatening indication if the palms are opened and facing upwards. This individual is accessible and can be perceived in essence as welcoming. The palms switch, therefore, totally alters the manner we are viewed by others.

Don't Cross the Arms

While talking, the arms ought not to be crossed and the hands must not be caught. Fastened hands show the absence of responsibility and the absence of certainty. Crossed arms show guarded or anxious position. It has likewise been seen that on when an individual stand with his arms crossed, at that point he gets little on of the discussion when contrasted with an individual with great affection with open arms. Additionally, protective non-verbal communication likewise prompts lower maintenance control.

It is in our normal nature to fold our arms to feel great. Be that as it may, thinks about have demonstrated that such a non-verbal communication is seen as adverse by individuals. Besides, held clench hands are additionally a major no during discussions. The arms ought not to go underneath the midsection level and should consistently be raised over the abdomen while talking. The arms can at times go down however it ought not to be so all through the discussion.

Do Not Grip Your Arms

While addressing somebody, don't grasp your arms by intersecting them. It is an indication of being insecure. Continuously abstain from holding your arms together before your crotch region, as it shows frailty too. It is known as the Broken Zipper posture. This is one stance that shows weakness and accommodation simultaneously and henceforth, must be maintained a strategic distance.

Try not to continue modifying your sleeve buttons in general public location as it again shows you are a lot of worried about your weaknesses of turning out in broad daylight. The women must make a note that they ought not to grasp their bags near themselves as they talk as it shows their cautious position and their uncertain nature.

Zero Arm Blockage

At the point when you are in an eatery, don't grip your espresso cup away from plain view. There ought to be no arm boundary when you conversing with someone else. Keep open non-verbal communication and hold the espresso cup aside.

Use the Parallel Over Perpendicular

In bunch talks, it is a command that when you need to point towards somebody, don't utilize the hand that will be opposite to them. Utilize the other arm that can point to them and can be parallel to your chest as well. Having the arm opposite to your chest to indicate out others is commonly an inconsiderate motion. Continuously attempt to have the arms parallel to the body.

Arms and hands must be utilized cautiously in discussions. The development of your arms and hands can make or blemish your exchange and can change the results fundamentally.

Head Action

We use the head, as much as any other part of our body, to communicate actively without using words. There are a few basic head gestures you can learn to recognize and use to express different emotions and thoughts.

117

The most common one is nodding. In most cases, it is a sign of agreement although it is often culturally bound. For example, people in Bulgaria nod for "No" and you may get confused if you are in a meeting with a representative of this nation.

Nodding often prompts your counterpart to talk more because you are sending them signals of agreement. During a meeting, the more you nod, the better and more relaxed a person would feel because you express agreement with their statement and are of the same opinion. You show support. However, don't overdo it because you risk looking funny.

On the other hand, head-shaking is considered a refusal, a literal "No". In business body language, shaking your head would mean you do not like the proposal being made. You may come up with a counter-proposal or refuse the deal altogether. If you see your counterpart shaking his head during your speech, change the direction of the conversation and try to understand their intentions and meet halfway.

Leaning forward or tilting your head to the side can mean that you are listening carefully and/or are focused on what the other person is saying.

During meetings or in your personal life you may see a person scratching their head. This may mean that they are trying to remember something, or feel uncertain. It may even mean lying. However, you must always be careful to watch for other gestures to support your opinion because scratching can be purely physiological – the person may have dandruff or is just sweating.

More often than not, head gestures and positions are tied to gestures with hand or the position of the body and facial expressions in the so-called clusters that map to interest or boredom, for example.

One of the gestures that most authors advise us to avoid is touching your face during meetings or dates. In most cases, this means that you are either lying or you feel insecure. Such gestures are often involuntary, but you can exercise at home and try not to use them. If you cover your mouth during a meeting, it will signal your partner that you are lying. The same applies if you touch your nose or rub your eyes.

Some simple rules to follow include the following:

Covering Your Mouth – you can cough, this way camouflaging the real gesture;

Touching Your Nose – if your hand or fingers involuntarily go towards your nose, you can either stop and put your hand under your chin and lean forward to show investment in the discussion or just run your fingers through your hair. It may show nervousness or confidence depending on your facial expression and the tone of your voice;

Rubbing Your Eyes – try instead to stop right before you have reached your eye and turn the gesture into one of interest – support your head with your palm rested on one of your cheeks and your index finger pointing up. This shows interest and assessment.

All of these are effective when you are listening. In case you are the speaker, try to avoid them altogether.

Not all gestures like touching your face or head are negative. As mentioned above, resting your palm on your cheek with your index finger pointing up means you are interested in the conversation and listening carefully while assessing the situation. However, the moment you start supporting your head with all fingers, it signals boredom.

Women often use hair-flip or hair-toss unconsciously to show they are attracted to a man. In a business environment, the hair-toss may mean that the woman feels confident about herself. In rare cases, when the hair-toss is preceded by touching or playing with her hair, it may mean nervousness or insecurity. Therefore, during business meetings, it is best to avoid touching your hair. A piece of advice – if you have noticed that you touch your hair often, go to the meeting with your hair tied to avoid unwanted body language signals that may ruin your position.

Another gesture is rubbing your chin. This usually means reflection and is used before you reach a decision. The same applies to rubbing your neck although it may also mean that you cannot make a decision, you are still not convinced.

If you want to exude confidence or even arrogance, you can put both your hands behind your head. This gesture, however, can only be used amongst equals or if you are surrounded by people on lower positions than you. Do not use it in front of your manager or people holding higher positions.

It Is Important to Understand Body Language

Most individuals rely on social networks and texts to connect in the modern digital age, and this is a very reliable way for doing so.

While digital communication enables people to speak at convenience and can reduce stress on certain individuals, something can be lost in so doing, and because you are incapable of recognizing the person when you speak to them, you can miss key non-verbal signs in addition to verbal ones such as vocal inflections. Digital communication has become the main method for people around the world, and to satisfy this, there is the likelihood that body language will proceed to develop. Most of the time you may hear the negatives of body language. Maybe you are told not to twist in a certain way, sit this way or that way. However, body language can influence your life positively. Let us look at what you should do to maximize body language.

Non Verbal Communication

Body language refers to the nonverbal cues they are used for communication. Such nonverbal cues, as per scholars, constitute a major part of your daily interaction. The things we do not say can still express volumes of knowledge from our facial expressions to our physical movements. It was proposed that facial expressions can speak for 60% to 65% of all interactions. It is important to recognize non-verbal communication, but it is also important to listen to other signals such as meaning. In many situations, instead of relying on a single event, you must look at signals as a band. You may be wondering what you should look at as you interpret non-verbal cues. Well, this chapter is going to fully answer your queries and leave you enlightened.

How to Use and Improve Body Language

After getting the tips, you may be asking yourself whether indeed body language influences your life positively. I am here to prove to you that indeed, your life is bound to transform if you take your time to nurture your body language and its relevance in each and everything that you do. You should know what to use where to be organized and articulate. This book will focus on positive body language. That includes; good eye contact, effective engagement, targeted gestures that make your message more understandable and effective. In essence body language has been found to create and enhance your confidence, influence, and all-round success. More studies have revealed that the people who know how to use their body language are more likable, persuasive, competent, and also possess a high level of emotional intelligence. That means that they can command presence and manipulate their way into various platforms and win people's hearts. That also explains the success in negotiation which we shall look at later in the book.

Let us go ahead and look at the ways that body language will transform your life.

Positive non-verbal communication changes your frame of mind. The research found that deliberately changing your non-verbal communication to make it increasingly positive improves your demeanor since it powerfully affects your hormones.

It leads to an increase in testosterone. At the point when you hear of testosterone, your mind can easily be swayed to focus on athletics, yet testosterone's significance covers substantially more than games. Regardless of whether you are a man or a lady, testosterone improves your certainty and makes other individuals consider you to be progressively dependable and positive. Research shows that positive nonverbal communication builds your testosterone levels by 20%.

Body language leads to a reduction of cortisol. Cortisol is a pressure hormone that blocks execution and makes negative wellbeing impacts over the long haul. Reduction of cortisol levels limits pressure and empowers you to think all the more plainly, especially in troublesome and testing circumstances. Research shows that positive non-verbal communication diminishes cortisol levels by 25%.

It makes a ground-breaking blend. While a reduction in cortisol and an increase in testosterone is incredible in its special ways, the two together are a ground-breaking blend that is normally observed among individuals in high positions. This blend makes the certainty and clearness of mind that are perfect for managing tight deadlines, intense choices, and huge amounts of work. Individuals who normally have high testosterone and low levels of cortisol are known to flourish under pressure. Indeed, you can utilize positive non-verbal communication to make yourself like this regardless of whether it doesn't occur normally.

It makes you progressively attractive and likable. During a study in a university, students watched soundless videos of doctors having an interaction with their patients. Just by watching the doctors' non-verbal communication, the students could conclude the doctors wound up getting sued by their patients. Non-verbal communication is an enormous factor by the way you're seen and can be a higher priority than your manner of speaking or even what you state. Figuring out how to utilize constructive use of body language will make individuals have confidence in you, like you and trust you more.

It shows capability. In an investigation, scientists found that a one-second video of candidates in a campaign was able to pinpoint the potential candidate that was voted for. All this because of their body language. While this may not build your confidence in the democratic procedure, it shows that the view of capability has a solid establishment in non-verbal communication.

Body language improves emotional intelligence. Your capacity to viably convey your feelings and thoughts is vital to your passionate knowledge. Individuals whose non-verbal communication is negative have a dangerous, infectious impact on everyone around them. Attempting to improve your non-verbal communication profoundly affects your emotional intelligence.

Chapter 4.   Public Speaking

The Importance of Public Speaking

Most people cringe at the thought of giving a speech in public however, the spoken word has so much power over written speech. Therefore, whether you are a teacher, student, business owner, employee or leader, public speaking is a very important skill to master and have.

You can be required to make a project presentation at school, make a presentation at work, pitch a product or service to a client or deliver a speech at a family gathering all of which requires you to be conversant and comfortable with public speaking. For those who are not good at it, it is a skill worth learning. Here are some reasons why the skill is important:

Public Speaking Increases Self-Confidence

Our self-esteem, in most cases, centers on what other people think about us, which should not always be the case. Through public speaking, we are able to increase our communication skills and thus become more comfortable around people and talking to them. The better you become at public speaking, it is likely that your self-confidence will only increase and this will, in turn, make you an even better public speaker.

It Increases Knowledge

Event organizers do not ask just anyone in the crowd that is interested in delivering a speech to stand up and do it. Before a public speaker stands up in front of a crowd to deliver a speech, he or she must do research. Therefore, over a long time, a person is bound to improve his or her research skills and gather an immense amount of knowledge. The preparation process also helps the speaker to understand the topic even better.

It Is an Opportunity to Show and Share Knowledge

When a speaker is standing to speak in front of a group of people, he or she is transferring information from him or herself to the audience in attendance. Therefore, taking up speaking roles positions an individual as an expert with knowledge in a particular area. People in the audience will, therefore, look up to a speaker not just with regard to the content he or she is sharing, but also with all the aspects surrounding the topic he or she is sharing on.

Public Speaking Delivers a Message to a Larger Audience over a Short Period

Speeches allow speakers to deliver one message to a large number of people over a short period. It would take a very long time for all the people in the audience to get down, conduct the same research, and come up with the same or even similar findings. Furthermore, the audience at an event where a speaker is giving a speech can also play the role of spreading the message to other people they know that could not make it to the event.

It Provides a Platform for Advocating for Certain Causes

If an individual has a certain cause that he or she holds dear, he or she can make it known to other people by holding public speeches and telling people about it. Some of the greatest revolutions in the past have gained massive followings after expert orators have charged people up with their speeches. People who deliver speeches in a great way convince their listeners to buy into the cause and in the process lead to positive social change.

It Brings People Together

Speeches foster cohesion because they present an opportunity for people to come together to share ideas. Politicians running for public office always call their supporters together to listen to them speak, and the more they address big crowds the better they become at delivering speeches and the more people want to vote for them. Such a public gathering will force human beings to interact with other like-minded people, and these interactions can foster the development of a community.

It Helps Develop Other Skills

Public speaking not only improves the speaker's communication skills but also helps to develop other skills in them such as leadership, negotiation skills, and people skills. You might discover that the people who are the greatest public speakers end up making some of the best leaders because of the leadership and interpersonal skills they develop in their quest to becoming expert public speakers.

Public Speaking Advances You in Life

Public speaking makes you more noticeable and can, therefore, fast track you to a promotion. Public speaking puts you in a position of influence, which means you can make a difference in your workplace and community. With this skill, you can negotiate for a job and better terms. Business owners with good public speaking abilities can also close deals quickly.

Principles of Public Speaking

As mentioned earlier, public speaking is the process of standing in front of a crowd and relaying information. Public speaking is not as easy as many would think and most people who are good at it have received training, or have done it so many times. Here are a few guidelines on the foundations of public speaking and the steps an individual can take to become better at it.

The principles of public speaking include:

1. Perfection - It is almost impossible to speak in public and not making any mistakes, even the gurus of public speaking sometimes make mistakes. You can stutter, misspeak or find yourself saying a couple of "umms" which make you sound less confident. However, when you make a mistake no one actually knows or cares but you. Therefore, keep going, only apologize if the mistake was momentous. If anything, the audience relates to you more when you make a mistake because it shows that no one is perfect.

2. Perception - Every day we hold routine conversations with people either at work or at home and we do it by being ourselves. However, when it comes to public speaking, something changes. We forget about being ourselves and concentrate on the public. Public speaking is all about being relaxed, holding an interesting conversation and being comfortable but most importantly being ourselves. Do not try to change the process through which you arrange your thoughts and how you normally speak just because you are addressing more people than you normally do.

3. Visualization - Visualization is key in public speaking. Practicing and creating images and technique in your mind can help you communicate the message. It is also a good way to get rid of panic and anxiety when speaking in public. You can also visualize the audience applauding at the end to keep you motivated.

4. Discipline - In order to be an effective public speaker, you have to keep practicing. Practice makes perfect or in this case efficient. Someone who has been speaking in public for years will be more efficient than the one just starting out. Even the best musicians in the world, have to practice every day. Even if they have been singing for years, they still need to practice in order to sound good on stage.

5. Personalize the Message - It is important to tailor your message to the audience. When you generalize, the audience has no way of relating to the message and may even stop paying attention. The audience usually relates to you more and even warm-ups to you when you personalize the message and share your own personal experiences. People like to hear about other people's victories and tragedies because they have probably gone through the same thing.

6. Inspiration - A good twist to public speaking is to take the focus off yourself and shift it to your audience. After all, your message is supposed to benefit them and not you per se. When creating your speech know the end purpose and always have the audience in mind. Keep the focus on the audience, look at their reactions and adjust your speech accordingly. You can even engage them while speaking.

7. Anticipation - When speaking in public, avoid making long boring speeches. People tend to drift away when the speeches are too long and wonder what you have just told when it is too short. Always make it shorter than anticipated and leave them wanting more. Leave the audience wishing that you had spoken a little more. It means they enjoyed every bit of the speech.

8. Authenticity - Authenticity is vital. When speaking in public you are only as good as your speech. Great speeches do not just happen; the best ones are perfect for the person who makes them. Your speech should have something that makes it unique to only you. The audience prefers listening to a speaker who connects with them personally and emotionally than the one who is just blunt and gives a great speech.

9. Authority - When you are on that stage or platform, you are in charge. Speaking in public is already an act of leadership and therefore you should ensure you are guiding the audience. When you lose your authority while on stage, the audience will stop listening to you. Being in authority, however, does not mean you cannot be vulnerable or share your mistakes.

10. The Purpose of Your Speech - Before you make a speech, you need to know the basic purpose of the speech you are about to give. There are three general reasons why people give speeches:

- To inform, you want to pass on some information to the audience that they do not currently have.
- To entertain, you want to keep the audience lively and laughing. This kind of speech sometimes may contain important information but delivered in an amusing manner
- To persuade, you want to change the audience's opinions or perceptions about something.

Know Your Audience

A good way to better your public speaking skills is to speak to familiar faces. If you do not have friends or people, you know there, talk to one or two people in the audience when you arrive. They become your allies in the audience. As you speak, it is also important to watch for feedback and adjust your speech accordingly. At the same time, when you speak, ensure that your speech moves people to action, if that is never the case, then it will have zero effect.

Capture Their Attention

You have to be relaxed when speaking in public, so avoid arriving late and rushing to the stage without giving yourself time to relax. Start with a personal story or quote, it is a good way to capture the audience attention and calm your nerves.

Strategies: How to Talk in Public with Confidence and Overcome the Fear

Here are a few tips on how you can start your journey to overcoming glossophobia:

Research on Your Topic

The trick to giving good speeches is to prepare well for them at least a week before the actual day you will stand to deliver them. This means getting as much information as you can about your topic and understanding it so that you are confident enough to present your material and to answer any questions that may come up. Knowing your topic also enables you to engage better with the audience in case a discussion arises. If you can, anticipate some of the questions the audience might ask and come up with answers.

Practice Makes Perfect

Once you have your speech drafted out, practice it as much as you can because the more you practice the better you will become. Do it in front of a mirror or in front of your pets if you have to since doing so will help you to visualize how you will feel on a material day. Ask a few family members or friends to listen to it and give you feedback. You can also practice in front of complete strangers who will not mind listening to you. Giving frequent motivational speeches at local groups can also improve your public speaking skills.

Give Shorter Speeches at First

Overcoming glossophobia might take some time, though it is always different in different people. More often than not, this process requires individuals to take baby steps to overcome it. With this in mind, you should try giving shorter speeches before you move to longer ones. A good way to practice this is to open the podium for another speaker. Knowing that you are not the main attraction will somehow put you at ease. Such speeches should also not go longer than three minutes.

Give Your Speech in Familiar Locations

If you have to give a speech and you happen to have a say in where your presentation will take place, choose a place that you are familiar with. For example, if you are supposed to give a business presentation choose to do it in your conference room, which you are familiar with. This way you are aware of the sitting capacity, the sitting arrangement, the lighting and the section of the room to plug in your electronics for the presentation. Doing this also removes the stress of setting up and the risk of something going wrong or not working.

Engage the Audience

Engaging with the audience can help make you less nervous. There are a number of ways you can do this; you can great a few of the people who come in before the presentation starts, you can start the presentation by asking your audience a question or you can invite the audience to comment on a few points in your speech. Doing this gives you an opportunity to take a break and reorganize your thoughts as well as to give your audience an opportunity to open up to you as well.

Be Vulnerable

Depending on the crowd you are addressing, you can get real with the audience and admit to them that you are nervous or have forgotten what you wanted to say. Chances are the audience will laugh when you say such things and this will put you at ease. It is also okay to request a minute to recompose yourself.

Use Props

Props can be anything from a video, to a PowerPoint presentation, to another speaker, to a person in the audience who can help you read points on the screen. If you are nervous about speaking, using props lessens the time you have to speak. Audience activities, a question, and a discussion session take the attention away from you.

Darken the Room

If your audience's sharp stares and stern faces make you nervous, forget about imagining them in their undies and dim the lights. If you must give an excuse for doing so pretend that you cannot read the screen properly with all the glare from the lights. This way you are less distracted and intimidated by people's facial expressions that can focus on delivering your speech. However, this mostly works if there is a stage and the lighting is separate.

Breathe

It is normal for people to speed through their speeches when nervous. Reading a speech at lightning speed will sure not help in keeping you calm. Improper breathing can affect your speech and make you sound out of breath or less confident. Instead, you should strategically pause in between sentences or engage the audience in an activity so that you can catch your breath and take a sip of water.

Celebrate the Success

Once you have gotten through what might have been the biggest challenge of your life, reflect on how you performed. You can ask a friend to sit through your speech or ask them to record the speech and then review it later. Applaud yourself for the parts that went well and polish up on the areas that need improving. With time, you will master the art of public speaking.

Manage Shyness

The ability to maintain a good pattern of conversation skills is one of the many reasons why we are tagged as humans. It is often said that humans are social beings; however, how does one buttress this obvious fact if one does not know how best to maintain a conversation with anyone?

One of the many rules of communication with anyone is said to be the fact that the decoder has to understand the encoder in other that communication is made perfect.

While this is the case, this might prove a lot of difficulty to a lot of people who are shy, because they feel that people might see the flaws in them and major on them. This leads us to the question of, "why do some humans feel shy?"

WHY DO PEOPLE FEEL SHY?

A lot of people feel shy for a number of reasons, more often than not, it is said that the major reason why a lot of people feel shy is because they have the low self-esteem, while this might be true, there are a plethora of reasons why people would feel shy, and it does not necessarily have to be because they have a low self-esteem about themselves.

In a recent survey which has been conducted on a set of shy people, as regards the reasons why they are shy when communicating with people within their social setting, we were able to outline some reasons why people are shy, and they include:

Private Upbringing:

Some people are shy because of the way that they were brought up. It would be interesting to know that some people were brought up by their parents in such a way that they do not interact with people on the outside, and this is owing to a lot of reasons.

The major being the fact that they do not want their wards to make friends with bad companies, and this ends up making them feel like they need to have their lives in private. For such kind of kids, when they eventually have the need to go outside of their home, they might have a reason or two to hold back and not communicate with the people that they find within their social setting.

Social Factors:

There are a lot of things that could contribute to the social factor, which makes a lot of people shy. One of such reasons is because of one thing or the other that such people have been made to come in contact with.

A lot of people become shy because of a desire that they had which made them disappointed or because they were turned down by someone that they admire. All of these a part of the social factors that could make people shy

Fear:

Some people also become shy because they are scared of being under the spotlight or being seen by people. There are tons of people who become shy because they are scared of what people might think of them, but they also fail to understand that regardless of wherever it is that you are, you would always attract some kind of attention to yourself.

Validation:

A lot of people are shy because they do not get validations from those that they expect it from. They presume that the only way that they can know that they are doing things the right way is when people acknowledge them for doing it that way, they do not realize that a lot more people feel the need to do the right things because it appeals well enough to their conscience.

Kindly note: Whether a person is shy or not, there would always be consequences for one's actions or inactions. Regardless of this fact, one must strive at every point in his or her life to make sure that they are in the best part of whatever it is that they do.

CONSEQUENCES OF BEING A SHY PERSON

Many people might say that it is okay to be a shy person, especially because it allows you to be at the safe side of things, but in more ways than one, being shy could cost you a whole lot, and this leads us to some of the consequences of being shy. To mention but a few of those consequences would include:

When You Are Shy, It Gives the Wrong Impression of You:

There are people in the world that we live in today that didn't mean to give the impression that they gave to others, but because they are receptive and shy, they gave those impressions.

One of those impressions is the fact that people would assume that you are proud, just because you are a shy person, and such kind of impression would have been easily refuted if you are the kind that is vocal about their intents. Nobody really wants to be involved with one that they assume to be proud, and this leads us to the next consequence of being shy.

When You Are Shy, People Will Not Approach You for Something That They Feel That You Can Do:

Research has it that people that are shy are those that seldom talk about their abilities. When people do not know that you are capable of doing something, you don't get the best of your relationship with people, whether it is official, social, or any other kind of relationship.

When You Are Shy, You Are Bound to Be Stagnant:

When you are shy, you are bound to be stagnant because you do not know how best to express yourself so much that you can bring people to find interest in the work that you do. Many people who are shy are always people who are multi-talented, but they do not make the best of their skills because they chose to be mum when they could easily have spoken their minds about a particular situation.

You Can Be Cheated:

People who are shy are people who can be easily cheated because people assume that regardless of whatever it is that they do to such people, they would never talk or complain about them.

There is nothing to be admired about a shy person, and this is what leads us to our next topic.

Chapter 5.   How to Talk to Anyone

Relationships Talk

The foundation of all human relationships is how well you can bond with another person. Two people start off as strangers, and how do they form a bond from there? They start communicating. They interact, they start talking and start getting to know one another and slowly, a relationship begins to form, and it begins with being able to communicate effectively with one another.

Confidence   and   Have   Great   Success   in Relationships

It is one thing to be confident, and quite another to show it. Can the listeners tell that you're confident? That will inform their expectations. There are those speakers that make a poor first impression and are dismissed from the start. You can see it in the demeanor of the listeners. They sink back into their chairs and look bored. Such a speaker will have a hard time salvaging the situation.

How people perceive you affect how you behave. If the listeners sit up and look eager when you begin to speak, you'll feel energized to do just that. Once you portray confidence from the onset, you raise the expectation, and that perception bounces right back to you.

Enjoy yourself as well. Be excited about the opportunity to speak and the topic at hand. Speak with enthusiasm. Smile. Once you radiate these traits, the crowd will follow suit to the end. Make sure that you have some actionable points at the end, something the listeners can go try out on their own.

Strategies of How to Talk at Work with Confidence and to Have Success

Good communication is imperative in any environment where humans interact, but when it comes to the workplace, communication is even more critical because it is a crucial influencer of the success of the business. Success in business refers to having an organized team working to attain the organizational goals, meeting production targets, keeping costs of production down, having healthy in-house relationships, and relating well with customers. Securing a market share is also part of business success, and it is a result of all systems working together well, often because people are communicating properly.

Other benefits derived from good communication include:

- Makes employees more engaged: Communication connects persons in the organization towards a single purpose and goal. If the goal is clear, employees understand what they must do to reach the goal.
- Causes the workforce to be more productive: Communication is a key contributor towards the

productivity of the workforce because it promotes an understanding of each member's skills and talents, and encourages creativity and innovation. Hence, the organizational planning is done in consideration of each employee's points of excellence. If the results are all excellent, then the company and its workforce will be productive.

- Prevents misunderstandings with the clients: With excellent communication, the needs and preferences of the clients will be clear, the customer will feel heard and understood, new information will be presented in a form that all parties can understand, and existing conflicts can be straightened out quickly.
- Alleviates conflict: Misunderstandings, feeling disregarded and misunderstood often result in conflict. People also conflict when they fail to understand how others communicate.

How to Resolve Conflicts

Below is a step-by-step tool to help you resolve conflicts that come up at the workplace, and in other forums that involve interaction with people.

Do Not Burry The Conflict

When conflicts arise, do not assume that they didn't happen, or burry them to avoid talking about them. Unresolved issues are ticking time-bombs that build up pressure, and the situation only gets worse with time. Therefore, conflicts should be dealt with as soon as they occur so that there are no problems or hurt feelings as people perform their duties at work.

Speak With The Other Person

Reach out to the other party and let him or her know that you are interested in speaking about the problem. Invite them to choose a time and place that you would conveniently meet to discuss what happened. Ensure that the location has minimal interruptions, if any so that you have ample time to speak and iron out your issues.

Listen

Listening is quite essential because it allows you to see the issue from the other party's perspective. Therefore, listen to what the other party is saying, and get ready to react. Do not interrupt him. Once he is done talking, summarize and rephrase what he said to seek confirmation, so that you are sure that you understood all that was said. Where you need clarifying, ask questions.

Take Note Of The Points Of Agreement And Disagreement

With the other party's help, take note of the issues you agree or disagree on. At the end of it, ask the person to confirm your assessment. Ensure that both parties agree on the areas of conflict that need working on.

Discuss Behavior Not Individuals

As you try to figure out the causes of conflict, it is easy to start attacking each other's personalities. Some people say, "I do not like it when you leave papers containing sensitive information on top of your desk when you are out." Instead, say, "When papers containing sensitive information are left lying on a desk without supervision, the company stands to expose our clients' personal information, and we could wind up with a lawsuit." The first statement addresses the weaknesses of the person, while the second statement attacks the deed itself.

Develop A List Of Priority

Decide on the issues that are of greater significance, and purpose to work on them first before you move on to those of lower consequence. As you start to discuss the issue, let your focus be the future of the company, and how you should work with one another to actualize company goals.

Follow Through With The Plan

Stick to the list of conflict areas, addressing them one-by-one until you get to the end. Ensure that you come to a consensus on the solution to a particular issue before you move on to the next. Through it all, maintain a collaborative attitude so that you remain united, focused, and committed to working out your conflicts.

Forgive Quickly

When conflicts are resolved, the natural thing is to acknowledge that feelings were hurt, assumptions were made, and ignorant words were said. Acknowledge also that your perspective was wrong (if it was), and thank the other party for helping you see from a new perspective. Tell the person that you are sorry, and forgive the person too. Superficial forgiveness is not good enough because it causes grudges that worsen with time, and undermine every progress you had made.

How to Increase Your Self-Esteem

Self-confidence shows in the way you speak. You either have it or you don't; and it shows. People flock to those who are steadfast, while they tend to shy away from those who are weak. If you don't have it, then get it. Yes, it's that easy. You hold the key. You are in charge if you chose to be. Here are some great things you can do to boost your self-confidence:

- Make a conscious decision RIGHT NOW to become self-confident.
- Change what you don't like about yourself. If you think you are rude, work at being a nicer, more

considerate person. If you don't like your looks, do what you can to improve them and also determine to focus on inner-beauty as well.

- Make a daily list of ten things you like about yourself. Grab a pen and paper and start RIGHT NOW!
- Ask a trusted friend 10 things they like about you.
- Every day, recall 10 things you have done successfully.
- Praise yourself for every step you take forward.
- Treat yourself to rewards like a special coffee, a good read or a long soak in the tub.
- Verbally tell yourself in the mirror that you are a good and worthy person.
- Forgive yourself for shortcomings.
- Know that you are as good as everyone else

OK, so, if you truly do the steps above, you are well on your way in becoming more confident. You will begin to see yourself in a whole new light and others will see you the same way. You will learn to respect yourself more and others will follow suite. As the famous psychiatrist and television talk show host, Dr. Phil McGraw says, "You teach people how to treat you." It's true. You are in the driver's seat.

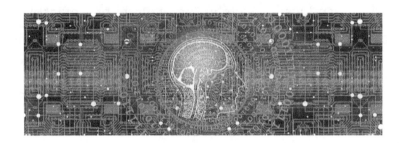

Chapter 6.   Conclusion

It doesn't take rocket science to figure out that effective communication is the most important skill to learn and master as a human being. I truly hope this book was able to bring you closer to this goal and to inspire you. Remember, the most effective communicators on this planet (historical, spiritual and new movement leaders, politicians and dictators with big impacts, hero spies, the best teachers, legendary seducers, celebrities loved by masses, big company owners, good parents, popular YouTubers, writers, journalists, psychotherapists, stand-up comedians, actors...) were not usually just born that way! Communication is a skill like any other and it can be trained. If others can do it, so can you!

I wish you all the best on your journey and hope you will get there soon! Remember: you are who you stick with, so the sooner you start socializing with people who also want to be effective communicators, the better. Look for your local Toastmasters or rhetoric group, practice with a mirror and camera, read more books about social psychology and body language and never stop growing! The main prize is totally worth it! I believe in you!

OVERTHINKING

How to Stop Worrying, Relieve Anxiety and
Emotional Stress, Stop Negative Thinking.
Use Positive Energy To Control Your
Thoughts change your habits and mindset

MIND CHANGE ACADEMY

2

Table of Content

Introduction

As the name implies, overthinking simply means thinking too much. In reality, when you spend more time thinking instead of acting and engaging in other activities, then you're overthinking. You can find yourself analyzing, commenting, and repeating the same thoughts over and over again, rather than taking action, then you're overthinking. Such bad habits can hinder your progress, leaving one unproductive.

Each individual will experience overthinking differently and no two people overthink the same way. But generally, all those who overthink will agree that the quality of their life has been affected by their inability to control their negative thoughts and emotions. Such habits make it very difficult for the majority of the individuals to socialize, be productive at work, or enjoy hobbies due to the enormous amount of time and energy their mind consumes on a specific line of thoughts. Such uncontrolled emotions can be very harmful to the individual's mental health.

Overthinking makes it more difficult to make new friends and to keep friends; you will find it difficult to converse with them because you're overly concerned about what to say or what to do to keep the conversation going. Some individuals who are affected by this disorder may find it challenging to participate in general conversations or to interact with others even in a normal environment. In addition, some may have trouble keeping an appointment or going to the store. This kind of thinking wastes time and drains your energy, thereby preventing you from taking action or exploring new ideas. It also hinders progress in life. This can be compared to attaching a chain that is connected to a pole around your waist and then running in circles you will be busy but not productive. Overthinking will disable your capacity to make sound decisions.

Under such circumstances, you're more likely to be worried, anxious, and devoid of inner peace of mind. However, when you stop overthinking, you will become more productive, happy, and will enjoy more peace.

Chapter 1.   Overthinking Disorder Defined

What is Overthinking?

What exactly overthinking is? Experts overview overthinking syndrome as spending much of your time thinking of anything and something which causes stress, fear, restlessness, concern, dread, unease, and many others. This mental condition is not just about too much thinking of something, but also about spending more thoughts, which affects the capability of the person to work and finish the daily tasks.

If you worry about your friends, your job, your family, your boyfriend, and girlfriend, your life and anything else; You believe that you do not have overthinking condition; No matter what you are thinking about, perhaps concerns you for a moment, then a short span of time, you continue with other parts of your life. Yes, you return wondering every so often. However, you do not continuously wonder, and you do not find it getting in the way with the rest of your life. With this kind of mental condition, however, the troubled is all that you can think of. Even if you may not be troubled on the same thing regularly and repeatedly, you always worried about something.

To know if you are overthinking everything, you may experience one or more of these cases:

- Complexity in following and participating in a discussion.
- Constantly evaluating yourself to those around you as well as how you match up to them
- Giving so much time on worst-case scenarios involving members of the family or yourself
- Reliving previous mistakes and failures time and again, so you are not capable of moving past them
- Worrying too much about your objects and dreams or future tasks until such time that they are not viable to achieve
- Reliving your previous traumatic experience, which includes the loss of parents, or any members of the family, abuse, which leaves you not capable of dealing with it?
- Lack of capability of slowing down the flow of vague thoughts, emotions, and worries

No two individuals will suffer from this kind of mental issue in the same way. But people who do suffer overthinking will find that their daily living and lifestyle is at stake. This is due to their lack of capability of efficiently and successfully controlling negative thoughts as well as emotion. Thus, they find it hard to hang out and socialize. They also find it hard to enjoy their sidelines and hobbies. They are not helpful and not creative at work. All these happen since their mind spends an inconsistent amount of energy and time on particular lines of thoughts. There is a feeling that they do not have complete power over their emotions or minds that can be extremely destructive to mental wellbeing.

Making friends, meeting up with someone as well as keeping friends is hard with this mental condition as you resist interacting with them. You will experience difficulty in talking to the people that surrounds you. This happens because you are too much trouble with the things you do or say. You are also too much concerned about what will happen or how you will do it. If you, your friends or any member of the family experience, this mental disorder might struggle to make general conversation with others. It will also be hard to interrelate in a typical setting. You might find it so hard to go out to the department store or to your appointment, which affects your whole life in general.

The reality is that this mental condition can affect almost all aspects of your life. This can also change the way you communicate with others and the way you perform. What is more, it can also affect your personal life, social life, work-life, and of course, your love life. It can ruin your relationship to your partner, and people surround you and your entire life in general. Overthinking is a tough condition. It can create problems in your life.

Overthinking is a chaos which can happen to anyone and at any time. If you have anxiety or any form of anxiety disorder, it can become overthinking chaos too. The worry and the anxiety which you have on diverse life conditions can become overthinking quickly. You must think about what you must carry on or how you stop bad things from taking place. The reality is that you are not able to stop horrific and terrible things from taking place. Also, you are not able to stop yourself from each bad decision. So, the best thing to do is to ask assistance from friends, family members, and professionals.

Do you worry too much, even on simple things? Are you an extreme worrier? Maybe you automatically think that when you wonder/worry enough, you are able to avoid bad things from taking place. However, the reality is that worrying and wondering are able to affect your system in so many ways which might astound you. If you think too much on everything or if you have excessive worrying, it can result in feelings of high stress and even lead to a serious health condition.

What Causes Overthinking?

Overthinking is an indication that something is bothering you. Know the culprit of your agitation and cope with it immediately. Declutter your mind through meditation. Through this, you can organize, prioritize as well as analyze effectively and evidently in your head. The moment you distinguish the issue; you can work on addressing it. This will assist in avoiding winding amidst a host of unconnected and negative thinking.

Mental Clutter Explained

- Mental clutter is a boundless list of "what if's, shoulds" – all those things which should be accomplished
- Feel sorry for missed chances of the past
- Scared of things which might never occur
- Unfinished business, phone calls to make, emails to sends, and bills that need to be paid
- Criticizing and grumbling- these are habits that people get into that, in turn, drain our physical and mental energy.
- Trying hard for perfectionism: beating yourself up for not reaching your goal.

Mental clutter leads to a high level of stress, and stress is the leading cause of overthinking that can lead to various medical issues. So, instead, you can:

Change should to could: taking the burden off having to get things finished. Make it an option to do or not to do. An understated language change can make an empowering difference.

Past is past. You can't change it. Instead, put your strength and energy into making a better vision for your prospect.

Get on and set aside time to finish remaining projects, clearing niggle mental lists.

Exchange troubled for utilizing your mind to make something valuable and stimulating. Worrying is not just a waste of time; it can also drain your energy.

Focus and speak on the good bits about your life and cut out bad habits.

Unleash the needing to be faultless; anyway who cares? Perhaps only you!

Below are the easy and practical tips to assist you in decluttering your mind:

- Set Priorities: Bill Copeland, a renowned American poet, commented, "the trouble with not having a goal is that you can spend your life running up and down the field and never score." Prioritizing is indeed a smart way to take control of your life proactively. First, you need to know the things that matter to you, your aspirations in life, and your long term objectives. Make a record of top priorities and ensure that you and the choices you make reflect these priorities. Secondly, create an action plan to reach your objectives and work on how you like to split your time to concentrate on every task on your list. It is vital to remember that the list of priorities might change as you age. That is fine provided the fact that you check in yourself regularly and make sure those priorities are serving you.

- Journaling: Keeping a journal is a smart way to calm your mind by organizing and analyzing your thinking. A study posted in the Journal of Experimental Psychology: General, meaningful writing gets rid of intrusive thought on negative things and enhances working memory. Experts believe that the improvements might free up your cognitive resources for other intellectual activities, which include the capability to handle anxiety more efficiently. Journaling can also help handle stress and deal with sadness and depression because it is an excellent outlet to let go of bottled emotions. You do not need to be an inexhaustible writer to make a journal. For starters, the most straightforward technique to follow is bullet journaling.

- Know-How to Set Free: Accept who you are, love yourself, and keep on reaching your goals. Want to fly high? Then give up things that stop you from soaring. In the book The Light in the Heart by Roy T. Bennett, there is a line that says, and it is vital to set free of the negative emotions and thoughts which make you feel depressed and sad. Getting rid of unnecessary thoughts, troubles, concerns, and fears help lessen stress, enhance self-esteem as well as ease up mental space. Check your thoughts daily and try to substitute negative thinking with positive and helpful ones.

- Multitask Will Do No Good: Multitasking sounds counter-productive. Preparing for your office presentation while checking your Facebook account and at the same time searching for a perfect gift for your friends online is not helpful. There is no harm in multitasking, but ensure it is occasional. Continuously juggling between tasks restricts your attention span, boost stress level as well as makes additional clutter through making it hard for the brain to sift through irrelevant information. A study performed by Stanford University revealed that serious multitasking lowers effectiveness and may damage your cognitive control. So, the best solution is to complete task one at a time. Create a list of the things that need to be done first on that Day. Keep your list realistic and straightforward. Begin with what is most vital.
- Take a Breathe: Take a long deep breath. Stop. Release slowly. Do it again. How does it feel? Isn't it great? Deep breathing is indeed a simple but very efficient method to declutter your mind.
- What is more, this also induces tranquility and elevates your mood right away. It also lowers blood pressure, heart rate as well as motivates the

parasympathetic nervous system that helps a lot in keeping your body relax. Aside from being a stress-reliever, this exercise can also promote attentiveness and make your immunity system stronger.

- Be Decisive: Scott Roewer, a professional organizer, stated that clutter is merely delayed decisions. If you continuously suspend making decisions, your mind becomes overwhelmed by the clutter which is produced by those delayed decisions. Therefore, bring procrastinating to an end and make that call. It does not matter if it is about the new property you are planning to purchase or that call you are ignoring for so long. For a simple decision, carefully asses the advantages and disadvantages and never look back the moment you have made a decision. For essential decision, give WRAP method a try. This is a new approach discussed in Decisive: How to Make Better Choices in Life and Work by Heath brothers.

- Share Your Emotions and Thoughts to Friends and Family Members: Talking to your loved ones or a close friend on the things that troubled your mind is an excellent way to leave go of contained and unexpressed emotions. Sharing thoughts can help a lot in looking at things from a new perspective that can help in thinking clearer and make a smart decision.

- Limit Media Intake: Media has a massive impact on mental health. A lot of people spend lots of hours browsing online and their social network account. They give more time on reading blogs, watching viral videos, organizing Pinterest boards, and many others. This profusion of information can block your brain, which causes anxiety and stress. Limiting your exposure to social media is vital in getting rid of clutter related to media from your mind. Begin by setting a limit. You also need to be choosy on media consumption. You need to keep away from harmful content. Just follow dependable and trustworthy media outlets for fresh news and updates. Don't forget to recognize your email daily.
- Take Time to Relax and Unwind: Taking a break helps in decluttering your mind. Your mind just like your body needs time to rest and recharge to function smoothly. Therefore, turn off your phone and laptop, and do things which make you smile and happy. It doesn't matter if it is a short stroll in the playing field or a long nap.

So, what are fusty emotions and thoughts lingering in your mind? It is now the right time to make that junk out and eliminate them for good.

Social Expectation

Living and working in the world today is more demanding and challenging than ever before. Yes, we have the modern conveniences that make life more comfortable and convenient, but we also must contend with the structure of social life and the expectation that we follow a timeline that follows something like this: school, more school, entry-level career, climb the ladder, senior-level career, retirement.

For a long time, this was the norm for people living in countries of economic power. But a lot has been shifting over the course of the last few decades, and at an exponentially increasing rate. Finding a job in a lucrative career that will be enjoyable and satisfying for thirty or more years is not so simple anymore. The competition has grown right alongside the earth's population and the staggering advancement of technology. Many of the jobs readily available to our parents no longer exist, and nowadays, you would get a strange look for physically walking into a business and asking for an employment application instead of applying online. If you do manage to get that dream job right out of high school or college, then the real trial by fire begins. We could talk office politics, competition, and rivalry all day, but for right now, let's focus on some of the core triggers for overthinking in two of life's most influential domains: work and school.

We've started to discuss the challenge of finding gainful employment as a young adult in the modern age, so let's continue exploring where overthinking may come into play here.

Following the effect of globalization, the world is now overrun with advertisement and marketing schemes. From the very beginning of your career, you've been told that you will have to compete with many other candidates, many of whom may be more qualified than you. The interview process challenges candidates to make a compelling argument for why they should stand out above all the rest. You may practice in front of a mirror at home or think about all the possible questions that may come up. It is here when you may start thinking about how you measure up next to others in your field. You've just graduated from college with a degree and, at the time, you felt like you were on top of the world with a million different prospects awaiting you (best case scenario, of course). Fast forward a few months, and you start to realize that the job market is a tad more competitive than you thought, and you haven't proven yourself to be a shoo-in to some of your dream companies who have already passed on you. Many young adults in the millennial generation can attest to the challenges of having graduated during a recession in the US and having trouble finding any reasonable employment at all, let alone a prestigious start to a career in their fields.

The pressure of the social expectation that you can and will find a great job if you are smart and work hard enough becomes a great burden if and when things don't work out the way you'd imagined them throughout your time in school. At this point, you may begin to wonder if it is some fault or deficiency within yourself keeping you from your dreams.

The truth is, there are countless factors at play when it comes to finding or landing your "dream job," and sometimes, hard work and a positive attitude are just not enough, despite what your parents or teachers told you. This is why many young adults begin the cycle of overthinking that is dominated by questions of self-worth and adequacy. If society says I'm supposed to be here or there at this point in my life, that means I've failed and there is something wrong with me.

Once this conviction takes root, it is very hard to ignore the myriad images, slogans, and advertisements all around us which display the ideal professional man or woman in their nice corner offices, dressed in the latest fashions, sharing how they've made it this far because they work for this or that company, attended this or that school, bought this or that car, bought a house in this or that city, etc. This is when you may start to compare yourself to the success of others, which simply adds to the merry-go-round in your mind that feeds a feeling of inadequacy and low self-esteem.

But now let's say you've landed a decent job. It's not your dream job, but it may be a good start for you and your career. Now it's time to prove yourself. You immediately look around at your coworkers, boss, and peers to assess where you are on the ladder and how you measure up to your competition. Depending on the type of personalities surrounding you, you may feel a lot of pressure to do well and grow within the company. Society teaches us that being the best is the only way to grow and climb within your company, so professional life instantly turns into a competition. This pressure may manifest itself as overthinking every day as you constantly analyze how well you do your job. This is not a bad thing in and of itself—everyone wants to be good at their jobs. A problem arises when we begin obsessively comparing ourselves to others, and when the job is no longer an environment of several likeminded people working to build a better company, but a cutthroat competition to the top.

Once you've managed to break into the top echelons of business society, the competition turns toward other companies in your field—overtaking their market, putting others out of business, etc. And we've all heard the saying, the more you gain, the more you have to lose. This opens up a whole new avenue of worry and overthinking as you assess how far you may fall if you make a mistake or fall off the ladder!

Is this you? Do you experience constant worry about where you are professionally? Maybe you are underemployed and feel embarrassed, like you haven't gone far enough in life as you compare yourself to others. This may be one of the most common triggers for overthinking, but now it's time to move backward in time to examine how social expectation first takes root in our minds as kids. Let's take a look at social expectation in school.

As kids, most of us aren't thinking seriously about what happens after school. We may have some far-fetched dreams swirling in our brains, but mostly we just want to know what mom packed for lunch today and if that big kid is going to knock us off the swing at recess again today. (Hopefully not, but you get the idea.)

As we grow older and enter the realms of middle school and high school, social pressure and expectation become more central to our lives in an immediate sense. We may be thinking of our future careers from a distance, but most of us are preoccupied with whether or not people like us at school, how popular we are, whether or not we'll get a date for the dance, etc. Much of the social pressure at this age centers around physical appearance and either academic or competitive achievement. Sadly, most girls around this age start to become overly concerned about their physical appearance and may even begin to equate this with their self-worth. The trigger for overthinking has begun as these women look around at the beautiful women in social media and in magazines, and begin comparing themselves to those unattainable ideals. Similarly, young boys may have a role model in sports or even a father figure who has become very successful in their professional fields and begin comparing themselves as men, equating success in competitive sports or popularity or academics with their self-worth.

The pressure only gets stronger as we enter college, if that is your path. Balancing social life with academic life is a struggle that many lose, resulting in a student dropping out of college. Remaining focused and achieving good grades and that long-awaited bachelor's degree grants passage into the realm of professional work, where a whole new world of social pressure and expectation awaits.

As you can see, much of our overthinking may very well stem primarily from a distorted perception of ourselves in relationship to others in our professional or social environments. This pressure begins early in life and continues as we are constantly bombarded with images and messages in the media dictating what success should look and feel like.

Let's take a look at some more possible triggers for overthinking.

Afraid of Failure

Fear of failure is not a new concept to most people. In fact, this is what motivates most of us to work hard. Instead of working hard for a bright future, you find yourself drawing motivation from the fear you have developed inside you.

Irrelevant Decisions

There are times when we make irrelevant decisions because we force ourselves to make these decisions, yet we are not required to make them. For instance, when thinking about our future, there are instances where we end up making irrelevant decisions based on assumptions. Getting married, for example, based on the assumptions you have, you might conclude that you need to get married because you're getting old.

Afraid of What the Future Holds

Then, there is the dreaded future. When you overthink the future, you are often invaded by thoughts of what could be, or what might not be. You might find yourself constantly concerned about events that, upon rational examination, are unlikely to happen. Yet, your mind is overly active, worried about grave consequences.

In the present, overthinking might take the form of waiting too long to make a decision. You might find yourself being hesitant about what to do, or what to say. Then, before you know it, your opportunity has passed, and you are left with nothing but regret about having missed an opportunity due to your inability to act.

For example, you have been offered the job of your dreams, but it requires you to move to a new city. Naturally, you are inclined to do your homework and conduct research on the new city and company. However, you become paralyzed by thoughts about not having enough information on the new job. You are overly concerned about making the wrong move. Then, you think about past situations in which you may a wrong choice. Soon, you are so hesitant to act that you simply cannot work yourself up to saying "yes" or "no". In the end, your inability to act has led the company to pass on you and give the job to someone else.

As a result, thinking things too much, dwelling on the past for too long, or concerning yourself with the future in excess may lead you to miss the wonderful opportunities that life has for you TODAY.

Again, there is nothing wrong about thinking about your problems so you can think of a solution for them, it becomes worrisome when you have a bad habit of twisting narratives around in your head until you can see every angle and side to it. Overthinking is not productive as it just makes you dwell over your problems; you are not looking for a solution for them and you are only making yourself feel miserable.

In order to find an effective way to break your overthinking habit, you need to find out what caused it in the first place. Below are some of the more common reasons as to why people tend to overthink their problems rather than actually find a solution for them.

Information overload

If you are not self-confident, you tend to doubt every little thing that you say or do. When you hesitate, even a little, about the things that you want to do, you are letting uncertainty and fear creep into your mind, and it will be very difficult to get them out of there. You can never really tell what your decisions will take you; even if you planned every little detail, the outcome will still not be exactly what you hoped for (it could either be better or worse than what you planned). This is why you should learn to take risks and not torture yourself when you did not get the results you wished for.

When You Worry Too Much

It is only natural to worry when you encounter new and unfamiliar things and events. However, if you worry too much that you cannot even imagine a positive outcome, then it will trigger you to overthink. This is problematic because worry attracts even more problems; sometimes it creates ones out of thin air, which cause overthinking to go even deeper. Instead of mulling over how things could go wrong, it is better to entertain thoughts that are more positive, like how much better you would feel if a certain even turns in your favor.

When You Overthink to Protect Yourself

Some people believe that they can protect themselves from troubles whenever they overthink, but the truth is that overthinking is a trap that kills your progress. Overthinking and not doing anything to change the status quo might seem good, but stifling your progress is never a good thing at all. In addition, when you overthink, you are not really staying at the same position, you are actually undoing whatever amount of progress you achieved thus far.

You are Unable to "Turn Off" Your Mind

Many over thinkers became that way because they cannot seem to get their minds off their problems no matter how hard they try. People who are sensitive to stress live as if they are constantly wound up tightly, they have somehow forgotten how to relax and change their chain of thoughts. Overthinking happens when a person stresses too much on a single problem, and he could not turn his focus away from it.

You are Always Chasing after Perfection

Being a perfectionist is not necessarily a good thing. In fact, one could argue that being a perfectionist is not good at all.

Most people who struggle with perfectionism are constantly anxious. They often wake up in the middle of the night thinking of the things that they could have done better. Being a perfectionist causes overthinking because you are always trying to outdo yourself.

Overthinking is Your Habit

Overthinking is not always caused by a person's bad habits; sometimes overthinking IS the person's bad habit. For some people, it does not take much for them to overthink; they usually default to overthinking the moment that they encounter even minor inconvenience. This bad habit prevents people from living their lives the way they actually wanted to.

Fear

You can never completely curb your anxiety unless you face the fears it is rooted in. You can only feel strong when you master your emotions of fear and apprehensiveness, and this can only be possible if you actually face that to which you are afraid.

Now that you are aware of how to control your negative thoughts and be mindful of how you feel, consciously make a list of everything that you are afraid of doing. Things such as confronting your feelings to your crush, starting your own business, publishing your book, trying adventure sports, and anything else that you feel is holding you back can go on that list.

Once your list is ready, pick any one fear that you would like to overcome first and create a plan of action to curb it. If you are afraid of speaking publicly but have always wanted to pursue it, prepare a short speech on a topic you are passionate about and practice speaking it for a minute or two in front of the mirror, close friend or just by yourself.

Once you have command over it, speak on the topic in front of 2 to 3 people. You may stumble and make mistakes, but if you do manage to stay strong in that time, you will overcome a part of your fear. Slowly keep speaking in front of more people and soon enough, you will have overcome your fear.

After overcoming one little fear, take on another one, and then another one. Keep combatting your fears this way and thwart them one after another to have better control of your emotions and master them. Remember to record your daily activities and performance in a journal so that you can go through the accounts time and again. This gives insight into your strengths, mistakes, setbacks and accomplishments so that you feel motivated on acknowledging your accomplishments, learn from your mistakes, and improve on them to only do better the next time.

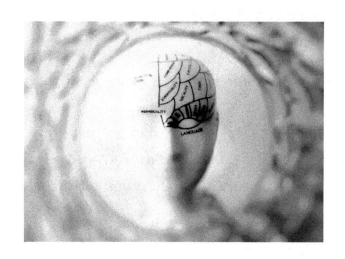

Chapter 2.   How to Declutter Your Mind

How to Stop Worrying

We all worry from time to time. You worry about yourself and others on a daily basis. This is normal, to an extent. You may worry about the potential of failure, about your safety, or other possible factors. It is instinctual, as animals must worry about their hunger until they feed themselves. However, there is a certain point where worrying is unhealthy. If you find yourself constantly worrying to the extent where it takes over your life, you need to take action. You must be able to enjoy your life. While you will certainly worry occasionally, it should not prevent you from completing your daily tasks. When worrying becomes severe, it needs attention.

You must learn to stop worrying. There is always the chance of a negative event occurring, but you must be able to find positivity and hope instead of dwelling on the potential for something going wrong. You must be able to live in the moment and focus on enjoying yourself instead of worrying about what you did incorrectly in the past and what could go wrong in the future. You must be able to enjoy your life, not spend every minute of it worrying. It's important to be able to stop the "what-ifs" and develop the ability to focus on the best possible outcome. There is a good balance between being realistic and being positive, and you must be able to find that balance. You should also become more aware of yourself and your emotions.

Stop Worrying

It sounds simple enough: just stop worrying. Although this seems easier said than done, it is possible to train your brain to worry less and be able to enjoy yourself more. Worrying can be lessened, and you may greatly minimize it and even prevent it from occurring. However, this will take a lot of practice and patience with your progress. If you tend to worry naturally, this will be an ingrained habit that will take time to replace with better habits. You must be able to change your mind so that you may reduce the amount of worrying that you do.

There are a few ways that you can reduce the amount of time that you spend worrying. One way is to simply set aside time to worry. Instead of suppressing your worries and ignoring them until they reach the point where they overwhelm you, set aside time each day to simply let your emotions happen. Instead of fighting against them, allow yourself to feel everything. You may even imagine yourself overreacting; this will allow you to see how beneficial (or not) it can be to allow your emotions to take over. Spending some time each day just letting it out will help you. You may choose to keep a journal or simply write everything down. Perhaps you type it out all of your thoughts and erase it right afterward so that you can see a clearing of your thoughts right in front of you. You may choose to confide in someone you trust, allowing yourself to rant for a few minutes to get it all out. Regardless, it is healthy to let your emotions out instead of suppressing them.

Determine the root of your worries. Perhaps you have too much free time and simply need something else to occupy your mind. You may choose to take up a hobby to keep yourself busy. There may be a particular event that triggers your worries. You may feel worried while scrolling through social media, as you compare yourself to others and worry that you aren't good enough. Perhaps your worries are the result of a past trauma that you still haven't moved on from. No matter the cause, it is important to take some time to reflect on why it is that you worry and work on a solution for that.

Another aspect to consider is whether your worries are solvable or not. If the worry has a solution, come up with a way to solve it and get it done. Instead of dwelling on it, solve it so that you may have more peace of mind. For worries that are unsolvable, you must be willing to accept that fact. Instead of trying to predict negative events or worrying about possibilities with a low likelihood, accept the uncertainty. Will worrying solve it or change it? The answer is most likely "no." Worrying won't prevent unpleasant surprises. You must be willing to accept the fact that life constantly changes. Finding the good in these changes can really help you to be happier and stress less.

Live in the Moment

Learning to live in the moment can really help you to stop worrying. Often, worrying is a result of the past or future. We don't typically worry as much about what we are doing in the present. You must be willing to accept the past and live without regrets. Every mistake is a learning opportunity, and every issue will only make you stronger. The future is unpredictable; the best you can do is to work your hardest towards making it a future you want. However, that's pretty difficult when you spend your time worrying!

You must learn to enjoy the present, or else you will never enjoy your life. Otherwise, you will always wish that you are in the past or be hoping to have a better life in the future. Tomorrow never comes, though. It will always be today. As a result, you must learn the importance of living today. Focus on the present. Be aware of all of the positive aspects of the present. To do this, you may have to shut off your electronic devices and really take in your surroundings. Take a moment to realize how great the present is and be more mindful. Accept your thoughts of the present, while allowing yourself to shut off thoughts about the past or future. Become aware of your senses. What are you seeing, hearing, smelling, feeling, and tasting? Instead of constantly multitasking, take a moment to appreciate what you are doing.

You may appreciate the finer details in life. Be thankful for small moments and what you may have previously neglected. There is much more to life than the obvious. The smallest details can make the biggest difference in your happiness. Appreciate everything, even the smallest aspects of life.

You may live in the moment by being happier and bringing joy to others. Remember to laugh and smile. These can really boost your happiness and help you to enjoy life more. Bring happiness to others, as well. Volunteering and performing small acts of kindness can go a long way. You will feel happy knowing that you made a difference and have a purpose. Be thankful for everything that you have and be sure to help others that may need help as well. Occasionally take a moment to realize everything that you are thankful for. Find positivity every day.

Take small moments to yourself. Perhaps you may choose to meditate. You may also simply breathe and focus on your breath. Focus on how your body feels and take some time to relax. You may feel that you can't enjoy the present because you are too overwhelmed. Check with yourself regularly and remind yourself to live in the present. You will have to make a conscious effort to do this at first, as it is natural to visualize the future or dwell on the past. When you can live in the present, you will learn to enjoy life no matter how it is.

Stop the "What-Ifs"

There are so many possible "what-ifs" that you can have. If you tend to worry constantly, you are bound to believe that the worst will happen. However, this thinking does not get you anywhere. If you constantly assume the worst and expect the worst, you will lack the motivation to continue on. You will feel like there is no point, as you will expect the worst to occur. It is therefore important for you to stop this cycle and to view life in a positive way. Although it is important to be realistic, you can't always expect the worst.

There is a proper balance between being realistic and being positive. You can't always get your hopes up for everything; it won't help you to have wildly unrealistic expectations, as you will feel disappointed constantly. However, you also can't approach life as something that's pointless and think that something will always go wrong. Although you may feel that this is more realistic, you must be willing to accept that life will be full of both challenges and successes. If you only focus on one, you are missing out. Mistakes and hardships will teach you more about yourself, others, and life in general. If life didn't have problems, the good times wouldn't be as great. You must be willing to take the bad with the good, and it's important to accept that both of these will occur. Doing so will allow you to live a life that is less worry-filled and full of more happiness.

Everyone experiences "what-if" thoughts from time to time. This is normal and can help with the decision-making process. However, they can harm your daily life when they start to interfere with your routine. If you struggle to go about your everyday routine because you are too focused on the potential for negativity, you need to make changes to yourself regarding your worrying. When you can't control your thoughts, it's problematic.

To control these thoughts, you can try a few methods. One way is to write down these thoughts when they occur. By doing so, you are becoming more informed of how you think, and you may realize that these thoughts lack logic behind them. It will help you to realize what you are thinking, and you may understand why you think that way as a result. You should also take action on these thoughts. If there is a way to solve the problem that you are worried about, do it. If there isn't, find a way to let go of that thought. Talk to someone, write it down, or think it through. You may also take a moment to understand what the thought is, how it makes you feel, and what your reaction to it is. This will help you to have a better emotional response to it and behave properly to solve the issue. You must also become more comfortable with change and uncertainty. Recognize that some things will simply remain unknown until they occur and worrying will not alter the outcome.

Become More Aware of Yourself

Self-awareness can really help you. It can make it much easier for you to understand your emotions and feel more in control of your mind. You will realize why you act and think the way that you do. You can understand what your strengths and weaknesses are. It will also help you realize what motivates you. You will become more aware of your purpose and goals in life. It can even help you to understand others better and improve your communication skills. By increasing your self-awareness, you will have a healthier mind and feel much better about yourself and your emotions.

To become more self-aware, you will have to make a conscious effort to do so at first. Take some time each day to really reflect on how you are feeling. Understand your current emotions, the causes of them, and the effect they have on you. You may also reflect on your day as a whole. Did you accomplish what you set out to do? If not, what held you back from doing so? Use this time to constructively criticize yourself. Do not simply criticize yourself, compare yourself to others, or think about how you failed. Instead, realize what worked for you and what did not. Doing so will benefit you, as you can learn from that and apply it to the next day. You will not be perfect at first, but if you can make improvements each day, you will be much better off. Only compare yourself to who you were yesterday. You should always be learning, improving, and changing for the better. This is a natural way to progress in life, and it's important to do so to be the best person that you possibly can be. Remember to think about both what can be improved and what you did well, as it is important to remind yourself of your successes and remember that you are capable of success.

You may ask others to help you in several ways. One way is to talk out your emotions with another that you trust. This can help you to verbally express your thoughts. You may also ask others for feedback, as they will be able to give you an opinion outside of yourself. However, this must be healthy. You should trust the other person's word and ensure that you take everything they say as a way to improve, not as an attack on the person that you are.

It's also important that you are able to write down your values and goals. This will make you more aware of what you're working towards. If you don't have goals to work towards, you will lack both direction and a sense of purpose in life. Understand what is important to you and what gives you a sense of importance. If you don't have goals, you won't be able to reflect on your progress towards achieving your goals. As a result, you won't be able to be aware of how you are doing.

Worrying can really hold you back from your full potential. Instead of living your life enjoying it, you will be spending your time worrying. For this reason, it's crucial that you work on minimizing the amount of worrying that you do. In addition to feeling happier, you will be less stressed and anxious. You will feel a weight lifted off of your shoulders as well. It will be easier for you to focus on what matters instead of dwelling on what doesn't matter. You will find greater importance in life and be able to concentrate on what matters to you. At work, you will feel more capable of accomplishing your daily tasks. At home, you will feel a better connection with those around you. While you are out and about, you will be able to go about your day without feeling overwhelmed with worries.

It's important to stop your habit of worrying, and there are a few ways that you can work on it. You must, however, keep in mind that it will take work to stop yourself from worrying. It's also important to discover how to live in the moment so that you can enjoy life and feel greater happiness. Stopping the "what-ifs" that you think can really help you. Most of these are unnecessary, and you will feel better for not thinking these thoughts. Finally, you must become more aware of yourself to worry less.

Practicing Positive Mindfulness

Have you at any point felt pushed, restless, or overpowered by life?

We live in a bustling world. With messages and messages flying all around as you are venturing over your kids' toys and attempting to get the canine sustained while the nourishment on the table is getting cold, you most likely get a handle on worried consistently.

Done effectively, mindfulness will enable you to diminish your pressure and nervousness, limit the measure of time that you spend feeling overpowered, and help you value every little minute as it occurs. In a universe of confusion, mindfulness may very well be the stunt you have to figure out how to have the option to adapt to the frenzy.

Luckily, there is a straightforward propensity you can use to normally quiet yourself down and acknowledge life more. It's called mindfulness. Mindfulness is the act of deliberately concentrating the majority of your consideration on the present minute and tolerating it without judgment. This is an incredible spot to begin if you are searching for the key component in joy.

If these sound like results you'd love to involvement, at that point I prescribe perusing this extreme manual for being careful about the duration of the day. First up, we'll spread the advantages of mindfulness—specifically, how it can decidedly affect both your mental and physical prosperity.

Advantages of Mindfulness

Mindfulness diminishes uneasiness

Research has discovered that mindfulness is particularly useful in diminishing nervousness. Rehearsing mindfulness consistently revamps your cerebrum so you can refocus your consideration. As opposed to following a negative and stressing thought down a way of every single imaginable result, you can figure out how to see the truth about your contemplations and simply let them go.

Mindfulness improves memory, focus, and execution

Focusing and focusing on the job that needs to be done might be one of the most significant psychological capacities individuals have. Mindfulness is one of the not very many strategies that function as a remedy for mind-meandering and the negative impacts that losing focus may have on you. Truth be told, inquire about understudies has demonstrated that there is an association among mindfulness and focusing both all through the study hall.

Extra examinations have demonstrated that ruminating over a standard premise causes the cerebrum's cerebral cortex (which is answerable for memory, fixation, and figuring out how) to thicken.

Mindfulness gives relief from discomfort

Around 100 million Americans experience the ill effects of ceaseless torment each day, yet 40% to 70% of these individuals are not accepting legitimate medicinal treatment. Numerous investigations have demonstrated that mindfulness contemplation can decrease torment without utilizing endogenous narcotic frameworks that are generally accepted to diminish torment during subjective based systems like mindfulness.

Oneself created narcotic framework has as a rule been suspected of as the focal piece of the mind for mitigating torment without the utilization of medications. This framework self-produces three narcotics, including beta-endorphin, the met-and Leu-enkephalins, and the dynorphins. These work together to lessen torment by rehearsing mindfulness.

Mindfulness assists with passionate reactivity

Of the considerable number of reasons that individuals more often than not have for learning contemplation, being less sincerely receptive is normally high on the rundown. Being careful or "Zen" compares to moving with the punches in life and being non-receptive to things that may come to your direction.

What's more, there's unquestionably something to this. Mindfulness contemplation has permitted study members to remove their feelings from upsetting pictures and spotlight more on an intellectual errand, as contrasted and a control gathering.

Mindfulness decreases rumination and overthinking

One of the most well-known manifestations that join tension is rumination or overthinking. After you start to stress over something, your mind will clutch that firmly and make it difficult to give up. It is anything but difficult to get into an idea circle where you keep on replaying every single awful result possible. We as a whole realize this isn't valuable since stressing over something doesn't keep it from occurring.

One investigation really demonstrated that individuals who were new to mindfulness and started to rehearse it during a retreat had the option to give fewer indications of rumination and uneasiness than the control gathering.

Mindfulness makes more joyful connections

Scientists are as yet uncertain this works, yet rising cerebrum studies have demonstrated that individuals who take part in mindfulness all the time show both auxiliary and useful changes in the mind locales that are connected to improved sympathy, empathy, and generosity.

Another advantage of mindfulness is in its impacts on the amygdala, which is the cerebrum's enthusiastic preparing focus. Mindfulness is connected to decreases in both the volume of the amygdala and its association with the prefrontal cortex. This recommends mindfulness may bolster feeling guidelines and lessening reactivity, which are two significant devices for making and looking after connections.

Mindfulness improves rest

The unwinding reaction that your body needs to mindfulness reflection is a remarkable inverse of the pressure reaction. This unwinding reaction attempts to ease many pressures related to medical problems, for example, agony, wretchedness, and hypertension. Rest issues are regularly attached to these illnesses.

One investigation of more established grown-ups affirms that mindfulness contemplation can help in getting a decent night's rest. As indicated by this examination, mindfulness reflection can expand the unwinding reaction through its capacity of expanding attentional components that confer command over the autonomic sensory system.

Mindfulness eases some pressure

Since individuals are looked with an expanding measure of weight nowadays because of the mind-boggling nature of our general public, they are regularly tormented with a ton of stress. This adds to a wide assortment of other medical issues. Mindfulness can diminish worry by going about as a precaution measure, and help individuals overcome difficult occasions.

Mindfulness advances mental wellbeing

Specialists have discovered that IBMT (integrative body-mind preparing) starts positive auxiliary changes in the cerebrum that could help secure against mental infection. The act of this strategy helps support productivity in a piece of the cerebrum that enables individuals to direct behavior.

Mindfulness advances intellectual adaptability

One examination proposes that not exclusively will mindfulness help individuals become less receptive; it may likewise give individuals progressively intellectual adaptability. Individuals who practice mindfulness seem, by all accounts, to be ready to likewise rehearse self-perception, which consequently withdraws the pathways made in the cerebrum from earlier learning and permits data that is going on right now to be comprehended in another manner.

Reflection additionally enacts the piece of the mind that is related to versatile reactions to push, which compares to a quicker recuperation to a benchmark line of reasoning in the wake of being contrarily affected.

Mindfulness in Everyday Life

As we have pointed out earlier, mindfulness is not some practice limited to monks who have taken a vow of silence. This is the type of practice which virtually anyone can do, at any time, and anywhere.

So, here are some additional strategies to implement mindfulness in your everyday life:

Sit with your experience

At the point when you center around being careful, you can sit with your experience.

Rehearsing mindfulness through concentrating on your body, psyche, and soul will enable you to turn out to be all the more dominant. The more you do this, the more you shut out the sense of self and the better you will feel in all pieces of yourself.

With shut eyes and a casual body, center around your relaxing. Tune in for sounds that are close by or even far away. Output your body to get a feeling of what is loose and what is holding strain. If you have a tingle, see the tingle however don't attempt to transform it. Simply travel through it.

This is a great practice for simply being careful without attempting to take care of business.

Once in a while, life is awkward like a tingle. Sitting with the experience will enable you to see that things go back and forth.

Nervousness can sneak up in your paunch or you may encounter a snugness in your throat while you reflect.

The brain is telling the body that there are such a large number of activities. At the point when you do encounter strain in the body, you can contact that zone with your hands and inside the state, "This as well." You're recognizing your full understanding without attempting to transform it. This is mindfulness.

Let's assume you're sitting outside in a recreation center; all is well until you see two individuals unmistakably enamored. Abruptly, dejection kicks in and no one is around to facilitate the inclination. This bit of dejection has consistently been in your heart.

It's not constantly enacted however can emerge at any minute. You become feeble and it feels like your heart is sinking. Different occasions you've felt alone are activated and put away vitality from the past strikes a chord.

How would you take care of the issue without calling somebody or utilizing an old device to calm down your contemplations and sentiments?

Basically, see that you took notes. You are the subject and you are what takes note. Those sentiments of the void are objects. Out is to see who is feeling the torment and depression. Give the emotions a chance to go through without fleeing or staying away from them.

Mindfulness doesn't mean getting to be associated with the show of the psyche. It's tied in with seeing the manner in which the psyche and body are reacting with full acknowledgment.

The touchy individual in you who has had numerous encounters will feel apprehensive, destitute, and desirous every once in a while. This is the mind and the conscience affecting everything. You are the person who is careful, you are the inhabiting being who knows.

To take advantage of the piece of you that sits looking out for this human experience, you simply need to remain completely focused.

All of what I'm stating may appear to be exceptionally perplexing for some who have never polished mindfulness. It just requires some investment of not responding and rather watching your experience to comprehend the procedure I'm discussing.

Reflection is an incredible practice for minutes that bring awkward feelings.

Attempt this activity

Make proper acquaintance with the one in your brain. Just inside make proper acquaintance. Who makes proper acquaintance and who hears hi? It's you who's talking and it's you who's tuning in.

The most ideal approach to turn out to be free from the steady prattle that is bolstering your horrendous thoughts is to step back. Take a gander at it dispassionately. Musings are only an object of the psyche, something that should drift by and not be clutched or dismissed.

As you're careful and watch the voice, you'll start to see that the greater part of what it says has next to no significance. It complains about the past and utilizes old encounters to attempt to control present and future encounters. This causes a wide range of issues in your life.

If you need to turn out to be free from your own brain, you must be careful enough to truly observe what's happening up there. At the point when you discover that a lot of your activities originating from some nonsensical voice that wants comfort, you can start to settle on different choices.

All in all, mindfulness can mend numerous things yet how would we accomplish it? One of the pathways to calm the psyche and go within ourselves is through contemplation.

Everyday contemplation

Contemplation isn't difficult but then its effortlessness threatens many.

This is on the grounds that your self-image wouldn't like to be calmed. It reveals to you that you're excessively occupied, that reflection is inconsequential, and that it's excessively unusual and otherworldly for you.

What's truly going on is that the self-image is terrified of ending up calm. Backing off and going in methods there's the capability of standing up to awkward sentiments. You gave your sense of self the activity of keeping away from distress or saw peril.

At the point when we ponder, there is incredible danger of running into past torment.

Mindfulness through your contemplation enables you to at long last manage old injuries so you don't need to live with them any longer. That implies that they never again have power over you.

To develop mindfulness, you'll need to invest significant energy consistently, yet this shouldn't be a task. The mind will prattle and reveal to you it's exhausted. Simply continue watching the objects of musings and emotions traveling through you.

The more you practice, the more you'll anticipate having that uninterrupted alone time. Consider it daily in the spa or getting a back rub. When you get into it, that focused inclination makes you feel as loose as 40 minutes in a sauna.

While you'll start to experience benefits practically immediately, the more you practice mindfulness, the more noteworthy the advantages will be.

In both the Buddhist ways of thinking and present-day psychotherapy, mindfulness is accomplished through reflection.

There is a wide range of approaches to reflect as well, so don't sit in lotus posture and consume those incense sticks at this time. Reflection is the umbrella for mending and inside your contemplations, you can accomplish numerous things for the body, psyche, and soul.

Mindfulness contemplation isn't tied in with changing or modifying yourself in any capacity. It's tied in with getting to be mindful of what your identity is. As you sit peacefully, things will come up. As you search inside yourself, recollections may come up as if they are a motion picture on a screen.

If you remain in the seat of cognizance without getting sucked in, you can become familiar with a great deal. You'll know if you get sucked in on the grounds that you won't let pictures go. You'll get genuinely included and pressure will begin to develop.

Buddha said that the wellspring of your enduring is attempting to flee from your immediate experience. Remaining in a lovely minute from your past is equivalent to pieces of torment. Clutching things keeps you before and it's essentially not beneficial for your mind.

Meditation (Reflect On Your Own Thoughts)

We are instructed to move away from dread—to pick comfort and quick fulfillment over the hard way. But then, we who ruminate are continually picking the hard way. Confidence is a position of a riddle, where we discover the boldness to have faith in what we can't see and the solidarity to relinquish our dread of vulnerability.

Each time I go into contemplation, it is a demonstration of trust, of squeezing into dread and drawing nearer to reality. It is the act of contemplating that has enabled me to look for that reality, to pick the harder way, and to discover sympathy for myself all the while.

As the years progressed, I've gone over a couple of sorts of contemplation that have helped me in the most dread ridden times of my life.

Qigong Meditation

In Traditional Chinese Medicine, it is accepted that dread is put away in the kidneys. In Western medication, it is realized that frightful considerations are minimal more than compound and electrical sign, activated through a mind-boggling system of correspondence in the body's cells. With enough reiteration, those neural pathways are framed and established, causing a similar reaction each time a danger is recognized.

Sit with your shoulders and your feet level against the floor. Spot your hands over your kidneys (at your back under your lower ribs). Picture them and the little adrenal organs over them in your psyche.

At the point when the psyche is looked with a danger, regardless of whether genuine or saw, it revisits those pathways to do similar activities. Furthermore, that is the place qigong contemplation steps in. By rehashing positive musings, you can make and fortify neural pathways, and clear up the kidneys, to assist you with more noteworthy authority over your feelings.

After a couple of breath cycles, lean forward a little as you breathe in, catch your hands beneath your knees, open your eyes, and envision breathing out dread, making a "choo" sound.

Closer your eyes, grin, and breathe in your stomach out envisioning dull blue light and harmony encompassing your kidneys and adrenal organs. Breathe out by driving your stomach back in.

Lean In

The act of reflection is intended to be down to earth in helping us travel during our time with a touchstone of harmony and mindfulness. Similarly, as with any feeling, contemplation can help balance out us notwithstanding trepidation to enable us to comprehend it all the more unmistakably.

As the day progressed, you can enable yourself to meet dread in an increasingly positive manner with the intensity of reflection.

Check-in with your feelings consistently. At whatever point you feel dreadful, let the inclination remain.

Rather than running, adopt a full breath and strategy your contemplations of fear and stress with neighborliness and interest. Be thoughtful to yourself in dread, as you would for a confided in companion.

If you have the opportunity and space, plunk down and inhale into your dread for ten breath cycles.

Dread AS POWER

Dread is stating that this is the ideal time to have the option to do what you're attempting to do. Your body is really setting you up to have a positive result. When you can truly comprehend that dread is a feeling like some other feeling, you can figure out how to oversee it. And afterward, you can accomplish things that the vast majority consider to be exceptional.

To beat my dread of statures, I have grasped the fear, taking a lead shake climbing class where I need to move to the highest point of the divider and free fall mostly down the divider before being securely gotten with a rope.

Through training, receptiveness, and cheering companions and teachers, I have figured out how to inhale through the dread and let go again and again. The dread remains, however my response to it has changed.

Practice it yourself — what is your dread? What little, safe advances would you be able to take to work on disapproving of your breath in that dread? As you practice, what changes do you see after some time?

Life consists of thousands of moments, but we only live one moment at a time. When we start changing this moment, we start changing our lives. Are you somebody who likes to overthink things? Trinidad Hunt. Nonetheless, what exactly is overthinking? According to psychologists, who have done extensive research in the field, rethinking is' too much, needlessly and passively thinking; always pondering the significances, triggers and consequences of your personality, your emotions and particularly your problems.' It can mean lying awake at night thinking, "This economy is terrible; my savings are not worth it; I will probably lose my job and, I will never be able to send my kids back to college." Or it can mean thinking about how unattractive your delicate and wispy hair is several times over the day.

In Gail Blankets post on 'How to avoid overthinking and starting a life' told a story about being invited to the 2007 annual dinner of the Financial Women's Association and how she was fascinated with choosing the' right outfit to wear in the knowledge that she was going to meet some very prominent, probably very good-playing women. She admits that she was actually thinking about it for days, even making lists and sketches of all the options and trying to look wear the right thing, before suddenly, her friend, who was 25 at that time, asked her,' Why are you working so hard?''. The invitation says 'Business attire,'. Dwelling on the situation and feeling like "Does that mean that she thinks my reasoning is dumb?" or, "Why didn't he answer my e-mail? I sent it three days ago. Is he be mad about something? Is he punishing me? Am I too insignificant to bother?" Someone who spends a lot of time wondering why a friend or boss hasn't made eye contact or spoken to them in a room, sits down to feel bad and then doesn't think it's worth putting in the effort or taking risks involved in top performance.

Most people think that if they feel disappointed or depressed by certain things, it will encourage them to think deeply and examine the situation to sort it out. When we look at science, the truth is just the opposite. Instead of being supportive, constant ruminations about possible adverse incidents tend to make people worse. Yes, according to Lyubomirsky, there is widespread and significant evidence that thinking about a painful or troubling situation is terrible for us over and over (also called "rumination"). It can be so harmful that it prevents us from taking significant pro-active steps to improve the condition and can lead to an increasing deterioration of attitude, cynical distortion of reality and even clinical depression in those who are vulnerable.

Life and the world around you are all full of problems, from minor annoyances, mistakes, and imperfections to major tragic events and frightening threats and possibilities. It does not make us more stable or somehow less vulnerable to any of these innovations. Actually, it makes us feel worse and makes us less likely to take constructive action to improve our attitude or to reverse those changes.

There is none other than during this period of terrible financial news, a volatile economy and increasing disillusionment with the government and the corporate Americas, when the confidence in their capacity for providing adequate, fair services and the protections and leadership need to ensure that the country runs smoothly is continuously small.

How can your job, your personal goals, your family and your relationships be overlooked? This can make you feel so pessimistic that you avoid taking risks, reaching out to others and making significant efforts to be successful. It can make it hard and even frustrating to be around for those who most matter to you. Ultimately, rethinking, with its forecasts of inevitable failure and terrible consequences, can drain the optimism required to work hard, speak up and spread good thoughts.

Have you ever done this? What can you do to stop it?

Tips for coaching: 1. To reduce and avoid overthinking, use validated techniques. Surprisingly, one of the simplest is the most effective. Distract yourself. Choose to turn your mind literally into something else, ideally absorbing and enjoying and/or exciting and optimistic thoughts. Instead, many people find a stop sign and say either in their heads the word, "stop!" whenever the situation loudly requires to be ruminated.

2. Offer yourselves to excellence. Learn to laugh at errors and challenges, welcome human error, and find irony and fun in it as it happens. Suppose people's lives are full and there are likely alternative explanations for what could be seen as a snub or power play otherwise. Realize that it's not about you most of the time.

3. Prevent causes. Keep away and limit your time to people or situations that lead you to feel depressed and think again as much as possible. Identify who and what and how your sensitivity to these stimuli can be reduced.

4. Go to "stream." Find areas of your life where you get so lost, whether it is playing the piano, shooting hoops, reading, walking, or kayaking. Schedule the stream times for events in your life every week, if possible, daily.

5. Learn, learn, practice, practice! Ultimately, pick some of these tips, training and practice. Study shows that its take a lot of practice to "hardwire" a new habit, so be patient with yourself and just continue to use your unique strategies to turn your mind in an overthinking way. You should be both happier and more productive with time and practice.

You can practice a relaxation method like progressive muscle relaxation because people who display generalized anxiety often have high levels of responsiveness.

Take up short-term activities that are captivating and enjoyable to take your mind off certain things and distract it from certain negative thoughts. These could be activities that have been useful in the past. Exercise is a vital tool for managing worry. When you exercise, brain chemicals are released that counteract low moods, worry and anxiety. Exercise also acts as a distraction from worries and reduces nervousness. Exercise at least once a day for half an hour, with cardio exercises at least three days a week.

Incorporate organized problem-solving strategies to handle stressors that contribute to your worry. When challenged with a difficult situation or life problem, most people often don't know how to handle these difficulties and lack enough coping skills; they feel as if they're incapable of controlling what they're faced with. Such feelings cause people to worry.

Everyone has problems and challenges in their lives, but they are more visible and difficult to handle if you always get worried. A useful strategy to combat this is training in organized problem-solving. Efficient problem- solving techniques minimize, reduce, control and even prevent worrying in our daily lives.

Avoid activities and situations that foster anxiety by confronting your fears and facing them directly but gradually. For instance, you could place them in a hierarchy, depending on which step you fear the most. These fears could be:

- Arriving late for a meeting
- Not checking your mobile phone for one hour
- Going grocery shopping without a shopping list
- Planning a birthday party
- Accepting an invitation without checking with your calendar
- Going out without your mobile phone for the day

Adopt Cognitive Interventions

There are two errors that those who have GAD tend to make:

Overestimation: They are always on edge, overestimating the likelihood of catastrophe. For example, they think thoughts like: "This will be a disaster!" or "I had better prepare for the worst scenario".

Underestimation: They are often underestimating their ability to cope with their problems. For instance, they might think thoughts like, "I will have a breakdown." or "I won't be capable of dealing with this situation".

If you have a problem with thoughts like these, what can you do? Simple! Challenge these negative thoughts by mastering how to recognize thoughts that are distressing and whether these thoughts are realistic.

For example, you may have to ask yourself what evidence you have to support these thoughts. If you can't find any, you may not need to dwell on it. Also, it might be that the best thing to do is to identify how likely it is that your fears for the future will come true.

Furthermore, folks with GAD should also continually work at challenging their beliefs and assumptions regarding themselves. For instance, a person's worry could be that he will never get prepared on time, and this might be followed up with the assumption that if things go wrong, he should be blamed and the creeping belief that he or she is a failure. Even though some believe that worry prevents harmful occurrences, this is inaccurate. Instead, it increases one's level of anxiety.

Well, as soon a person has been able to identify and question his or her negative thoughts, then the next line of action is shifting attention away from the negative thoughts. Cognitive Behavioral Therapy assists in identifying and challenging these assumptions and helping individuals to develop alternative beliefs that are healthier and better for their personal well-being. Experiences have shown that mindfulness-based interventions will also aid you to remain focused.

Adopt Emotion Regulation and Mindfulness

Recent studies have suggested that worry may present itself as a way of doing away with emotional processing. Involve yourself in what is called emotion-regulation strategies and mindfulness skills, as these will boost the form and manner in which you identify and experience underlying emotions.

Do away with the use of medications that will sedate you. Don't binge to relieve your anxiety. They may provide temporary relief from anxiety, but frankly, it will come back later. Instead of doing these, set up a time to consult a specialist or go for CBT if symptoms occur for longer than three months regardless of the above measures.

Realistic Ways to Cope With Symptoms of Anxiety and Excessive Worrying

It's great to learn tips and tricks that we can use to wrestle anxiety and excessive worry. Each time that you find yourself in an unpleasant situation, ask yourself these simple but effective questions.

- Is my worry reasonable?
- Will what I fear actually happen?

- How can I be sure that what I fear will happen?
- Could there be any other plausible explanation or outcome in my situation?
- Am I trying to predict things in the distant future that I am unable to do something about?
- If this worst-case scenario occurs, will it really be as bad as I think that it will be?
- Is it worth worrying about?
- How would someone else view my worry?

What is the Effect of Thinking the Way That You Do?

What will be the effect of thinking the way that you are thinking right now? Do these thoughts make you feel empowered to solve the problem at hand or do they discourage you from believing in yourself and feeling capable of facing the problem at hand? Are there instances where your worries are valid? Yes! Sometimes we worry about things that are likely to happen. In this situation, what you will need to do is to face your worry and do something about it if you can.

If not, you may need to let it go. For those who are experts when it comes to worrying, this may seem impossible. However, you could say to yourself, "There is absolutely nothing that could be done to alter this right now". Then you can find some other activity to occupy your mind and distract you from this situation that you have no control over.

Is There a True Problem to Solve?

If there really is a problem to solve, then you might have to focus your attention on a practical solution for it. In this case, you might turn to problem-solving skills to deal head-on with the things that are worrying you.

Below are six structured problem-solving techniques that you can use to do this:

- Write down precisely what you think the real problem is.
- Write down all the possible solutions that you could think of; don't eliminate the bad ones yet.
- Consider each solution carefully and logically.
- Select the most practical solution.
- Plan carefully how you will work on that solution.
- Do it.

Note: Anxiety is not your fault. Daily life and comes with stressors that can affect a person's thoughts, feelings, and everyday functioning!

Anger Management

Just like all other basic emotions, anger is designed to convey a specific message to us. That message could be our disapproval of something that has happened or something that someone has done. However, if our first response when angry is to vent or become raging mad, then the message gets lost in translation. For this reason, a calm mind and level-head are essential when dealing with anger. Being in a calm state of mind allows you to take a step back and objectively evaluate your anger from the point of reason. It also allows you to acknowledge your feelings and validate them without letting them control you.

Keeping calm when angry, however, is easier said than done. It takes a lot of practice, patience, and maturity to keep yourself from acting out of character when something that triggers rage in us happens. If someone offends you, it is much easier to revenge. In a way, we derive some pleasure from causing suffering to perceived opponents when we feel like they have wronged us. In reality, however, these solutions are illusory, since they do not deal with the real issues and cause of our anger. In fact, they can be more detrimental to us and our relationships in the long run. In light of this, we must find healthier ways to control our anger, even when we feel justified in it.

So, what is anger management, and what does it entail? Essentially, anger management is the process of identifying signs that you are becoming angry or frustrated and taking the necessary steps to calm yourself down in order to deal with your anger more productively. Many people have the misconception that anger management is meant to keep you from feeling angry. Others even think that it is designed to help them suppress feelings. Both of these are poor understandings of the role of anger management. Like we found out earlier, anger is a universal human emotion that all living humans experience at some point in their lives. Also, we already saw why suppressing anger is counterproductive as a long term strategy to manage anger.

The role of anger management is to help you become better at identifying signs that you are becoming frustrated and equip you with the necessary skills to keep your anger under control. A lot of literature has been written about anger and how to deal with it more effectively. One can, therefore, learn the right skills for dealing with frustration from reading books such as this one. However, the most common way through which people learn anger management is by attending an anger management class or therapy with a counselor.

You will get to learn how to identify the warning signs when you get frustrated, and how you can effectively calm yourself down in order to approach your anger from the point of strength.

You may be wondering to yourself right now, " How do I know if I need anger management classes?" Here are some of the signs that you may need to attend anger management classes in order to keep them in control.

- You Constantly Feel Like You Need to Suppress Your Anger

While expressing your anger through fits of rage is not the appropriate response for anger, hiding your anger is not a healthy way of coping either. If you constantly feel like you need to bottle up your anger, this may point to a lack of proper coping strategy. It may also be that you are afraid of being vulnerable with other people and showing them your true feelings.

Vulnerability is very important in any relationship, as it helps to build trust among individuals. Refusal to be open about one's feelings usually leads to isolation, fear, and distrust. These are not only weak foundations on which to build a relationship, but they can also trigger more feelings of anger and frustration. It is, therefore, essential to take it upon yourself to learn the right coping strategies instead of hiding your feelings of rage.

- You Always Focus on Negative Experiences

Granted, life is very challenging, and everyone will experience negativity in their lives at some point. However, it is important not to allow the bad things that happen in our lives to rid us of our joy and vitality. If you constantly focus only on the negative experiences in your life, you get distracted from actually living your life to the fullest potential. You may also find it a lot harder to appreciate the simple pleasures of everyday living, such as having a comfortable roof over your head, and people who love you.

You, therefore, need to learn the right coping strategies when angry in order to prevent your anger from becoming habitual.

- **You Constantly Struggle with Feelings of Hostility and Irritation**

If you constantly struggle with uncomfortable feelings of irritation and hostility towards others, then you definitely need to learn anger management skills. While life is not perfect every day, there are many things that make it worth the experience. If you are perennially irritated by the state of affairs in your life, this may point too deep-seated anger issues that need to be resolved as soon as possible.

- **You Constantly Find Yourself in Arguments which Further Trigger Your Anger**

There are many instances in life when you will find yourself justifiably angry at someone for something they did. However, if you always find yourself in heated confrontations with people, this could be a sign of an underlying anger problem. It could also simply be a sign that the strategies you use to deal with your anger are ineffective. Perhaps your first response when angry is to blame the other person or throw a temper tantrum. Maybe you even find yourself engaging in abusive exchanges with the objects of your frustration. All of these strategies of coping with anger are very inappropriate since they only trigger more angry reactions from you. It is important instead to find a way of calming yourself down enough to deal with the issue with an objective mind.

- You Engage in Physical Violence when Angry

While anger is a very normal reaction which may provoke feelings of aggression, using violence to deal with anger is very inappropriate. As a matter of fact, physically abusive responses when angry can be very damaging to your health, reputation as well as relationships. It can also lead to very serious legal consequences, such as getting sued or imprisoned for abuse. If you find yourself prone to committing acts of violence when angry, you should seek professional help immediately. Through counseling and attending anger management classes, you can break this cycle of poor anger management and learn to express your frustration in healthier ways that do not involve the use of violence.

- You Manifest Out-of-Control Behavior when Angry

Perhaps you are not outrightly violent towards other people when angry. However, you may have a tendency to smash or break things when angry. This is still not an appropriate response or strategy to deal with anger and frustration. This type of behavior fails to address the real cause of the anger, and only reinforces the idea that showing aggression is going to make the anger go away. The truth is that it doesn't work.

The only effective way of dealing with anger is by getting to the root cause and harnessing the emotion in positive ways.

- You Avoid Certain Situations Because of Fear of Getting Angry

Another tell-tale sign that you need lessons in anger management is you find yourself constantly avoiding scenarios that may trigger your anger. Perhaps you don't like going to parties with your spouse because they always leave you alone to go chat with the other people. Or maybe, you avoid talking to one of your close friends because you feel they are too judgmental.

Whichever the case, the temptation to avoid any scenario that may trigger your anger can be too strong to resist. However, opting out of certain situations due to fear of getting frustrated is not an effective way of dealing with your anger. For one, it shifts the responsibility to the other person, thereby diminishing your power to take responsibility for your emotions. It also only covers up pent up frustration, which continues to simmer slowly without your awareness. This can eventually erupt in very damaging ways, both to you and your relationships.

Anger management classes are typically designed to help people develop the skills to notice when they are getting angry and take the necessary steps to deal with the emotion appropriately. Usually, the classes are conducted as one-on-

one sessions or group sessions with a counselor or therapist. Depending on your needs, the anger management program may take a few days, weeks, or even months in some cases. It is, therefore, essential for you to be patient and consider the whole experience as a learning process.

When you first begin attending anger management classes, the first thing you will learn is how to identify stressors and triggers of anger. By identifying the early warning signs of anger, you can begin to understand its causes and figure out how to control it. Stressors are typically those things that cause frustration in your life and trigger pent up anger. These may include frustration with a child who behaves poorly, financial problems, or coworkers who constantly gossip about you.

Apart from identifying the triggers, anger management classes will help teach you how to pick up on symptoms of anger. As we found out earlier, physiological symptoms of anger vary between individuals. You may, therefore, not manifest the same symptoms as someone else when angry. While one person may experience an increased heart rate and sweat when angry, another person may feel a tight-knot in their stomach when upset. Anger management classes will help you identify the physical symptoms of anger as they present uniquely in your body.

Beginner's anger management is also meant to help you recognize the signs that your anger is on the rise. Perhaps you may feel like you want to yell at the perceived object of your anger, or you feel the need to keep quiet in order to avoid a heated confrontation. Being aware of the physical reactions happening in your body will allow you to take a step back and carefully evaluate your anger before proceeding with an appropriate response.

Getting Unstuck from The Past

The ghost of the past is tough to go. The harder we try to push it, the more resounding it gets. It comes to haunt at the most inconvenient times. It should come as no surprise that you always remember everything bad that has happened in your life. Your mind is a terrific storage device. It has unlimited storage ability. Scientists believe that you can record more than 2.5 petabytes of data in your brain and still have space left for more. It actually translates to 300 million hours of video recording space. This is huge.

It means that all the things that have happened in your life, positive or negative, are recorded in your mind. However, your mind also has a strong response to negative things as it feels the need to keep playing them, again and again, to keep you safe from falling into the same kind of situation. It is a survival mechanism designed for good.

The problem begins when your mind starts playing the negative things obsessively and makes it impossible for you to start fresh. It makes wiping the slate clean tough. Your mind clutter has an important role to play in this. You let your past remain heavy on you. The solace of victimhood, the desperation to remain safe and vulnerability are some of the strong reasons. These feelings encroach your productive space. They leave no room for positive thinking.

This all happens because you are not being mindful. You have allowed your mind to remain cluttered by negative experiences and want to be in a safe sanctuary.

Let's consider a small story. Once there was a farmer. He had a big farm but he had bad luck in the past harvests. Sometimes the harvests got affected by droughts and sometimes pest attacks killed the harvest. The farmer decided he had had enough of this nonsense. He wouldn't bear this nonsense again as his harvests were getting ruined anyway. So, he decided to play it safe and planted nothing. Was that a solution? It was definitely not a solution. Earlier the farmer had a fear that his harvest would get affected by rain or pests. There was a possibility that he may not get the full harvest. But, his actions made it a certainty that he will not get anything at all. Playing safe is sometimes the worst move. The baggage of the past does this to you.

If you let your mind and thoughts rule your world then you will rot in a corner without ever seeing the light of the day. It will keep telling you that the world is full of dangers and risks.

Learning from the mistakes of the past and letting it go is the only way to excel in this world. If your mind is cluttered with worries it will never be able to learn and succeed. It will lack the required potential. A cluttered mind is never able to make the distinction between a safe decision and a fearful decision.

Safe decisions are based on reality. They have their basis on the possible consequences of decisions and they invoke remedial precautions. The farmer could have made alternative irrigation arrangements. He could have employed pest control measures. Even if he hadn't done any of these the probability of getting a harvest was 50-50. But, he took a fearful decision of doing nothing. The result was a guarantee of having nothing at all. Fearful decisions come from your insecurities and they keep getting stronger. If you do not learn to fight them, they will degrade you and make you sub-human with no capability to enjoy this life.

How to Stop Negative Thinking

The power to think is what makes humankind superior to other species dwelling on this earth along with us. If you look closely, they do all the things similar to us. They are born, eat, grow, reproduce and die, just like us. There is effectively no difference between us and other species. The only thing that makes us different is our ability to think.

However, this boon easily turns into a bane when our brain starts indulging in negative thinking. If you feel that most of your thoughts are negative, depressing, and self-destructive, you are not alone. This is a malice that troubles most of the human race. But, negative thinking has deep roots in the survival mechanism of mankind and it has taken millions of years of careful evolution.

Humankind hasn't always been at an advantageous position in this world. We were weak and vulnerable. We had no protection from the climate. We were ill-equipped to arrange food and were practically defenseless against the beasts. Carelessness could have got us killed any minute. To survive, our mind developed a negative thinking process in which it could play all the negative scenarios to devise a safe outcome. It is more of a protection mechanism.

If one person in the clan got killed by a beast the scenario wouldn't simply end there. Our mind would keep playing the scenario so that you can formulate a strategy to avoid such an outcome again. The mind played the same scenario; it invoked fear so that we didn't make the same mistake. It helped in our survival. This mechanism of having negative thoughts has protected us for thousands of years against all odds.

If today you are having a similar negative thought process going on in your mind, then it isn't baseless. It has its roots in the very same survival instinct that enabled you to survive even in the fiercest situations. However, there is a line beyond which anything becomes toxic. If you let your brain run loose without any control, then it will keep playing fearful scenarios to prevent you from taking action. Your mind knows that the safest bet to survive is to remain in the shell. The outside world is unpredictable and the forces are beyond control. However, becoming the slave of this mentality is dangerous.

Negative thought patterns arise in your mind as your natural response to certain situations. The extent of negative thoughts depends upon your threat perception. Most of the times, there is no threat at all. You are simply scared to take an action and your mind starts showing you the worst possible consequences. This leads to inaction, procrastination, fear, and anxiety. If you fall into this trap, you are destined to fail. Inaction will take you nowhere. We have come a long way ahead of the vulnerable times. We are beyond the age of savages. This is a world that runs of dialogues, policies, and frameworks. There are calculated outcomes of actions. Even if all hell breaks loose, there is an extent of damage that can occur. If you do nothing, the damage is already done.

Excessive negative thought patterns forming in your brain are a part of mind clutter. Your mind is filled with too much negativity and it reflects the same in negative thinking. This can be a dangerous thing if it goes unchecked. It can make you indecisive, frightened, and weak. You will never be able to bring that winning edge in yourself. Your risk-taking abilities will end and you will become a fearful decision taker which means you will take no decisions at all. This is a pathetic state to be in the first place. You will lose all the control over your life. Your imagination and past scenarios will start deciding the way of your life. It will take a toll on your personal and professional life, health, family, relationships and career and more.

Become Conscious of Your Negative Thought Patterns

As said earlier, having negative thoughts is not a problem, but not being conscious of your negative thinking patterns is a big problem. Every person has negative thoughts. Only a toddler or a madman can be free from fear and negative thoughts. They are free from fear and it has no real meaning in their experience. You, as a sane person, have experience and hence, your mind will play negative thoughts about things, relationships, and events. The important thing is to remain conscious of the negative thoughts. If you keep ignoring the negative thoughts, they'll become stronger. Even a small mistake will get played repeatedly and frighten you.

We all get negative thoughts either we are awake or sleeping. Your subconscious is always playing the scenario. Your job is to play the scenario with a conscious mind and rationalize. If you do that once in a day, you will be able to calm your subconscious. You would have quelled all the fears.

If you have negative thought patterns and the fright is overpowering, you and clouding your judgment then start consciously analyzing your negative thoughts daily. Every day devote a fixed amount of time to ponder over the problematic situations at hand and the best possible way out. This will ease your negative thinking pattern and you will be able to work constructively.

Can't Undo Spilled Milk; Make Cheese Out of It

You can't remove negativity by negativity. If there is a problem, then brooding over it will not help. Think of the ways to overcome it.

On day to day basis, we come across several situations which have gone beyond our control. Crying over them will not help our cause. The only way to deal with such situations is to devise ways to nullify their effect. If you are late to work, then either choosing a fast transport could help or think of a better excuse. Brooding over getting late is not going to be of any help.

The same goes for negative thinking in real life. If you are having negative thoughts then in place of going deep into the repercussions, think about the ways you can deal with the situation. If a negative thought pattern has started and it is bringing in front all the bad things, start thinking of the good things you want and list the ones you can make happen. You can only kill negativity with positivity and you will have to make do with the things at hand. Try to make the best of it.

Stop Punishing Yourself

Negative thoughts are a torment. They lead to stress and anxiety. It is well known that stress and anxiety have a detrimental impact on your physiological as well as psychological health. They act as triggers that begin several negative processes. Your body starts releasing stress hormones that lead to fat accumulation, lethargy, and heartburn, stiffness in muscles and the works. Your body reacts poorly to these triggers.

Trying to ignore these thoughts is going to make you even more anxious as your mind knows that you are avoiding them. You should adopt a 3-step approach to deal with such negative thoughts.

Vent: Give a vent to these thoughts. Do not be scared to think about them. Let them come out in clear. It will help you in clearly understanding the extent of the negative thoughts. Nevertheless, do not remain immersed in them. Simply ponder over them and get over with them.

Cap: Once you have acknowledged the full scale of the negative thoughts, it will be easier for you to understand their extent. They will be less scary. This is the time you can put an end to them. Devise plans to counter these negative thoughts.

Strategize: You have the scale of the problem; you have an understanding of it, now you simply need a strategy to overcome it. This is the stage where you can get help from several directions. Think of the ways to deal with the problem. You can take the help of your family and friends in dealing with the problem. You can look for solutions on the internet. You can read about the possible solutions. It will widen your perspective.

If you keep punishing yourself with the negative thoughts, they will keep intensifying. Do not do that to yourself. Deal with the problem in an organized manner. Clear the clutter of your mind and you will be able to think better.

Write Them Down

Writing down your negative thoughts is a good way to clear the clutter of your mind. If you keep playing the negative thoughts in your mind, they'll keep getting stronger. The same scenarios will keep getting repeated over and over again.

Write down the negative thoughts and get them off your mind. It will help you in sorting your mind. When one thing is less to mix, your mind is better capable of thinking. Nothing helps in de-cluttering the mind better than jotting down your thoughts on paper.

Consciously Embrace Positivity

Negativity is a strong emotion. It gets expressed in a very visible manner and engulfs your thought process. The best way to deal with negativity is to embrace positivity. There may be a dozen negative things going around in your life at a particular moment but it doesn't mean the absence of positivity. You will need to remind yourself of the positive things happening around you. This will help in fighting your negative emotions. You should constantly remind yourself of the blessings in life. Think about the pleasant things in life to come. The things that you love or that infuse positivity. Take a break from the negative routine. Indulge yourself with some light moments. This will take off your brain from the negative thoughts. You will be able to break the negative thought patterns in an easy manner.

The negative thought process is very imposing. It has a very strong impact on your psyche. Simply trying to dodge this state will not help you. You will have to make conscious efforts to lighten up the moments. Positive things around you are very helpful in the process. Remove clutter around you. Organize your surroundings, as it also leads to negativity. Cherish your small accomplishments. These tiny steps to embrace positivity will help you in overcoming negative thought patterns.

Ponder Over the Merits of Negative Thought Patterns

Most of the times, negative thoughts are very imposing. They take off our mind from everything else. They instill fear. We are so frightened that we never pay attention to that extent. Fear has a gripping quality. It keeps us immersed. It has our unwavering attention. However, most of the times we are so engrossed in the fear that we overestimate its potential. If negative thought patterns are arising and fear is gripping you, evaluate its merit. Look closely if it can cause the amount of damage that you think.

Negative thoughts are there to caution you. There is no reason to become inactive. If you have a negative thought that makes you feel scared, then evaluate if it qualifies to put you in danger. Most of the times, the situation isn't that serious. You can easily overcome it. There is always a risk to reward ratio. Measure the risks and answer your fears. Do not take negative thought patterns on their face value. Think of the positive outcomes of your actions and compare if they are greater than the risks. You will have a better clarity of mind. Remaining lost in negative thoughts is not going to help your cause.

Stay Away from Negative Information Overload

We live in the age of 24 X 7 news channel age. Most of the times, the news is not positive as negativity sells fast and has great resonance. It is intriguing, and you feel like looking for more. This is the biggest reason, why most of the news items are negative. From social media platforms to the internet in general, negativity is widespread. The reason is simple, negative news has a greater impact than positive news. It creates curiosity that will lead to more TV time, more searches, more interest and ultimately more revenue. But eventually, you are at the receiving end of this negativity. It gives a bad start to your day. One negative news can shift your mind to the negative gear. You can start reflecting on all the things going wrong in your life and relate them to the news.

You live in an age where information access is instant. Do not begin your day with news. If you must, then look only for the news that concerns you.

Positive Thinking

It is important to replace negative thoughts with positive ones; however, it is not as easy to do as it sounds. Actually, most people misunderstand the whole idea of negative thinking. Happiness does not depend on a few negative thoughts; rather, it might depend on how one handles these negative thoughts.

In spite of any setbacks and obstacles, it is important to try to maintain one's sense of optimism. The benefits of avoiding negative thinking are greater than most people think. Actually, within the field of psychology, positive psychology is slowly gaining more attention. It involves the study of the physiological and psychological effects of positive thinking, behavior, and habits.

Research suggests that positive thinkers enjoy life more than pessimists do. Actually, when it comes to physiological and psychological health, in addition to stress levels, optimistic people are way ahead of the game. Thinking positively is a good way to heal; however, people need to understand that they should stop listening to the falsehoods their mind is telling them.

They should also try figuring out the origin of their negative thoughts. The first thing to remember is that negative thoughts stem from wrong assumptions and beliefs. Therefore, ignoring these thoughts is not good enough.

Everyone is worthy of love and happiness, and people should always remember this fact.

Some of the reasons to stop having negative thoughts include:

Ability to Cope with Stress

It is natural for human beings to face stressful situations, such as job loss, domestic conflict, and more. How people deal with stressful situations makes all the difference. According to research, however, people who have a more optimistic outlook tend to approach difficult situations in a more positive way.

Instead of wasting energy on negative thoughts that one cannot change our thinking about things that went wrong, people who think in a positive way take the opposite way. They understand they cannot change certain situations and find ways of dealing with life in a more positive manner.

Better Mental Health

Thinking more positively makes one less likely to experience problems such as depression and anxiety. According to experts, optimists enjoy a better quality of life, including psychological health, than pessimists do. Contrary to popular belief, positive thinking can cure certain mental behaviors and difficulties.

People who do not consider themselves do not need to worry. Overcoming negative thought patterns and starting to experience the benefits of positive thinking is not an impossible task. Stillness, for example, is a great way to overcome negativity. People can learn to break away from their negative thoughts through meditation.

Better Physical Health

Some believe that only people who think positively can engage in healthy behavior, such as regularly working out. However, this is not always the case. Although they tend to have a higher motivation to exercise, even those with frequent negative thoughts can learn to focus on their physical health by eating better and getting regular workouts.

According to another theory, optimistic people tend to have better physical health because they are better able to handle stress, or maybe because they experience less stress. Thus, the negative effects of stress on their physical health are significantly less. It is important, therefore, to stop worrying about one's negative thoughts to enjoy the following health benefits:

a) Live longer

b) Prevent cardiovascular diseases

c) Recover faster from illnesses and injuries

d)   Gain a stronger immune system

e)   Better overall well-being

Reasons to Stop Worrying about your Negative Thoughts

It is common for people to believe that negative thoughts are bad or even toxic, which is why so many people worry about their negative thoughts. According to some "experts," negative thoughts lower people's positive vibrations, keep them stuck on negativity, and so on. Essentially, they teach people to banish their negative thoughts to gain confidence and feel self-assured.

Some online articles and self-help books seem to suggest that getting rid of negative thoughts equals professional success, higher vibration, inner peace, better boyfriend/girlfriend, and much more. Consequently, people who constantly experience negative thoughts tend to wonder what to do with the thoughts running in their minds.

They wonder how to make such thoughts stop, or whether trying to force a positive thought over a negative one can really work. Unfortunately, most people tend to misunderstand the whole issue of negative thinking because they do not understand what thoughts, both positive and negative, are in the first place.

The negative thoughts that people have do not determine their happiness; rather, it is what they do with those thoughts. The good news is that people do not need to worry so much about their negative thoughts because of the following:

It is Normal to Have Some Negative Thoughts

Countless thoughts pass through the human mind every day, and most of them are negative. Actually, it would be interesting to meet and talk with a human being who never has negative thoughts. Most people carry tons of negative trash in their minds, even those that always seem positive.

For example, someone who is walking around congratulating himself/herself for buying a new car might really be trying to disguise negative thoughts and reinforce the idea that he/she was not good enough before buying the new car. Essentially, having negative thoughts is a normal part of being human; therefore, people do not need to worry about having them in the first place.

Negative Thoughts are not Always Based on the Truth

People do not have to believe in their negative thoughts. Contrary to what one's mind would like one to believe, not all thoughts are correct. A person's mind is just a part of him/her; therefore, it is important to separate one's thoughts from one's sense of self. Actually, the four components of a human being are:

a)   Physical body

b)   Mind

c)   Spiritual aspect

d)   Heart

One's mind, therefore, is simply a powerful tool for one to use, and one filters one's perceptions and thoughts through one's unique belief system. Negative thoughts stem from this filter because negativity is in the filter. Therefore, when people try to heal and grow, what they are really doing is changing their filters or belief system.

Everyone is perfect in his/her own way; therefore, people do not need to analyze and worry about their critical and nasty thoughts. They are simply thoughts, and the only way to overcome them is to stop listening to them. When one's mind is in the moment of calm, one will feel content and at peace. This is possible when one refuses to believe one's negative thoughts.

It is Possible to get Positive about one's Negative Thoughts

There is nothing wrong with choosing positivity; however, as discussed above, it is important to remember that negative thoughts do not really matter in the first place because they are often untrue. In addition, they do not make one a bad person or a lesser human being.

When people try to attack and reject their negative thoughts automatically, they are unconsciously telling themselves that they are not good enough. Essentially, according to them, good people should not have negative thoughts. This belief, however, is just as negative as their initial thoughts.

The small step of identifying the negative thought and refusing to believe it is an important step towards growth. Fortunately, the more one does this, the easier it will be to recognize negative thoughts when they appear, which will result in fewer negative thoughts.

Therefore, thinking positively is not the only way to find healing; rather, understanding that one is feeling bad because of entertaining and believing negative thoughts is the fastest way to heal and grow. It can also be helpful in determining the origins of one's negative thoughts. However, since most of them stem from untrue beliefs, it might be easier to ignore them.

Is Worrying Negative Thinking?

Worrying is a form of negative thinking. Thoughts tend to have powerful ramifications. When people have positive thoughts and stay positive, they tend to experience positive things. On the other hand, negative things tend to happen to people who entertain and believe their negative thoughts. By worrying excessively, people reinforce their negative attitudes and thoughts.

Unfortunately, the negative thoughts people focus on and worry about having a habit of coming true. People's thoughts and worries have a profound effect on their lives. By constantly worrying about a particular thing, people unwittingly spur it into becoming a reality.

Once people understand the correlation between worrying and negative thinking, they can begin to deal with their negative thoughts and change them. Consequently, they will begin to focus on things, which will lead to positive outcomes in their lives.

Identify Your Core Values

Core values are convictions and beliefs that people adopt as their guiding principles in their daily activities. They are behaviors that people choose to exercise as they pursue what is right and what humankind expects of them.

Core Values have the following characteristics: they can be specific, they can be different from culture to culture, they can bring disharmony between different people, a person can learn values early in life from family or friends, and finally values are often emotive.

Core values are of different types. Some of the classes include family, moral, social, socio-cultural, material, spiritual, environmental, intellectual, financial, and self-care values.

Examples of core values that emanate from the classification above include respect, honesty, freedom, fearlessness, dignity, loyalty, trust, cooperation, concern for others, initiative, justice, peace, humor, generosity, adventure, friendships, and excellence.

Core values are vital because they reflect people's needs, desires, and the things they care about most in life. Core values are remarkable uniting forces for people's identities. Core values are also decision-making guidelines that help people to connect to their authentic self.

Reasons To Develop Personal Core Values

Core values are vital factors that lead to the growth and development of individuals. The values help people to live happier lives, doing what is most important to them.

The following are reasons why it is essential for people to develop personal core values.

Core values promote self-awareness

Core values help people to acquire information about their strengths and weaknesses. That is because self-awareness comes from a person being honest with himself or herself about who he or she is.

Honesty is a value that facilitates people to talk about themselves truthfully. In that way, people can appreciate both their strengths and weaknesses. Honest people do not try to make themselves appear better than they might be.

The value of wisdom enables people to understand themselves better and to accept what they cannot change. It also helps people to realize that they cannot expect success if they do not know how to use their abilities.

Humility is a core value that brings a person to appreciate what other people are doing. A humble person allows other people to be in the limelight and to celebrate their successes. A humble person will not focus on himself or herself at the expense of other people.

Core values help people to learn about themselves so that people can live meaningful lives.

Core values give direction

Core values point the way a person should go. Core values are about standards that define who people think they are and what they hold in high esteem. While people cannot always measure up to these standards, the ideals tell them how they should think and act.

In the professional world, employers run businesses in unethical manners. Such unethical practices include lying about the effectiveness of a product or having mission statements that do not align with the company's conduct.

A person who follows his or her values will not do things just because other people think it is OK to do so. He or she can walk away from a situation that causes him or her to compromise his or her values. In so doing, the person allows his or her values to set the tone for his or her life, rather than blindly following other people's standards.

Core values help people to check whether they are consistent with what they believe is important.

Core values dictate behavior

Core values inform people's thoughts, feelings, words and, ultimately, actions. A person's values help to explain his or her actions. A person who values honesty strives to be honest. Accordingly, a person who values transparency will always try to be transparent.

When it comes to material things, a person who values his or her family dedicates his or her time to be with family members, and he or she encourages family relationships. Similarly, a person who values fitness will more likely develop daily rituals and long-term habits that promote fitness.

In the corporate world, a person may act in ways that are consistent with his or her values. Since people have different values, conflict may arise in the workplace. However, companies try to instill common core values that will guide every person's behavior.

For example, when hiring, a company may not control what shapes different people's values and behavior. However, the company may try to influence its employees through training programs and codes of conduct to get the employees to behave in ways that are acceptable to the company. Core values are thereby very crucial in determining and guiding behavior.

Core values unravel and boost individuality

Core values make people see how unique and special each person is. Some people value adventure, while others value safety. In addition, some people may value solitude, while others may value publicity.

For example, a person who values solitude may feel smothered if he or she allows his or her friend to influence them to go out for a party. The person may accept to go along, but they will not be having a great time. For the friend, people, drinks and endless conversations may be their lifeline.

Everyone is different, and what makes one person ecstatic may leave the other person feeling disconnected and uneasy. Consequently, a person has to know their values and live by them without fear of the unknown.

Therefore, when the person's values guide him or her, the person acknowledges his or her uniqueness and learns to respect and appreciate the individuality of others too.

Core values make conversations meaningful

A meaningful conversation is one where the parties involved are present in the moment and not distracted by thoughts or by other people's activities. In addition, a meaningful discussion includes people being open, transparent, and willing to share their honest thoughts and feelings.

When a person is not open to say what he or she thinks or feels, they are most likely not having a candid conversation. Values of transparency, honesty, openness, and genuineness help people to communicate meaningfully.

Meaningful conversations also value sensitivity. Sensitivity means that a person can sense people's needs to talk about painful experiences, and he or she is asking them about it. When a person opens up about an awkward situation, the listening party should sit quietly, listen keenly and offer a piece of wisdom when necessary. Care for other people is a value that can go a long way in making people feel better about themselves.

All it takes is one meaningful conversation to change another person's life.

Core values help to have wisdom in complicated situations

A person's core values affect every part of his or her life. The values are demonstrated in making decisions and in interacting with other people. Most of the time, a person's values come from their life experiences and the people closest to him or her.

If a person values spending time with his or her spouse, but he or she has to work for extended hours, the person will experience internal conflict and stress. In such an event, the person needs to go back to his or her values to seek help.

The values will help the person to understand his or her topmost priorities in life, and in that way, he or she will determine the best decision to make for himself or herself.

For a person to become the best person that he or she can be, the person has to live in agreement with his or her values. As a result, the values will be the foundation for the person's goals and life purpose.

Core values strengthen your confidence

Confidence becomes easy to achieve when a person is clear on his or her core values. When a person is not clear on what he or she values, they feel less confident to interact with other people.

Core values boost confidence in that they help a person to form ideas around what the person values. During conversations, people tend to have different opinions on the subject they are talking about. That is because people's core values shape their ideas and opinions about issues. Every person's 'point of view' usually emanates from his or her value system. That is what brings about bias in conversations and other aspects of life.

Consequently, a person's core values help him or her have an opinion, or to stand out in a matter, or to have interesting conversations and interactions. A person, who is not sure about his or her values, cannot have the courage and confidence to interact freely or to speak their mind.

Tips To Help You Discover Your Core Value

How can you find out and develop your core values?

Observe yourself and learn

You can begin by asking yourself the following questions: What two things were missing in my childhood? What two things do I spend most of my time thinking about? What two things do I spend most of the time talking about? What two things do I spend the most money on? How would I describe my ideal living space?

At the end of asking yourself and answering these questions, you will notice that you discovered at least nine things about yourself. With that background, it will be easy for you to know the memories or things that you value, or still hold to.

Think of people you look up to

Are there people in your life who you look up to? You could be looking up to a family member, a friend, a grade school teacher, a university lecturer, a celebrity, a famous personality, or even the person who works at your favorite restaurant.

Then ask yourself, 'why do I admire these people?' It could be that you marvel at the values they embody. For example, the person who works at your favorite restaurant is always smiling when serving others and you can see that the person genuinely loves his or her job. Your grade school teacher always listened to every student with sincerity, and you admired her excellent listening skills and charisma.

Identify the specific values that the people in your list exemplified. Those values can inspire you to adopt them.

Think back to the most painful moments of your life

Where were you? What made you sad? If you have experienced the pain of being excluded by others, then you may find that you value inclusivity and compassion.

Although pain is an undesirable experience, it helps people to learn the things that they would not want to re-live. As a result, they develop values about what they consider significant. From pain, you may have developed values of tolerance and resilience, humility, empathy, and independence.

Think back to the most joyous moments of your life

What were you doing? Why did that make you happy? Did other people share your happiness? Who were they? What other things contributed to your feelings of joy?

As you recall those moments, find examples from your school, career, family and personal life. You will discover that every experience is essential and valuable for the values that come with each lesson.

Make a list of your core personal values

First, write down a list of your core values. Afterward, go through the list, visualizing circumstances where each value may apply.

For example, when comparing the values of adventure and security, imagine that you have to decide to go to a different country to explore new opportunities, or continue to live where you are because it is a more familiar place. Continue working through your list until you identify values that resonate with you.

Change Your Habits and Mindset

There is a strong connection between confidence, emotional control, and the conquering of psychological habits. Over the years, through all of the surveys, interviews, and studies conducted, this is the most common and repeated truth from those participating in them and those performing them: no matter what a person is trying to attempt, confidence is key!

There are lots of different life factors that can affect a person's self-esteem and confidence, with adolescence taking the largest toll on a person's view of themselves. During adolescence, humans It is in these years that men and women receive the majority of their emotional education as it has the highest inclusion of factors like the following for most people:

First romantic relationships (often tumultuous with lots of highs and lows)

- First deep friendships that are tested by adjusting hormones, changing personalities and other life factors that may arise without warning
- First major successes and accomplishments like national awards and recognition, college scholarships and summer internships
- Learning to drive and understanding the responsibility that comes with getting behind the wheel of a car
- Developing decision-making skills that are shaped by how adolescents handle things like peer pressure, balancing their school, work, and social lives, and making their first life-affecting decisions like if they want to further their education after their required schooling is completed

With all of these exciting changes taking place, how could someone's self-esteem and confidence levels be hindered or even damaged? Unfortunately, for all of the positive events men and women experience during their teenage years, there are also a lot of negative events and factors they face (in their highest quantity and intensity than most people see throughout the rest of their lives) such as:

Learning to differentiate affectionate teasing from friends and loved ones with harmful teasing and bullying that comes from those to cause harm

- Physical changes to their skin, muscles and other parts of the body that may require attention from over-the-counter medical products or even prescriptions from medical professionals
- Emotional changes that are often unexpected and out of control as skills are developed through experience and education
- Lots of fear and uncertainty as everything seems to be changing around them without a sense of direction or stopping point insight

Not everyone has come out of adolescence with more negative memories than positive ones, but for those that did and find those negative experiences or memories affecting their adult lives, never fear! There is always action that can be taken to improve your self-esteem and confidence levels to improve your overall life satisfaction and path to reaching your goals!

Self-Esteem & Confidence Levels: How Are They Connected & How Are They Different?

Many times, when people talk about self-esteem and confidence, they speak about them as if they are one and the same. However, in truth, self-esteem and confidence are two separate personality traits that are often interconnected but can be damaged or weakened on their own and need individualized attention to help rebuild and strengthen them.

Pro Tip: Self-awareness is one of the skills people should try to master or at least become more familiar and practiced before turning their energies to self-esteem and confidence. Without knowing where you stand psychologically, mentally, and emotionally, it is difficult to determine where your focus should be aimed and what kinds of goals you should set to reach your ultimate hopes and aspirations.

A Self-Awareness Exercise: Listen to Your Self Talk & Learn from What You Say

One of the best ways for someone to understand their emotional status and why they are feeling a certain way about something is to listen to how they are speaking to themselves, either vocally or in their minds. Everyone has a little voice in their thoughts that voices their opinions about what they are thinking or what they are doing honestly, even if sometimes it can be discouraging or even cruel. The reason this voice can be trusted as a person's most honest thoughts is because these are the thoughts, ideas, and opinions that only circle through someone's mind when they are alone (especially if they are voiced audibly) or whenever they have the opportunity (for those who play the voice in their minds where only they ever hear them).

Those with lower self-esteem and confidence levels often find that their private voice is a negative one, repeating Self Talk that further damages their view of themselves or opinion of their abilities. For this exercise, the goal is to teach individuals how to be more aware of this Self Talk and its tone so that they know how to change their current thought process or emotional status any time their Self Talk takes a negative turn.

When you feel yourself inner voice becoming negative, whether this is because you are unsatisfied with something about your physical appearance or because of a broken sentence in an earlier social interaction, it will start to make critical comments or try to target other fragile or underdeveloped aspects of your personality to bring your mood further down.

- Self-depreciation and attacks on one's own status or abilities are some of the most damaging behaviors someone can take part in, and in many cases, this voice develops subconsciously, only voicing fears and concerns when the brain knows the person is emotionally vulnerable.
- When this behavior starts to take over your thoughts, take a step back and calm your mind. Listen to those thoughts and how your inner voice sounds (or your vocal tone) when the Self Talk starts.
- What kind of tone does your voice or inner voice take?
- Is it angry, sad, or hurtful?
- Does it express any kind of emotion, or does it come across as a more neutral side to your character?

- What kind of words is that voice using?
- Are they offensive?
- Are the words you do not normally use when talking to other people?
- When is this voice most active?
- Does the Self Talk get most negative or most targeted during times of stress? Or any time you are not thinking about something else?
- Do your own thoughts, actions, and behaviors determine how active the voice is? Or is it more active after encounters with others?

Why This Exercise Works: This exercise works because it is based around a natural human behavior that all men and women have in common, an inner voice that takes charge of conveying our deepest and most private thoughts about the things we do and say each day. When regularly practiced, it has proven to be one of the most effective exercises in helping people expand their emotional intelligence and their understanding of themselves and how they view their private thoughts.

Whom This Exercise Works Best For This exercise has proven the most effective for those who are dedicated and motivated to take control of their emotional and psychological health. Anyone ready to better understand who they are and what makes them tick to improve their interactions with others or saying yes to more opportunities will also see noticeable progress when this exercise becomes a habit and makes its way into their daily routine.

Once a person becomes comfortable with self-awareness habits and has a better understanding of where their emotional health is, they are better able to make an actionable plan for how to first improve their self-esteem and confidence levels before moving on to more stubborn and difficult to break psychological habits like compulsive overthinking and procrastination. But what is self-esteem, and why is it such an important element to master when it comes to expanding emotional knowledge and health?

What Is Self-Esteem?

Self-esteem is most commonly defined as how a person feels about themselves as a whole. There is often an emotional connection to a person's self-esteem that is not shared with someone's confidence levels.

This trait is one that covers how an individual may feel about:

- Their current life status
- Their current job status
- Their relationship status
- Their main hopes and how they are working toward them
- The people around them like friends and family

- Their physical strengths and where they want to work more

These are just some of the individual factors and variables that can go into shaping a person's view of themselves and their self-esteem. If everyone in the world made a list of the points and traits they think about when they think about their view of themselves, you would most likely see a lot of repeated important factors. However, another certainty that many experts and professionals who study the effects of self-esteem on people are that there will also be as many differences as there are similarities. The reason for this is that everyone has different values or expectations for themselves based on an additional variety of factors such as:

- The environment they were raised in
- The family values instilled in them throughout childhood
- Their personal beliefs and values that have developed throughout their individual life experiences
- The expectations they set and the standards they hold themselves and those around them

These are just some of those additional factors that can help to shape an individual. The more in-depth someone looks into their own thoughts, feelings, ideas, hopes, and dreams, the more they will know about themselves, and the higher their self-esteem will grow to be.

Where It Comes From: A person's self-esteem is most commonly shaped by their emotional experiences and encounters. The mistakes, triumphs, accidents, and successes that come throughout life all carry their own emotional and psychological influences with them. It's these influences that are most powerful when it comes to shaping how a person views themselves and their current lifestyle or life situation. The more positive influences and experiences a person can collect, the better their self-esteem will be, and the more emotionally in control they will find themselves when stressful situations arise.

What Is Confidence (or Self-Confidence)?

Confidence (particularly when described as self-confidence) refers to faith a person has in their own knowledge, experience, skills, and abilities. Depending on how much belief someone has in the things they know, the things they say, and the things they do during their personal or professional interactions, the higher a person's confidence levels will be.

Where It Comes From: A person's confidence comes from their opinion of and trust in their own strengths and abilities. This trust and faith most often are the result of positive experiences such as promotions at work or awards at school. The more experience they have and proof they have been able to collect that they know what they are doing or what they are talking about, then the higher their self-confidence will be, and the more that will start to affect other areas of their life positively.

There are lots of people who have a high level of self-esteem but find that they lack confidence, especially in certain situations like when they are asked to do something without time to prepare or when they want to ask a question, but are concerned with how others will react to it, so they decide just to keep their hand down. Alternately, people may have high levels of self-confidence and belief in their personal abilities, but also have poor levels of self-esteem from having their heart broken in a failed relationship or from trust issues that developed after being double-crossed by a friend or a co-worker.

Why Are These Traits So Important for Men & Women to Embrace, Develop & Strengthen?

As different as they can be, there are also plenty of situations and experiences that can be caused by interconnected levels of self-esteem and confidence. The more understanding, experienced, and control a person has over their personal self-esteem and confidence levels, the better off they will be in all opportunities they attempt or goals they strive for throughout their life.

Strengthening these traits not only helps with improving a person's overall mental, psychological, and emotional health, but it also comes with a variety of other benefits that can help improve someone's personal health and wellness in a wide range of styles.

The Many Benefits of Building Self-Esteem & Confidence

Even for those who are happy with their control over their habitual overthinking and procrastination, there are an endless number of reasons to keep focused on and motivated to work on for anyone and everyone building self-esteem and confidence levels. Here is a look at some of the most popular and widely reported benefits people have experienced in their quests for higher self-esteem and confidence!

Those with higher self-esteem and personal confidence are less likely to be people pleasers or develop people-pleasing habits than those with lower opinions of themselves or their abilities

They also tend to have better performance ratings and higher success rates in leadership roles

Not only are they more personable with customers or other audiences, but they are also more empathetic with employers or co-workers and better able to boost morale during times of high demand or increased stress levels

They are also more likely to have higher success rates with setting and reaching personal and professional goals because they are more self-aware of their mental, psychological, emotional changes and how it affects their daily performance

Those with higher self-esteem and confidence levels report more personal and professional satisfaction throughout their lives

They are more likely to take up opportunities when offered

They also tend to be bolder and more dominant in their professional teams and social circles as they are more likely to openly share their opinions and start conversations with even those they do not know with more confidence than those who question themselves and hesitate around others

These are just a handful of the benefits that study and research subjects of all ages and lifestyles have reported when tracked over time and throughout their personal improvement journey! Each person will find a whole new array of benefits and progress markers that are specialized and more tailored to their individual needs based on the techniques they choose to put into practice, how dedicated they can remain to their self-improvement plan and of course, what specific issues and concerns that are working to improve or eliminate.

Form Good Habits

One of the biggest problems with overthinking is that it leads to procrastination. In fact, the whole point of the brain for causing anxiety is to push you into inactivity. It wants you to stick to a corner so that the risk can be minimized. As we have already discussed, this can be a good strategy for survival in the wild. It is no way to live in this world where your contribution matters.

Procrastination is one of the most common side-effects of overthinking. It keeps you in a never-ending loop of thinking that has no scope of action. Your mind can keep forming strategies and then discarding them after a point to form newer and better ones. This process can be continued until the end of time.

What you really need is a plan to break the chain of thoughts and get into action. The longer you keep thinking, the harder it will get to stop overthinking about it. Even the best strategies in the world can get washed down the drain if they are not put into action.

Procrastination can be one of the biggest negative traits of an overthinking person, and it would also support your habit of not taking action on time.

Given below are 5 strategies that can help you in ditching the thinking mode and taking action. You can pick any of these as per the situation and break the deadlock.

Remember, the longer you remain in the deadlock, the harder it will become for you to get out of it.

The 5 Second Rule

Fear has a very deep-rooted relationship with postponing things. When you are afraid of doing something, its results, or have a distaste for it, the mind automatically starts overthinking about it. It makes you think about the consequences if things go wrong and would also make you believe that things would go wrong. Many a time, if you don't act on time, the mind will be able to convince you that the time has passed and there is going to be no use of taking the action then.

The mind likes to keep you sitting tied to thoughts. That's the safest playing ground as per the mind.

We only postpone things for the future that we don't like to do. The things for which we don't feel that passionately or the things that have been forced upon us. The things about which we feel passionate, we prepone them.

People don't want to get up in the morning even though the alarm clock rings several times and gets snoozed. The reason is their dispassion for getting up. They don't feel excited about the prospects of the day.

The same people would get up hours early if they have to do something about which they are really passionate.

However, you can't be passionate about everything you need to do. Especially not about the things you fear or loath. Yet, inaction will only push you into overthinking.

Make it a rule to get into action within 5 seconds of having the thought. It is a very short window. But, you don't need to finish the job in 5 seconds. You simply need to initiate.

For instance, if you need to go to the office, within 5 minutes of the rining of the alarm clock, you must be off the bed. Any longer you stay there, and your first preference would be to snooze it one last time.

Once you cross the 5 seconds window, your mind would start overthinking the whole process and would surely find things to prove the futility of the whole process.

Get into action before it is too late. This is a great way to break the shackles of procrastination.

Ditching the Autopilot

Most of the decisions taken by us are not conscious decisions. They are the decisions taken on instinct. We really don't put much thought into them. This happens because our mind remains on an autopilot mode most of the time.

If you have not been taxing it much about making real decisions, it likes to make decisions based on references. The things you did in similar situations earlier. Did they lead to any negative outcome? What probability of success does it see of for the actions in this attempt?

Your actions are guided by the autopilot in your mind on the basis of such questions. The situations are never judged on their merit. The mind doesn't like to see the probability of the success this time and the conditions that might lead it to the result. It wants to maintain inertia. This is the reason most people procrastinate and never take action. Their mind easily disqualifies most of the possibilities without even considering them a little. The remaining time you'll have at hand now will get utilized for overthinking.

If you want to ditch this trap of overthinking, you must ditch the autopilot. Look at the things mindfully. Take all the decisions consciously. Look at the merit of every situation, and don't try to assume things a lot. This will prepare a better ground for action, and it will also spare you from overthinking when you stop assuming a lot.

Starting Positively

One of the biggest reasons for our backing down from taking any kind of action is our tendency to look at things pessimistically. We begin on a negative note and then expect things to end positively. This almost never works.

The negative thought process is disheartening, and it is bad for the initiative. Chiding your own mind will not pump you up; it will push you into inaction.

Try to start anything new, even a day with positive intent. Don't weigh it down with expectations as that may also fill you with worries. Simply set out with a positive note that things would get better from where you start.

If you feel that looking at things in a positive manner from your perspective is not possible due to your limited view, try changing your perspective. Put yourself into the shoes of someone else you could imagine doing a better job at it. Think it through with a different perspective. Sometimes, changing the perspective can bring all the change in the work. The same things that may look very challenging from your angel maybe a piece of cake for others.

Once a man was looking for a famous church in a village. He had come walking from far and was getting grumpy. He saw a boy paying in the way and asked him the distance of the church. The boy thought for a few seconds and said 24,858 miles. The man was awestruck in disbelief. He said that the church couldn't be that far. I have come looking for it from so far.

The boy said that it was 24,858 miles as per the path he had taken; however, it was only 2 miles if he walked in the opposite direction.

Sometimes we simply look at things from a very difficult angle. Looking at it through someone else's perspective can change the whole story.

It can make the work easy and interesting. If you feel stuck at some work and feel that you don't have a going there, try thinking differently from the angle of someone else.

Acknowledging the Fears

Fears can push us into inaction. It has a very strong impact on our decision-making skills. If we don't address our fears, it will keep cornering us. Even if we keep avoiding the fears, our mind doesn't sit silently; it makes you think all the time only about those fears and consequences of the actions.

There is no escape from this cycle. If you want to avoid it, the only effective way is to acknowledge your fears.

The moment you acknowledge the fears, they lose the deadly impact they have. You are able to clearly understand the kind of impact they'll have. You also get a chance to look beyond the fears and assess the chances of success clearly.

This is a good way to break the deadlock and come out of the habit of procrastination led by fear.

Learning the Art of Setting Milestones

Our mind is constantly looking for the avenues to push us into inactivity. It seeks ways to push you into inaction, as that is the safest approach.

Many people who began working ambitiously at one point end up in failures not because they had put in the poor effort but because their mind was able to convince them of the futility of their actions.

For instance, you aim to lose 30 pounds and get slim. Your aspirations, external motivations, and inspirations can energize you to begin work in that direction. But, it is a task that requires constant motivation as you will be working against your own body. The body would make your work difficult. The mind would assist the body in it.

This means that after a few days, maintaining that motivation can get very difficult. The task of 30 pounds is not something that you are going to get within a few days or weeks, and hence there is a high probability that you'll surrender.

Many people surrender even before they have begun as their mind starts overthinking about the probabilities of success and find none.

Now, think if you had defined your goal in a more accurate way and broken it down into smaller milestones.

You'll lose 30 pounds in 6 months looks like a much well-defined goal. There is a target timeline so that you can't keep postponing it further. This is your first challenge to procrastination.

However, 6 months is a very long period, and maintaining motivation, even with a defined goal, can be difficult.

You also need milestones to help you in your pursuit.

Milestones help you in staging the results in smaller compartments so that you can track your progress.

You need to lose 30 pounds in 6 months means that you have 24 weeks to lose 30 pounds. It brings us to 1.25 pounds per week.

You will have a weekly target, and that can act as your constant motivator. You will have some weeks in which the weight loss would be slower. The milestones would push you to work harder the following week for making up for the deficit.

There will be weeks when your achievements will be higher, and the milestones will pump up to work harder for achieving the final goal faster.

Setting clear goals, dividing them into smaller milestones, and getting into action immediately can help you in breaking the chains of procrastination and inactivity.

Make a Habit of Writing a Diary

Keeping a journal is a great strategy to help organize your thoughts. People tend to underestimate the power of noting down their thoughts every day. Journaling helps you rid your mind from things that you might not be aware of. It enhances your working memory and also guarantees that you can effectively manage stress. Similarly, the habit of noting down your daily experiences in a journal helps you express your emotions that may be bottled up within you. Therefore, you create space to experience new things in life. The effect of this is that you can relieve yourself from the anxiety that you might have been experiencing.

Write Goals, Emotions, Results

It's been described in a lot of different ways with various terms—our reasons for living or the best part of living. The ideas or feelings or passions we wake up each day to pursue. Our purpose. Maybe just a hobby we get a lot of joy from practicing. However, you want to describe it, now is the time to start thinking about how you want to refill that empty space, where the cluttered thoughts of your mind had once taken root. It's time for another thought exercise.

Think back to when you were a child, or maybe a teenager. Was there something in your life that gave you joy as a kid? Was there a sport or a skill or a hobby that you spent most or all of your free time perfecting? Maybe you loved reading and simply read lots and lots of books over summer break each year. Did you enjoy swimming more than anything? Playing basketball or baseball? Riding a horse? Drawing and sketching? Maybe just getting together with friends and talking and laughing was what you looked forward to every day. Whatever it was, I want you to think back to a time when you were doing what you loved to do, if you can. What did it feel like to you? Do you remember the happiness it brought you?

A lot of adults live with this fallacy that the happiness we experience in childhood disappears forever once we become adults. This could not be further from the truth. Each one of us still has that child inside them, and it's not a necessary part of life that we give that up once we hit a certain age. Many people have turned their childhood passions into a lucrative and fulfilling career. They get to relive the joy they experienced as a child every day, only now, they're getting paid for it!

We don't have to give up freedom of mind, playfulness, curiosity, passion, all of the most precious parts of being a child just because we grow older. I want you to remember those things that made you happy as a child because now it's time to figure out how to manifest that joy in your life now. I'm not talking about trying to relive the past or turn into a child. What I'm saying is that it is possible for adults to experience joy and presence just like a child. It is just society and other cluttered minds telling us that there is no room for these things. Let's prove them wrong!

Get out that paper again, maybe just flip over the sheet you were working from before.

It might be helpful to first make a list of the things you loved to do as a child. Maybe go find those old home movies or pictures from your dance recital or boy scout troop, etc. Take some time to really remember how much joy these things brought you.

Now think about what you like to do now. When was the last time you had enough free time to pursue something you loved to do? If it's been a long time, it may take a little longer to think of what you like to do. Don't get discouraged. You can always pick out something you'd like to learn about, maybe this will become your new hobby!

Write down a couple of things you'd like to really concentrate on as a strategy to introduce happiness and relaxation into your life. There may be lots and lots of things you enjoy doing, but it's important not to overwhelm yourself. Most people are not going to be able to just drop their jobs and start pursuing all their passions full time (wouldn't that be the life!), so let's choose one or two things that you would like to start introducing into your life.

The last thing you want to do is turn your hobby into a chore, so when I say make some time to dedicate to your joy, what I mean is that you should try and prioritize doing something every day that is just for you. Maybe that is as simple as taking a nap! Making time for yourself is a great way to work together with that interruption technique we talked about earlier to reinvent the way your brain interprets your daily life. If you wake up every morning feeling that inner dread in your gut of having to get up and drive to work each day, then you are familiar with this phenomenon. It may seem like an impossible task now, but I promise, by the end of this book, you will have learned the important steps to take toward realizing a positive and fulfilled daily life.

If you're someone who needs structure, like me, consider finding and taking a class related to something you've always wanted to learn or try. If it's been a few years since you drew anything and you used to love drawing, find a class, maybe a free community class in your city, and you just may find some like-minded friends! You will find that the more you pursue personal betterment, the more it will naturally find you. Once you've learned to be aware of your thought processes, you will inevitably begin to notice things you hadn't before, when there were too many thoughts in the way.

Chapter 3. How to Declutter Your Environment

Principles of a Minimalist Approach

1. Less is more.

In his Nicomachean Ethics, Aristotle talked about how most of our relationships are based on utility and convenience and are empty of any value. However, when we hold on to the one or two valuable relationships, we place an importance on those relationships that contribute to our overall well-being. When you can focus on a few really good relationships, you'll enjoy your life a lot more because you'll worry less about what others think of you and think more about how you can live a happier life.

2. Let go of toxic relationships.

The second thing that you must do is get rid of every toxic relationship that is a bad influence in your life. One example of this kind of relationship is when a person sucks all the energy out of your life and plays the needy victim. Victims play the role of the victimizer, and they zap you of your needed resources. Eventually, they will take every trace of life from you if you are not careful. Victimizers can also become the center of our lives. And when that happens, you cannot do what you want to do because you have to take care of a very needy person. Instead of holding on to this toxic relationship, you should try to get rid of it as soon as possible. Surely, it will be difficult for you to relinquish your hold on this relationship because you may have invested a lot of time and energy into it, but it will be better to get rid of it sooner rather than later.

3. Be true to other people.

In today's world, an authentic man or woman is to be exalted. Being real is something that people in society need to do to live better lives. Being a con artist and lying to others is something that is easy, manipulative, and evil; but our world is filled with such people. It harms your image, and it can also hurt your soul. One of the best things that you can do for yourself and for others is to be true to yourself and to other people. This way produces less stress and enables you to live a life that is going to bring you greater happiness in the end. If you want to be a true leader or manager, authenticity is increasingly important because people look up to you and trust you to do your job the right way. If you don't do that, they may look elsewhere for work. The basic principle that should underlie all of this is to never compromise on principles in your life.

4. Live your life in relation to the here and now.

Humans tend to look to the distant past and hold feelings of unforgiveness, or they think endlessly about the future. Both of these methods are not at all productive. We must keep our eyes focused on present circumstances, and this applies to our relationships. There is no better way to help a friend than to be for them here and now. Your friends need you now. Your wife or husband needs you now, and your kids need you now. Don't waste too much of your time surfing the web, working, or doing other things. Instead, you should prize the relationships that you have at this moment and not compromise on them for anything.

5. Get rid of unreasonable expectations of others.

Another thing that you need to do is to release the burdensome expectations that you have of other people. This is an essential part of your friendship or love relationship. When you maintain clear and reasonable expectations for your relationship, you will experience a smoother and easier relationship with whomever. Many people have unreasonable expectations of their spouse, significant other, or friend. This will only lead to heartbreak and friction in the relationship. Breakups and divorce can be the worst result of these expectations. Therefore, it is crucial to maintain good relationships with others while getting rid of the unreasonable expectations we may have of other people.

6. Connect with your friend or partner deeply.

In relationships, it is crucial that you go deep rather than seeking more. When you get to know someone deeply, it will require a significant investment of time and energy. Most of our relationships will be based on a shallow level, and they will disappear when the person goes out of our life. It could be that the person moves away from us or a work situation changes. In true relationships with others, permanence should be a key marker of the relationship. Do you spend most of your time talking to your friend about sports, Netflix, or something else superficial, or do you spend more time talking about deeper and more philosophical things? It is worth finding out more about how you can spend more time on the deeper things of life, rather than dwelling on the fruitless and meaningless things that simply don't matter. Going deep will help you to have deeper connections with people.

7. Focus on shared experiences.

Spending time with friends, family, or other people in our lives allows us to have shared experiences that will last a lifetime. When you make the most of these times together, you can create amazing memories. Such memories will remain in your mind and heart for a long time. These memories are more important than the material stuff we acquire. They will point us to something deeper inside of us that we can share.

8. Intentionality.

Having intentionality is an important aspect of creating good relationships. When you are intentional about your different relationships, you can have smoother and more effective communication, which will help your relationships get off the ground in a better way. Find a purpose for spending time with your friend or partner, and you will find that the time spent will be helpful to get you in the right place. Intentionality is going to improve your friendships, love relationships, and family relationships.

9. Love your neighbor.

The way to pursue a meaningful relationship with another person is through love. This is not the kind of erotic love that we are accustomed to thinking about. Instead, it is a concept of human love that applies universally. It is a love for a brother or neighbor that defines how a person can live a more meaningful life. Love should permeate your interactions with other people. It also makes things a lot prettier and less messy because what defines your relationship is what you can give to the relationship rather than what you can get from it. This makes it a less stressful kind of relationship.

10. Pursue relationships with passion.

One final point is that we need to pursue our relationships with passion. We should not settle for less than excellence. Pursuing relationships requires dedication and commitment. Many people don't like to commit to things because they are afraid or too busy, but you can stand out from the crowd and commit to a relationship, whether that is with a friend or significant other, and that can be an amazing thing for your life. So find things that you can do to spice up your life by associating yourself with wonderful people who will be beneficial to you and who can help you down the road to success in your life.

Your Home, Your Digital Life, Your Activities

Now that we have looked at the benefits of decluttering your home, let's get creative about how to declutter your home. These simple, yet effective tips will get you started on how declutter your home.

Determine the department of the house you want to start decluttering.

This is the first and foremost step you need to undertake. You can't declutter all the areas of the house in a day. Even you do, that means you, leaving work, school or that vital task that you were supposed to handle for the day. It can be so overwhelming if you think you can declutter your home in a day, especially if it's your first time. It can also be time consuming, so you need to decide where you are going to start decluttering from. It could be your bedroom, bathroom, kitchen, sitting room, the dining or even the garage. Start with the easiest one so that you won't get tired easily. Then, ascend to harder areas. When you have chosen an area to declutter, it's time to move to the next step on this list.

Give yourself 5-10 minutes decluttering period.

Decluttering is a gradual process. A process that you ought not to rush. You can dedicate 5 or 10 minutes of your time every day to declutter your home. As you proceed, increase the time and add more tasks on your list as you go on. For example, the first day can be 5 minutes. The second can be 10, the third can be 15, and so on. Don't start decluttering with 10 minutes on your first day and spend 5 minutes the next day. It simply won't work. Before you realize, you are finding it hard to dedicate even a minute t declutter your home. Start with the lowest possible time (5 minutes at least) and ascend accordingly.

Get a trash bag ready

You would want to get rid of those items that are causing your home to be cluttered. Get a trash bag, throw them inside. Old items that you feel you don't want to get rid of, give them to charity. If you're going to store any item, get large boxes. Move them to the appropriate places and create space in your home. You will be amazed to see the number of trash bags that you have taken away.

Create a to-do list of items you want to throw in the trash

Surely, there will be a good number of items in trash bags that you would want to get rid of. Get a paper, write out all the items that you want to get rid of. Each item that you take to the trash cross them on your list. Also, it's important you create a to-do list of all your tasks, so that you cross each one you have accomplished. As you get rid of each item, the clutters get reduced. Creating these lists will help you keep track of tasks that you have completed and the ones that you haven't. It's easier to declutter if you have a picture of where and how to get started.

Dedicate to remove one item everyday.

Each day that you decide to clutter your home, try to at least get an unwanted item out of your home. Imagine doing this for a month? That's 30 items. Do this for a year, and you must have for rid of 365 items. How about you increase it to 2 items every day? In no time, you will be able to declutter your house and get those items thrown into the trash. Your home will stay completely clean and devoid of dirt.

The same thing goes for cleaning the house. Most people who do 9-5 jobs often have a hard time cleaning the entire house, and it's quite understandable. It will take your time. If you aren't able to clean your whole house, start from cleaning one part. You can just decide to clean your sitting room for that day and clean another room the following day. The most important thing is to establish a goal and stick towards it.

Take a picture

This isn't necessary, but it's quite helpful. You can decide to take a picture of a cluttered area, like your kitchen and then, take another picture of your kitchen. This time, a decluttered one. Observe those photos, and you will see how proud you have become that you have begun the step in decluttering your home.

Use the four-box system

Establishing a system will make it easier to declutter your home than having none. The four-box system is an example of such systems that will help you become more efficient in tidying up your home. Get four boxes and label them as follows with descriptions;

- Give away: These are boxes that should be filled with things that you don't need or use, but are still okay. In other words, these are items that you can either sell online or donate to some charity organizations.

- Keep: These boxes should contain items that you plan on keeping. They are items that you can't do without. That is the items that you use frequently. Examples of these items are your clothes, sound system, chairs, etc. They mostly have a fixed place where they are kept.
- Return: In this box, things that are misplaced in your house should be kept in this box. For example, your soap shouldn't be in the sitting room. Your cutlery shouldn't be in the bathroom, and so on. These items should be kept in their appropriate places and not the other way round.
- Trash: Items or possessions that are worthless should be kept in this box.

Each room that you enter identify items that should be placed in their respective boxes. Any item at all, irrespective of its size, should enter their appropriate boxes. It may take you some time, but it's worth it. You will discover items and will now what to do with them.

Don't be afraid to ask for assistance

Asking for help from a friend or relative is a cool way to get suggestions on how to declutter your home. Your friend or relative can go through all the items in your home and suggest which one is to be thrown, given out, or which one is to be kept. You might want to defend your reasons for keeping such an item, which is totally cool. If your friend or relative see the same reasons as you do, then your decision is valid. If otherwise, then it's wise to get rid of such item.

The best thing about this is that your friend or relative doesn't need to be a professional to help you get rid of any clutter. Just that having someone by your side all through the decluttering process will make it easier and faster for you to get rid of certain items that you have doubts getting rid of.

Chapter 4.   How   to   Declutter Relationships

The Negative Impact of Bad Relationships

The first step to breaking out of any toxic relationship is to identify the signs around you, acknowledge and then accept them as a truth that is negative to your health and needs to be amended. Everyone's relationships are different, but here is a closer look at some of the most common signs connection to toxic relationships:

- Emotional manipulation is one sign that is prominent in any kind of toxic relationship or connection
- The definition of this symptom varies because it can include a wide range of actions and behaviors that vary from case to case
- At its core though, emotional manipulation refers to the intentional alteration of behaviors or way of speaking in order to avoid or manage the emotions of someone else
- In the case of the toxic person, this can refer to an intentional intensification of tense emotions and responses when their friend or partner is talking in order to get them to leave the room or feel powerless in their current situation
- In the case of the victim, they know that when their friend or partner is in this mood that their tense

emotions will only intensify if they try to talk to them so instead they intentionally find something to do in a different room to avoid talking to their friend or partner until they are in a better headspace

- Isolating oneself from other close connections with family or friends to spend more time with their toxic friend or partner
- In many cases, this isolation is directly linked to and even the result of their friends and family seeing the way their loved one has changed in this relationship or connection and confronted them about it
- This confrontation is seen as an act of aggression by the individual and they get defensive, siding with their toxic friend or partner and hindering their relationship with their supportive loved one
- Being dismissed as overly emotional or overreacting to things whenever you voice your feelings or opinions (particularly if they are counter to the toxic friend or partner)
- In some cases, the individual is not dismissed but rather teased and ridiculed making them feel even worse about speaking their mind
- They can be accused of imaging problems that do not exist if there is an issue the toxic friend or partner does not want to deal with

- Some toxic partners might try to make the individual feel selfish or guilty if their thoughts, opinions or desires are centered around anything they need or want
- A variety of controlling behaviors have been associated with toxic relationships and connections
- Calling a person names and speaking with a sarcastic tone in situations where it is inappropriate or hurtful
- Endless and harmful criticism that is meant to damage their self-esteem and confidence so that they are easier to control and manipulate
- Using intimidation and fear tactics when the person becomes too bold or exploratory for their liking
- Blaming the person from things they had no control over or were not even connected to and throwing out unnecessary accusations in an attempt to make their partner feel guilty about something that may not even have happened

Whatever the specifics are with toxic people, they are unhealthy influences on men and women of any age or profession. The more toxic people that are around and the longer or more connected their relationship with the individual becomes, the more power and negative influence they will have on the person. These types of relationships are often neglectful and even dangerous, and they can be some of the most difficult to break free from.

Remove Negative Influences

Identify where your negative self-talk comes from if you want to truly beat it. Many times, it is people around us who condition us into thinking or believing something as the truth. Even seemingly harmless or subtle negative comments or pieces of criticism can impact our sense of self-worth. The voice of others slowly and insidiously becomes our inner voice of critical self-talk. Never let someone else's perception about you define your reality or become the foundation of your critical self-talk.

Are there people around you who view their or your life in a predominantly negative light? Are you an unwilling victim of someone else's negativity? While it isn't uncommon for the negative self-talk to originate within us, it can often be traced back to our conditioning or beliefs/actions/words of the people around us. Negative critical talk originating from another person's low confidence or self-esteem is highly challenging to deal with. Run miles away from such negative and destructive people to change your outlook on life, and view it more positively and constructively.

Avoid slipping into the trap of negativity laid down by others. Stay away from chronic, habitual whiners and complainers. Don't validate other people's complaints by chiming in or playing a willing party. According to a Warsaw School of Social Psychology study, people who are always complaining experience reduced life satisfaction, greater negative emotions, stunted positive thinking and lower moods.

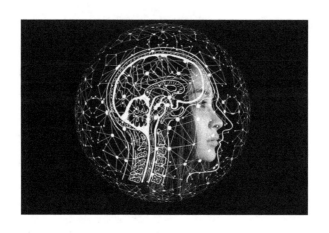

Conclusion

We have touched on a number of topics that can help you declutter your mind and reinvent the new you. The topics we touched on are what successful people do to focus their minds on their goals. Practice what is written in this book and you'll find out that there is nothing you'll aim for that is outside your reach.

The secret of harnessing the power of your mind is not in doing the right things once, it is in doing them consistently.